9/7/91

THIS BOOK IS DEDICATED TO THE MEMORY OF
PETER FLETCHER RIDDELL

MASTERPIECES · OF · PHOTOGRAPHY FROM · THE · RIDDELL · COLLECTION

INTRODUCTION BY SARA STEVENSON
CATALOGUE BY JULIE LAWSON
1986

SCOTTISH NATIONAL PORTRAIT GALLERY

ISBN 0 903148 64 1

Designed by McIlroy Coates, Edinburgh
Duotone Origination by Adplates, London
Typeset and printed by Blackwood Pillans & Wilson Ltd. Edinburgh

The Scottish National Portrait Gallery wishes to thank the following people who have given so generously of their time and expertise in assisting us: Norma Armstrong and the staff of the Edinburgh Room, Edinburgh Central Public Library; Bobby Burnett, Historian of the Royal and Ancient Golf Club, St Andrews, Fife; Ian Gow, the National Monuments Record of Scotland; Murray Johnston, Director of the Stills Gallery, Edinburgh; Patricia Kattenhorn, the British Library, India Office Library and Records; J W F MacKenzie, AIC Photographic Services; Dr Walter Makey, Edinburgh City Archivist; Alan Paterson, the Anglo-Chinese Educational Institute; Larry Schaaf, Carnegie Fellow at the University of St Andrews; Joan M Schwartz, the Public Archive of Canada, Ottawa; William F Stapp, Curator of Photographs, the Smithsonian Institution, Washington DC; the Technical Department of the National Galleries of Scotland. In particular we must thank the Portrait Gallery typists, Sheila Smith and Jessie Hassan for a meticulous typescript.

The research for the book was undertaken by the Scottish Photography Archive at the Portrait Gallery, in the person of Julie Lawson. The Archive depends on outside funding and we are grateful to the following for their generous support during the last year: Mobil North Sea Limited; the Calouste Gulbenkian Foundation; the Scottish International Education Trust; the Tarnie Trust; Scottish Television; the Royal Bank of Scotland; Adam and Company; and Barr and Stroud.

In June 1985 after the deeply regretted death of Peter Fletcher Riddell, Mr Riddell's family decided to give the Scottish National Portrait Gallery his magnificent collection of nineteenth-century photographic material. This extraordinarily generous gift transformed the Gallery's photographic collection overnight from a good but lop-sided one into one substantially representative of the best and most interesting nineteenth-century photographs. We owe an incalculable debt to Mr Riddell's enthusiasm as a collector and to his family's very great kindness in giving the collection to the Scottish nation.

Duncan Thomson
Keeper

Peter Fletcher Riddell was from boyhood a collector. His first interest was in stamps, then perhaps inspired by a bibliophile uncle he progressed to books, many of which he purchased during Saturday browsings in Glasgow's Barrows. It was in the 1950s, now living in Edinburgh, that he began his collection of old Scottish photographs. Many years later he confessed his regret at not having bought more while they were available at such comparatively modest cost, but at the time, with a young family to support, he felt some guilt at the shillings he did spend.

He was born in Langside, Glasgow on 14 December 1918, only son of David Fletcher Riddell, a manufacturer's agent, and his wife Edith Gerrie. The happiest memories of his childhood were the annual holidays spent at Millport on the island of Cumbrae. All his life he retained a love of the Clyde, and a special interest in the old paddle steamers once so abundant there.

He was educated first at Battlefield School, then at Queen's Park Secondary, both in Glasgow. For several years he was a keen member of the Boys' Brigade. In 1936 he entered the Commercial Bank (now Royal Bank of Scotland) as an apprentice, and five years later was transferred to Edinburgh. At the beginning of the war he served for a short time with the Argyll and Sutherland Highlanders, but was discharged on health grounds and returned to the bank. He became Staff Manager at the St Andrew Square office in 1959, and in 1968 Manager of the busy Nicolson Street branch. He retired in 1978.

Throughout his life Peter Riddell had many varied interests. Rock gardening and amateur photography were among his early pastimes, carried out with an artistic sense and conscientiousness which characterized his nature. He was a lover of classical music and used to attend concerts by the Scottish National Orchestra in Glasgow and Edinburgh. In addition to photographs and books his collections included old Scottish porcelain, prints and post cards.

He will be remembered by his friends as a kindly man with a shrewd sense of humour, well informed on a great many subjects, and with a particular regard for all things Scottish.[1]

Peter Fletcher Riddell collected photographs over a span of forty years, beginning at a time when there was little public or academic interest in the subject. Although he missed one or two important items—an album of Hill and Adamson's calotypes which was advertised in the United States before it was advertised in Edinburgh, a copy of P H Emerson's *Life and Landscape in the Norfolk Broads* which he much regretted sending back to the bookseller because the binding was imperfect—Mr Riddell's collection contains a substantial body of extremely important material. He described, for example, finding a cellarful of James Craig Annan's photogravures being sold for pennies, and the loss of the Hill and Adamson album was made up when he bought another which had descended through Hill's family and contained a surprising number of unfamiliar images.

It is impossible to categorise the collection in any simple way, except as a collection of photographic material relating to the period between 1843 and 1918. It includes about ten thousand objects: books, albums, prints, stereocards, cabinet portraits and cartes de visite, ambrotypes and daguerreotypes. The scale varies between the miniature tintypes and the two and a half-foot high copy of Francis Frith's *Photographic Views of Egypt, Siniai and Jerusalem*, and the importance of the material veers between the work of the lesser studio photographers and the work of the giants in the field. Geographically the photographers range across the world from Edinburgh to the Philippines, from Melrose to Trichinopoly, and the subject matter travels from peaceful domesticity to war. The wide scope of the collection means that it serves as an effective guide to the practice of photography in the nineteenth century: photography as an art and as a business, photography as a social and a psychological force.

The collection is a model and a test track for research into nineteenth-century photography. When a collection is made not just with a conventional regard for the well-known photographers but from pure affection for the medium, many of the photographers will be unknown and many of the subjects will be unidentified. We make no apology for including in this book some of these unidentified photographs: the pictures may be nameless but their striking character entitles them to immediate and serious consideration. The literary evidence for their importance will come later but in the meantime, they speak eloquently on their own behalf. By its very nature, the Riddell collection is a source of historical information and pleasure which will grow as the years pass.

The newly-discovered goldfield

The earliest photographers were mostly people with time and money at their disposal. The processes were laborious and expensive—few fortunes were made and photography stayed substantially the province of amateurs for the first fifteen years of practicable photography, during the 1840s and early 1850s.

In the mid-1850s the first flood of professionals moved in, lured by the apparently easier, quicker, collodion process.

> 'From every grade, from every profession, from every trade, and hundreds from no trade at all, a motley group—such formed our ranks at starting. A newly discovered gold field could not have called forth more excitement than did photography. Thousands threw aside their usual employments, tempted by the tales told of fortunes made in no time at this wonderful trade, photography. Like soldiering, love of art and a desire to excel actuated many; whilst others, like shadows, moved on in the trail for plunder and profit only. "It's so easy," said those who had got the "straight tip". "Why, with a cigar box and a spectacle eye you can get an impression," the knowing ones replied. The idea was that it cost little or nothing to get up the apparatus, little trouble and large returns; and so, many who had nothing to lose ventured their all in speculation.'[2]

Main streets and back streets of every city and town in the world were taken over by photographers. Photography was adopted as a sideline by a bizarre range of trades from glaziers to ice cream sellers. 'Into the practice of no other business or art was there ever such an absurd, blind and pell-mell rush. From the accustomed labours of agriculture and machine shop, from the factory and counter, from the restaurant, coach box and forecastle, representatives have appeared to perform the work for which a life-apprenticeship could hardly be sufficient.'[3]

Photography became in itself a source of social upheaval and a sharing of ideas and ideals—some admirable and some cock-eyed—which was both fascinating and alarming to contemporary observers:

> '. . . where not half a generation ago the existence of such a vocation was not dreamt of, tens of thousands are now following a new business, practising a new pleasure, speaking a new language, and bound together by a new sympathy. . . . The world was believed to have grown sober and matter-of-fact, but the light of photography has revealed an unexpected source of enthusiasm. An instinct of our nature, scarcely so worthily employed before, seems to have been kindled, which finds something of the gambler's excitement in the frequent disappointments and possible prizes of the photographer's luck. When before did any motive short of the stimulus of chance or the greed of gain unite in one uncertain and laborious quest the nobleman, the tradesman, the prince of the blood royal, the innkeeper, the artist, the manservant, the general officer, the private soldier, the hard-worked member of every learned profession, the gentleman of leisure, the Cambridge wrangler, the man who

bears some of the weightiest responsibilities of this country on his shoulder, and, though last, not least, the fair woman whom nothing but her own choice obliges to be more than the fine lady?'[4]

There were two great waves of enthusiasm for photography in the nineteenth century, one around 1860 when the flood of professionals overtook the amateurs and the second after 1880 when the amateurs caught up in force. The impact of photography was felt in more than the number of new photographers—the miniature painters' and silhouettists' trade was destroyed and many of the practitioners were absorbed into the business of hand-colouring photographs. Subsidiary industries sprang up—camera makers, album makers, suppliers of photographic materials, backdrop painters. Photography proved a substantial drain on the world's silver resources, posed its own industrial health hazards, and created its own forms of pollution.

One example of such pollution involved the albumen print which used a film of egg-white on the paper surface. A large photographic studio could use thousands of eggs in a day, and firms that prepared photographic paper commercially on such a scale faced a serious problem:

'Mr Spencer was, at one period in the history of photography, the largest manufacturer of albumenised paper in this country, and carried on his business at Shepherd's Bush. In 1866 he told me that he broke about 2,000 eggs daily, merely to obtain the whites or albumen. The yolks being of no use to him, he sold them when he could, to glove makers, leather dressers, and confectioners, but they could not consume all that he offered for sale, and he buried the rest in his garden until the neighbours complained of the nuisance, so that it became ultimately a very difficult thing for him to dispose of his waste yolks in any manner.'[5]

An appalling vision of Mr Spencer sneaking out at dead of night with buckets of decaying egg yolks to dump in the highways and byways of Shepherd's Bush is made yet worse by the discovery that another photographer, Valentine Blanchard, had a similar business in the same neighbourhood.

Any new, vigorous industry adopted by thousands of only partly-informed people will run into trouble. Photography had all the potential for fraud that the criminal world could hope for—excitement, profit and an ignorant public. So many remarkable discoveries and improvements were being made, that a few extra impossibilities could easily pass. Photography itself was such an extraordinary fact that gullible people could be sold photographs that were not there and photographic secrets in sealed envelopes for £10 apiece. Henry Mayhew's account of a fairground photographer who handed out completely black pieces of paper swearing that the picture would develop later, was a standard confidence trick.[6] A complaint uttered in 1857 described a slightly higher level of the business in equally depressing terms:

'Photography has become so far popularised that its practice may be at times considered a public nuisance. In the suburbs of London, particularly at the east end, the streets are impassible with 'touters' of rival establishments, who with showy gilt frames in hand, intercept all passengers, and almost drag them into their dens. An enormous trade is carried on upon Sunday at all hours, in defiance of public decency. It has really now become a matter for police interference, both on grounds of propriety and public comfort.'[7]

'Look happy!'

Photography had a reputation for ease and simplicity which was not at first the case. It is hard to realise at this distance quite how daunting the conditions could be. The early daguerreotypes were impractical for portraiture because the exposure times were still five to ten minutes in length. Even when the timing was reduced to somewhere between seconds and two minutes (depending on the strength of the light), the practical instructions for posing a successful portrait could be bizarre:

> 'Amongst the numerous improvements proposed in the Daguerreotype is the following by R Jobard of Brussels, for taking portraits à Heleographé: "Paint in dead white the face of the patient, powder his hair, and fix the back of his head between 2 or 3 planks, solidly attached to the back of an armchair; and wind up with screws."'[8]

Even the most hardened believer in the truth of photography must hesitate before accepting that the results would be natural.

The above quotation sounds like a joke at the expense of the early, primitive stages of photography. Within fifteen years there was a full-blown photographic industry at work, catering for hundreds of thousands of people anxious to have their portraits taken in the quicker and cheaper methods of the collodion and albumen processes. Greater speed and sophistication had found the way to take truthful, natural portraits in conditions of some comfort. Or had they?

> 'Furs, rocks, stones, hair, hands, or complexions, leaves, grass, earth, carpets, etc, may be lightened as much as necessary by a powder puff, directly applied, or shaken a yard or so above them, so that an atmosphere of extremely minute white particles shall settle on them—chalk or whiting may be lightly smeared on iron work, carved wood, or other surfaces, etc, or a stiff "hog tool" may be used to these or other surfaces with powdered chalk; large parts may be tinted wet with whiting and lamp black to any tone required; or to darken, take burnt umber and lamp black . . .'[9]

This advice was given by William Lake Price in 1858. By this time there were at least professionally-made clamps and supports and the wet collodion process was swift enough to reduce the exposure times to seconds. Unfortunately the precise demands of a shallow depth of focus, the need to pose the sitter, fix the clamps and dart about with a powder puff all took a great deal of time. The wet collodion negative, as its name suggests, had to be exposed in the camera while wet. So, unless the photographer had an active assistant, he would spend some time in the darkroom draining the negative while his sitter sat clamped into position, waiting. Lake Price remarked, *encouragingly*:

> 'Of course, it is in many respects better that an assistant should prepare the

plate, leaving the artist entirely free to arrange the picture; but to show the student that it is not absolutely necessary, it may be stated that groups of several figures have been arranged, the whole of the manipulation performed on plates of some size, and several negatives, with satisfactory expressions, produced entirely without assistance, within the hour'.[10]

Dr John Brown sat for his photograph so often that the *Caledonian Mercury* waxed satirical in 1864: 'When was there a photographic exhibition or a photographic showcase, for that matter, without a portrait of *him*? His benevolent countenance appears so frequently that one almost fancies that the photographers practise on it after business hours, as well as during the day, when sitters are few.'[11] He nevertheless described the process of portrait photography in unappealing terms:

> 'The truth is, that it is a distressingly mechanical, amental, almost fatuous state you get into when your cerebellum is gripped in a vice, and you are told to look happy and at your ease, with your eye fixed upon the idiotic head of a stag, or a *nail* in the wall—some friends asking you to think of your sweetheart! The consequence is, there is little between the extreme of glumness and the smirk—between fatuity and furiosity.'[12]

The 'Universal furniture Set'

The obvious practical difficulties presented by portrait photography especially did not hold back the crowds of happy optimists who contrived to believe that a few hours' lessons or a small book of instructions would put them in possession of all the necessary facts, and that a few commercial accessories bought from a catalogue would turn their portraits into masterpieces.

The first wave of studio photographers were mostly satisfied with an elementary set of properties to produce 'artistic' pictures. They followed the great portrait painters of the seventeenth and eighteenth centuries and bought large curtains for draping and columns for the sitters to lean on, followed by classical balustrades and backdrops of magnificent scenery. These splendid accessories, the argument went, would transform the most modest sitter into a person of high standing and wealth. Unfortunately, the results fell short of their aim. The close detail of the albumen print reproduced not just the nervous faces and every wrinkle in a sitter's trousers but the battered papier mâché of the column, the odd curve on the canvas backdrop or the way the view was nailed to the floor. Even handling a modest set of accessories was beyond the capacity of some studios.

After a steady trickle of new accessories through the 1860s and 1870s—little boats on ponds (fig 1), rustic gates and stiles, clumps of turf and dried ferns—the second commercial flood of photographers arrived in the 1880s and 1890s. By this time the support industries had grown in strength and firms like McGhie and Company of Glasgow issued illustrated catalogues of easy ways to brilliant photography. Studios were offered such wonders as 'The "Three-Back" posing Chair', 'Busts for producing statuesque photographs' (fig 2), 'Baldwin's Baby Holder (in the slot in the back is a spring clamp into which the operator may force a portion of the child's dress)', 'The "Renaissance Stairway"', and 'the most useful tree yet introduced'. Some of these accessories are of such comprehensive awfulness that they must instantly have wrecked any picture they were introduced into. J Fallowfield's 'Universal' Furniture Set, 'A very handsome and elaborate accessory in carved oak, representing as desired—piano, writing table, fireplace and mantel, and book-case' is a prime example of the kind (fig 3).

There can be no doubt that these devices worked, after a fashion. Splendid and elaborate backgrounds must have given nervous sitters some confidence because they then did not have to make the whole picture with their own face and figure. They introduced interest and pleasure into what is for most people an ordeal, and gave some spurious consequence to the resulting pictures. They made the standard business of photography less mundane and more entertaining.

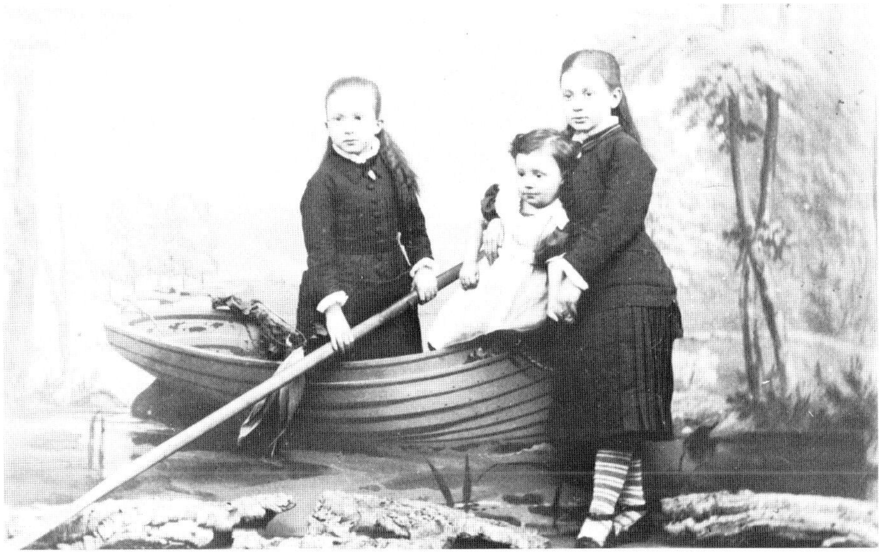

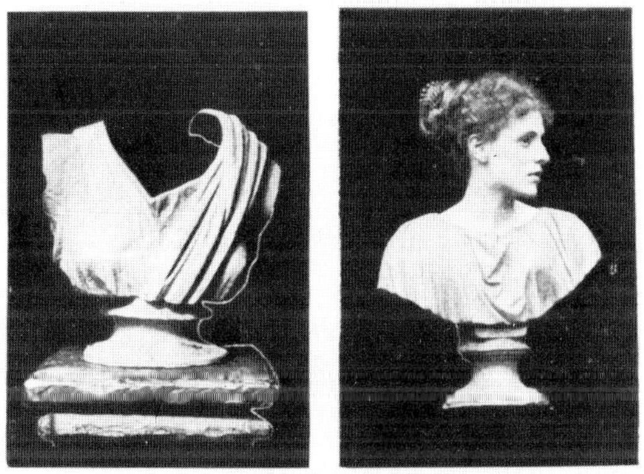

Fig. 1. No. 204. Fig. 2.

204.—**Busts for producing Statuesque Photographs** (W. Tylar, 41, High Street, Aston, Birmingham).

This article takes the form of a modelled shell of *papier maché*, or some such material, in which the sitter's head can be posed. The body of the sitter is covered with a piece of material that photographs the same shade as the background.

Price [illegible] each.

Figure 1
The popular boat accessory of the 1860s
carte de visite photograph by Turnbull and Sons, Glasgow

Figure 2
Papier mâché busts for statuesque photographs made by W Tylar

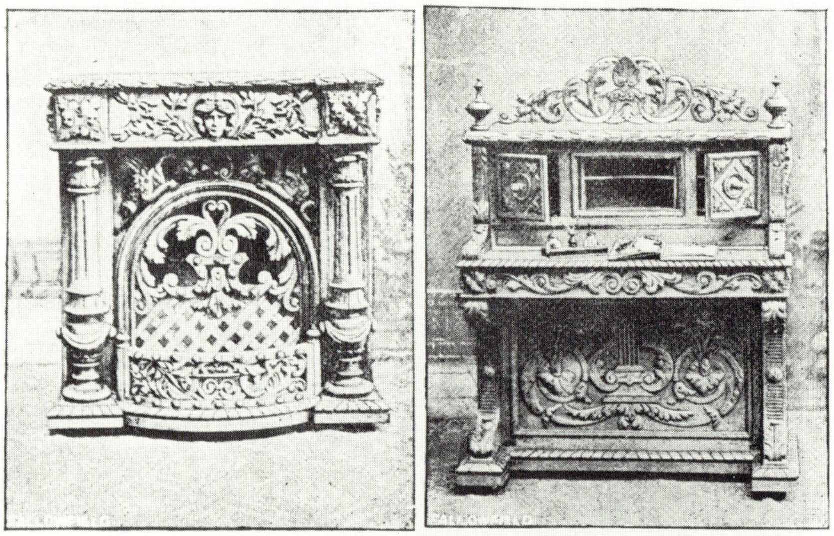

Fig. 1. No. 342. Fig. 2.

342.—"**Universal**" **Furniture Set** (J. FALLOWFIELD).

A very handsome and elaborate accessory in carved oak, representing as desired—piano, writing table, fire-place and mantel, and book-case. *Price* £12.

Figure 3
The 'Universal' Furniture Set, a piano, writing table, mantelpiece and bookcase in one
made by J Fallowfield about 1891

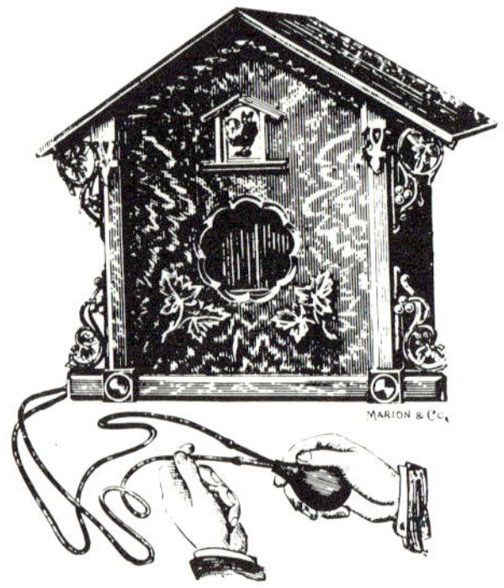

Figure 4
A cuckoo-clock disguise for the studio camera
made by Marion & Co, about 1891

In the painful business of photographing small children any method of tying them down and achieving a pleasant expression has to be regarded as a necessity rather than a frivolity. A photographer who found himself unable to handle children would reasonably welcome a cuckoo-clock front for his camera (fig 4) or a ploy with a musical box recommended by Mr Ingles Rogers:

> 'Having wound up the instrument, place it behind you out of sight, if possible, but conveniently near the camera. All being ready for exposure, touch it off. The effect is marvellous! The little creature at once pricks up its ears, assumes a radiant expression and becomes transfixed with joy at the strains of "Come into the garden, Maud. . . ." '[13]

'I thoughtlessly stepped back a few paces . . .'

The great commercial rush to photography found a peak of enthusiasm in the pioneering photographers. Photography like many other obsessions blinded people to danger in a remarkable way. The sentence quoted above was written by Herbert Ponting who was photographing alligators at the time and had forgotten the one lying behind him. It is one of many alarming stories told of people pursued by wild dogs, falling off precipices and blowing themselves up. The history of photography often takes on an adventure-story narrative style worthy of Rider Haggard, which crops up even in the advertisements: 'Will exchange Snider rifle with bayonet for background on roller, interior or exterior'. 'Wanted, modern half-plate camera, folding tailboard, three double dark slides and accessories (Ross's preferred); exchange, pigeons to value.'[14]

The photographers who laboured so hard to take the more remarkable photographs found it disconcerting that the results could look so calm and effortless. The public made the situation worse by congratulating them on their good luck and pleasant employment. Samuel Bourne, who set up a considerable expedition to photograph in the Himalayas in the 1860s, reacted forcibly:

> 'Ah! you gentlemen! and you, careless public, who think that landscape photography is a pleasant and easy task—a sort of holiday pastime—look at me toiling up that steep ascent in the grey dawn of a cold morning in fear and trembling that my labour would be all in vain! See me sitting for ten mortal hours, shivering in cold and mist, on top of that bleak pass waiting

for a "break" which would *not* come! See me descending, disappointed, at night to my tent, to return next day and go through the same again and say if *this* is a pleasant pastime!'[15]

Bourne's account of his sufferings struck a chord with George Washington Wilson—photographic conditions in the Scottish Highlands were clearly akin to those in the Himalayas (terrible). He wrote a letter quoted by Bourne on the same occasion:

'I can almost appreciate your amount of toil and trouble expended upon these views, but very few of the general public can do so, and I am often *riled* when I hear people speak of landscape photography as mere holiday work. I believe that the only reason why I have managed to get on here is that I have worked like a horse, and done things and suffered things that few people would submit to.'[16]

The stories told by the photographers were designed to counterbalance the calm, simple effects of the early photographs. John Werge, photographing Niagara Falls in the 1850s, can still make the hair rise:

'I remember, when we started, taking a hatchet with us, like backwoodsmen, to take a view of Prospect Tower, on the American side of the great Horseshoe Fall, how we had to hew down the trees that obstructed the light; how we actually hung over the precipice, holding on to each other's hands, to lop off a branch still in sight where it was not wanted. The manner in which we accomplished this was what some bystanders pronounced "awful". I hugged a sapling of silver birch, growing on the brink of the precipice, with my left arm, while friend Easterley, holding my right hand with one of the masonic grips, *hung over* the precipice, and stretching out as far as he could reach, lopped off the offending branch . . . To get a view of the Tower we wanted, we had to make a temporary platform over the precipice. This we managed by laying a piece of timber across a fallen tree, and, unshipping the camera, shoved it along the plank until it was in position, balancing the shore end of the plank with heavy stones. When all was ready for exposure, I went round and stood on the point of a jutting rock to give some idea of the great depth of the Fall, but I very nearly discovered, and just escaped myself being the plummet. In the excitement of the moment, and not thinking that the rock would be shiny and slippery with the everlasting spray, I went too rapidly forward, and the rock having a slight decline, I slipped, but was fortunately brought up by a juniper bush growing within a foot of the edge. For a second or two I lay on my back wondering if I could slide out of my difficulty as easily as I had slidden into it. In a moment I determined to go backwards on my back, hands, and feet, until I laid hold of another bush and could safely assume a perpendicular position. After giving the signal that "all was right", the plate was exposed, and I *cautiously* left a spot I have no desire to revisit.'[17]

It is clearly no slight coincidence that one of the acrobats who decided to cross Niagara

Falls on a tightrope (fig 5) was a photographer. Simon John Dixon was a Toronto photographer who first had the idea 'while crossing the suspension bridge on his way to attend the Photographers' Association of America at Washington'. On the first occasion Dixon indulged himself, in 1890, Mrs Dixon stayed in bed, on the second, she had hysterics on the river bank. Dixon survived.[18]

At home photography could be equally thrilling. The brothers Kearton made photographing nature an exciting business. Their picture of themselves up a tree with a ladder (fig 6) requires no commentary. Even without seeking risks, photographers regularly poisoned themselves or set their premises on fire. Valentine Blanchard described 'an event of a most unexpected character which took place in 1869'. He had filled four glass barrels

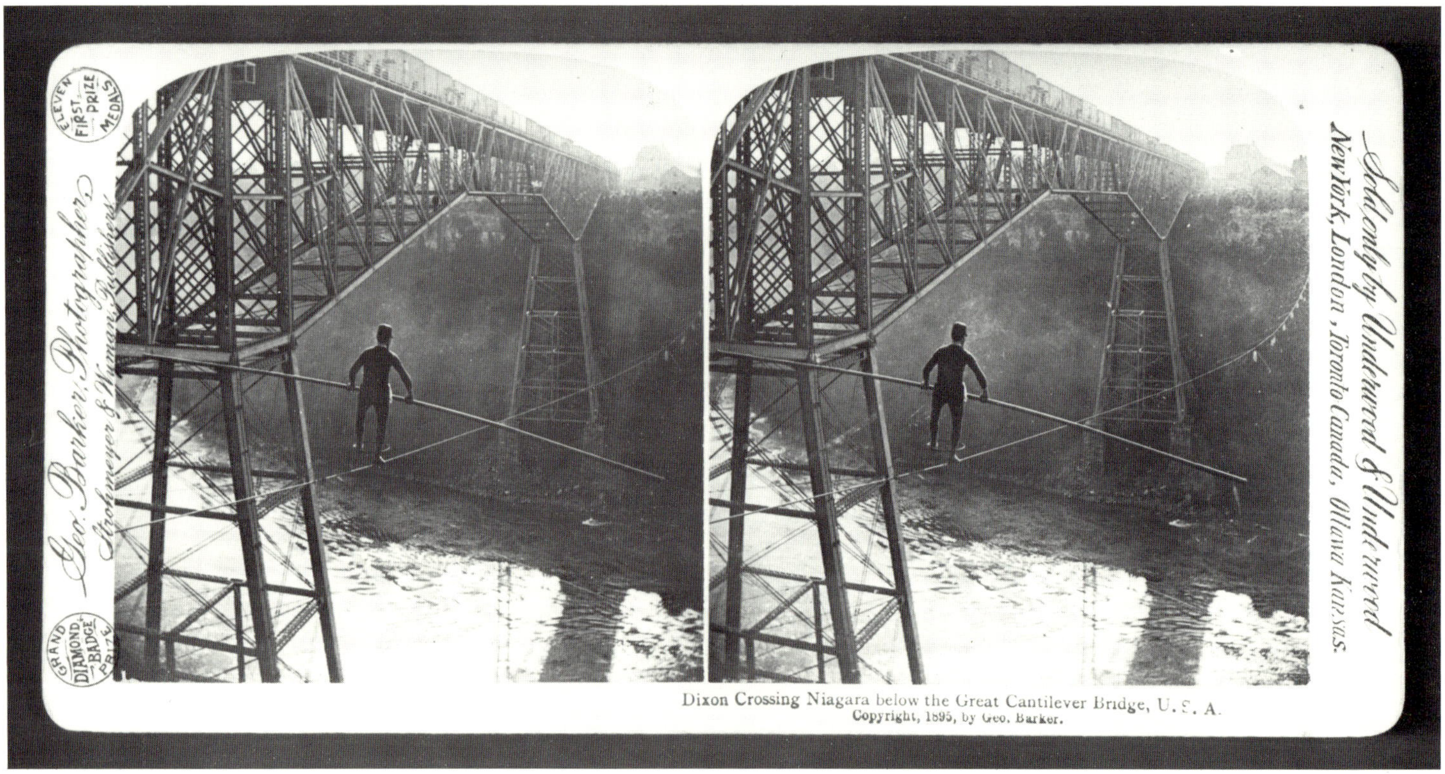

Figure 5
The photographer Simon John Dixon, crossing Niagara Falls, 1890
stereoscopic photograph by George Barker

with collodion in very cold weather and then stored them next to a warm room:

> '. . . the boy who assisted in printing came rushing in with staring eyes, and exclaimed that one of the barrels had gone crack! . . . I rushed to one of the windows, which fortunately opened outwards, and was in the act of pushing it as far open as possible so as to let out the fumes when — ? I cannot find a word to describe the sound. It was not like the sharp crack of near artillery, nor the roar of thunder; it was a hoarse boom, and instantly I was carried out with a force mightier than a gigantic wave of the sea, and deposited on a grass plot some twenty feet from the building. Immediately followed a series of thunder charges of artillery (probably from the explosion of the other barrels), and the sharp rattle of musketry, which was the roof of the studio sent flying skywards, and then descended a hailstorm of finely splintered glass. It was a great mercy to me that they were fine splinters for several entered the exposed part of my body . . . I picked out a few pieces of glass sticking variously in my head and my hands . . . I had now time to turn round and face the scene—and what a scene! The whole place was a raging furnace. There was no smoke; intensely white flames soared forty feet into the air, and through the openings in the wall formerly occupied by windows, I could see chairs, tables, cameras, stands, in fact, everything burnable, roaring away, each adding its contribution to the mighty blaze. In a very short space of time there were seven engines on the scene, but practically there was nothing to be done. They played upon the charred remains, but everything of value had been totally destroyed long before the firemen could commence action. A stream of gas from the place where the meter stood still blazed away and explained the cause of the catastrophe. I had altogether forgotten that gas arrangement.'[19]

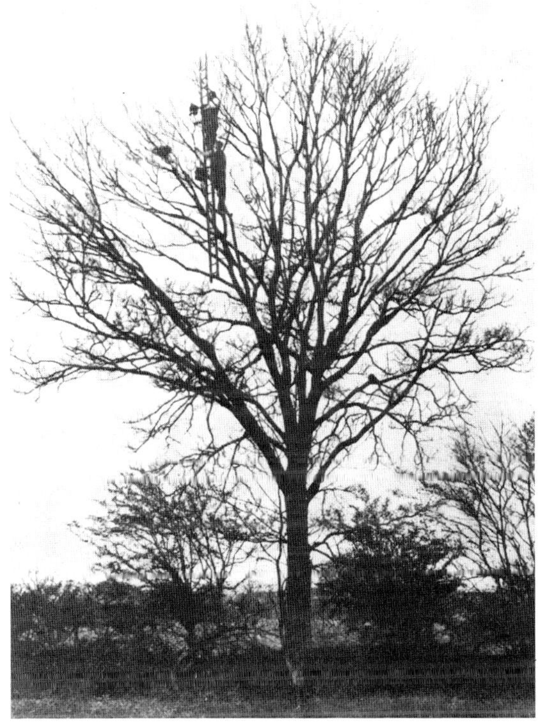

Figure 6
The Kearton brothers, natural history photographers, at work

'We have got the fruit of creation now and need not trouble ourselves with the core.'

The enthusiasm of the photographers and their readiness to ignore danger is a reflection of photography's importance as an extraordinary and exciting discovery—'sun painting', the 'divine art', the 'black art' (a pun on a combination of chemical stains and black magic). Above all it was 'the truth'. Early photographers were fascinated by the minute detail and the accidents of photography—the washing lines, the tiles on a roof or the chimney pots—all the details a painter might have omitted or drawn at random. Whether the photographer noticed them or not they would appear in the photograph accurately drawn. This remarkable fact has given photography a reputation for objective truth which would make the photographer merely a man who activates a machine. Joseph Ellis took this view in 1856:

> 'Many sit to the photographer as to a different kind of artist, without the slightest notion that they make their own portrait, express their disappointment that they are not presented with a handsome resemblance, and grumble both at the process and the photographer.'[20]

The belief that a photograph of a man contains some real part of him, his soul or his essence, is by no means confined to the 'primitive' races. A photograph can stand as a substitute for a person. In the Victorian age, a time of desperately high mortality, the value of the photograph could not be underestimated. Dr John Brown wrote of this in 1862:

> 'When death comes and you can never again see "him" or "her"—then how you take out these, it may be, wasted, shadowy, almost vanishing images—how you treasure them for ever, beyond all trim and graceful miniatures by man's hand. That is the very turn of the head, the shape of the bald head, the child's look you so well knew, the restrained smile, the waistcoat, the shawl—the *reality* you can never more forget or see—all are brought back to you, and in that *camera lucida* of your own brain, in that chamber of imagery, from out this poor, imperfect sun-sketch there blooms into life, untouched by time or change, your idea of that face.'[21]

In this way photography could halt the natural forces of time and decay. The same idea was at work in the commission given to Archibald Burns in 1871 (see catalogue entry) to photograph part of Edinburgh's Old Town before it was demolished. Several of the people involved in reforming the appalling slum areas of the city were antiquarians. To alleviate human distress, they advocated pulling down important historic buildings; to reduce their feelings of guilt about this destruction, they commissioned a series of photographs. By securing photographs of the buildings, they had preserved an accurate memory, a stand-in for reality.

A wholesale claim on the part of photography to be the truth did not, however, bear close analysis. Its limitations were obvious. For example, it was not until the end of the century that a practical method of colour photography was released to the public, so for a photograph to be coloured, someone had to sit down with a box of colours and paint on top of it. Again, it was impossible to take a photograph of a landscape with its true sky; the land was dark and the sky was light and the camera would take the one slowly or the other quickly, but not both together. Most nineteenth-century landscape photographs have a blanked-out white sky. If the clouds are there, they were probably taken on a separate negative and the two photographs combined to make one. Negatives of clouds were sold commercially for the purpose and by the 1880s the judges of photographic competitions were faced with walls of landscape photographs with the same commercial sky sitting neatly in dozens of different views.

Another problem examined in the 1850s, was an imbalance in the reaction of the photographic chemicals to the colours of a subject: the monochrome photograph would not record colours, as we would expect, in their equivalent tones. Robert Hunt in 1852 considered the problems of photographing a lady:

> '. . . possessing a somewhat jaundiced face and yellow hair—we will imagine her to wear a dark blue bonnet— and we will allow our fancied fair one to wear a violet silk dress, a purple mantle, and give them an abundant trimming of yellow or gold colour. The daguerreotype or calotype portrait of such a lady would have a *dark*—almost mulatto face and black hair, the dress and the mantle would be different tones of white, and the yellow trimming an *intense* black. This peculiar result—which we should never expect by any system of *a priori* reasoning, is proved to be dependent on the interfering influences of light—those colours which produce the most intense illumination giving the smallest amount of chemical action and the contrary.'[22]

Green trees were notoriously difficult to photograph: 'If done with the slower paper process, are black, and from the movement, uncertain webs against the white sky—if by collodion, they look as if worked in dark cambric, or stippled with innumerable black and white specks; in either case missing all the breadth and gradations of nature.'[23]

One of the curiosities of the nineteenth century is that a great deal of the naturalness and truth which we think of as the province of photography continued to be the province of the painters and draughtsmen for a surprisingly long time. Stranger than that, it is becoming clear that certain ways of seeing, which we think of now as photographic, were discovered by the painters before photography was invented.

The art critic, Lady Eastlake, was disconcerted to find in 1846 that Constable whom 'we had not sufficiently prized before'[24] had been producing true effects, which she had not recognised until the invention of photography proved him right. Constable's skill in painting shifting weather conditions, which he recalled by a concentrated effort of mind and hand was ahead of the camera's skill for much of the century. Similarly the ability to capture and record fleeting expressions remained in the hands of artists like Daumier. The ability to freeze a moment, to take a snapshot, was acquired by the realm of photography only about fifty years after its invention.

It was of course argued by the supporters of photography that the deficiencies of the photograph were temporary and to a great degree they were right. In 1884 Oliver Wendell Holmes predicted a future life in which *'Form is henceforth divorced from matter.*

In fact, matter as a visible object is of no great use any longer, except as the mould on which form is shaped. Give us a few negatives of a thing worth seeing, taken from different points of view, and that is all we want of it. Pull it down or burn it up, if you please—we have got the fruit of creation now, and need not trouble ourselves with the core.'[25] Holmes was talking about the stereoscopic photograph, popular from the mid-1850s through into the twentieth century, which was the kind of photography capable of the greatest illusion of truth. The stereograph was two photographs taken side by side at a distance from each other proportionate to the distance between the human eyes. When seen through a binocular viewer the photographs combined to give a three-dimensional effect.

Holmes was echoed with less wit but with an evangelistic salesman's belief in the great advantages of his product by M S Emery in 1902, introducing a set of stereographs of Mont Blanc:

> 'The cows feeding on a Swiss "alp" or mountain pasture experience all the physical facts of seeing Swiss scenery, but they never attain to the truer mental and spiritual reality of seeing Switzerland with the mind. The material facts are only the raw stuff out of which genuine realities may be wrought in the workshop of the receptive, active mind . . . There are people who make long journeys to famous places merely for the sake of being able to say they have been there. Stereographs will not satisfy that cheap ambition. There are people who go about writing their names on observation towers and chipping little bits of stone off famous monuments to carry home in their pockets. Stereographs cannot be of much use to travellers of that poor sort, either. But with most of us, the chief satisfaction and joy of travel consist in seeing the grandeur and beauty of "this goodly frame, the earth"; in seeing how the world looks in spots made famous by great events or by men who lived there; in seeing how other men live now, and what sights of earth and sky are woven into their daily life-experience. If this is what we want, the sensible, thoughtful use of stereographs cannot be overestimated as a practical means of enlarging our knowledge and multiplying our delight.'[26]

'Why, you little beauty! how long have you been our cook?'

The enthusiastic conviction in Emery's salesman's pitch makes the stereograph particularly interesting as historical evidence. The 'cleverness' of this kind of photography made it a natural source of education and entertainment because it could catch and hold the attention. It was one of the forerunners of the cinema, and series of stereo cards could act like a newsreel or as a way of telling stories. Like television it presented not only the supposedly virtuous educational programmes but the popular programmes, which are always defended so weakly as 'what the public wants'. The sale of stereoscopic photographs was a vast commercial business involving door to door salesmen selling hundreds of thousands of views. The photographs are, as a result, a fair guide to the way people thought, not just publicly but privately.

The stereograph was especially effective for wonderful ephemeral events. Because it had a greater illusion of reality than a single photograph, it had a natural affinity to the more bizarre truths—the people who crossed Niagara Falls the *hard* way (fig 7) or the Prune Knight at the Columbian Exposition (fig 8) on his boastful plinth, 'Horse and rider made of prunes. In 1891 Santa Clara County California produced 20,000,000 lbs of prunes—Balance of the United States—9,000,000 lbs.' Reason and good sense prevent us from believing that any woman in her right mind would cross Niagara Falls on a tightrope wearing buckets on her feet or that making a life-size statue out of prunes would strike anyone as a seriously good idea; but there are the photographs and it is indeed true.

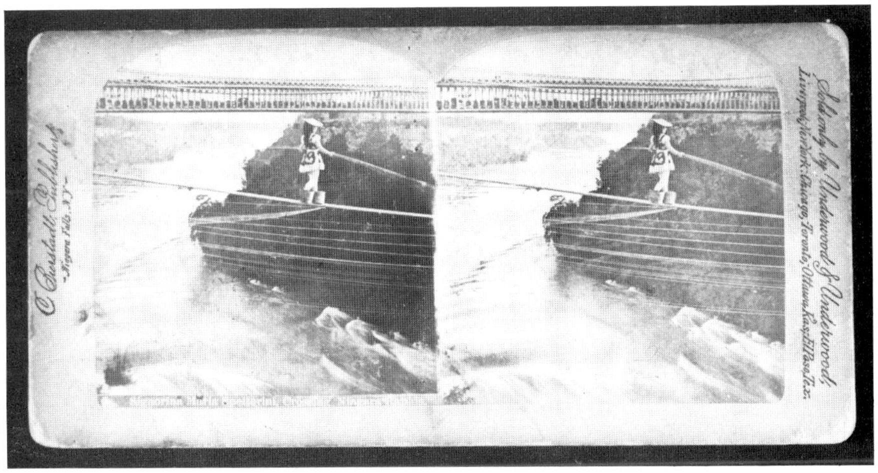

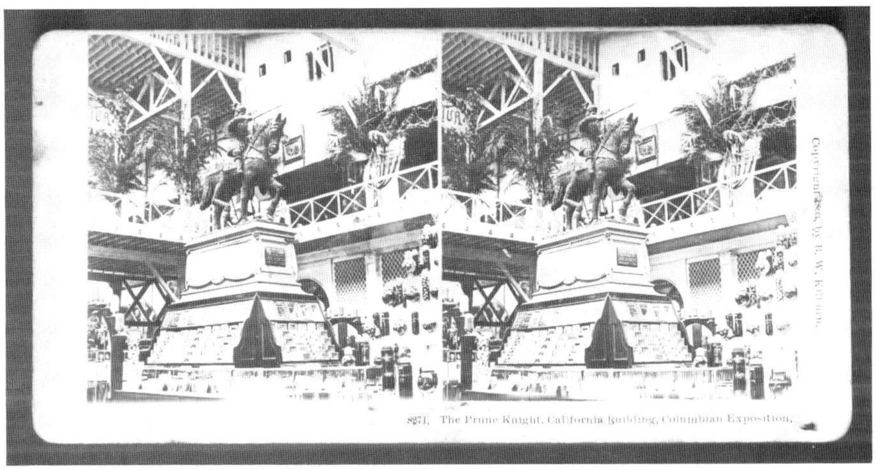

Figure 7
Signorina Maria Spelterini crossing Niagara Falls with buckets on her feet in 1876
stereoscopic photograph published by C Bierstadt

Figure 8
'The Prune Knight', made of Californian prunes for the Columbian Exposition in 1891
stereoscopic photograph by B W Kilburn

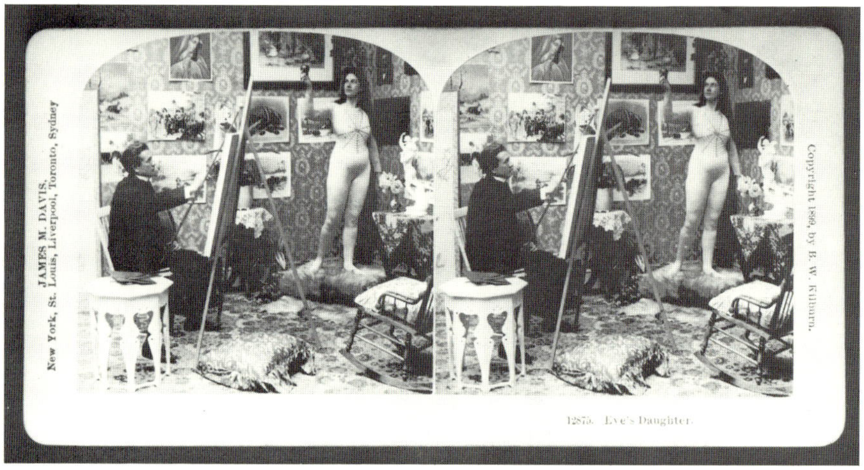

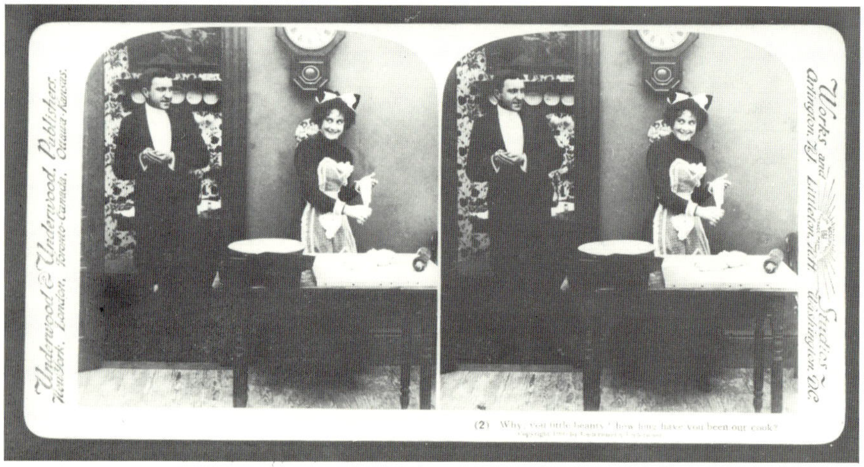

Figure 9
'Eve's Daughter' stereoscopic photograph by B W Kilburn

Figure 10
'Why, you little beauty! how long have you been our cook?' stereoscopic photograph by Underwood and Underwood

Stereocards were looked at through a viewer held up to the eyes. Effectively you were alone with the photograph. Not surprisingly, many of the indecent photographs came out in stereoscopic form. But the stereoscope was a family affair, suitable for the front room and Sunday viewing, so many of these photographs adopted a respectable gloss either by pretending to a jocular narrative reason for looking at women's ankles, such as 'An Unexpected Wave' or by surrounding the undressed woman with the intellectual respectability of art. A good example of this method is 'Eve's Daughter' (fig 9). The woman is in fact fully clothed in a close-fitting body-stocking but it conceals nothing of her splendid figure. She is respectable because she is a biblical subject and is posing for an artist. The artist's own respectability is manifest—this is no dubious Bohemian in a loose cravat—his dark suit, firmly buttoned up, his white, apparently clerical, collar, the Madonna on his wall amongst the singularly innocuous paintings, the fact that he owns *two* tablecloths and an aspidistra, the rocking chair conveniently placed for his mother are all evidence of impeccable moral purity. This photograph was clearly intended to disarm moral criticism before it was offered: a kind of parlour titillation.

Amongst the staged, humorous or storytelling cards certain themes predominate. There was a great deal of racial stereotyping: Scots meeting in the rye, saucy French maids (fig 10), Irish being illogical and negroes being cheerful against impossible odds. By the end of the century, stereoscopic photography was joining battle with the fearful dangers of the New Woman. These cards, like the one of 'Eve's Daughter' are notable for the wealth of meaningful detail, the care with which the

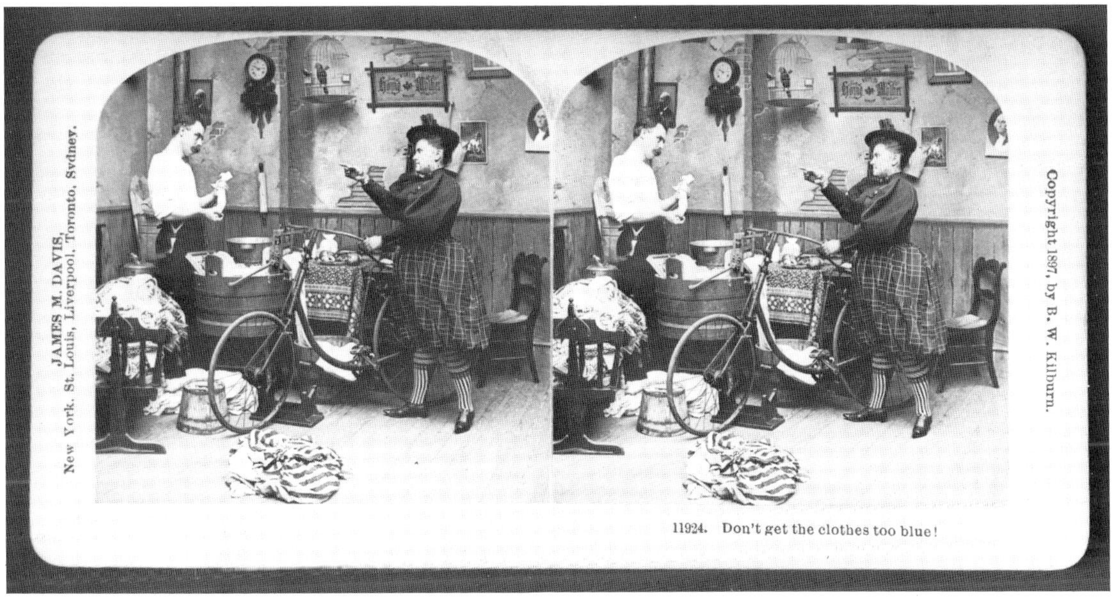

Figure 11
The New Woman, 'Don't get the clothes too blue!' stereoscopic photograph by B W Kilburn

image of the mannish, neglectful woman is built up (fig 11). The house is disordered, the woman is either reading in the middle of the day, or about to leave on a bicycle, plaster has fallen from the walls, a rolling pin and a parrot figure prominently, and in case the viewer misses those, a plaque on the wall snarls, 'What is home without a mother?' Worst of all, the sad, drooping husband is either cooking the dinner or washing the clothes. Womanhood could sink no lower.

The careful elaboration of such stereocards, the crowded stage sets and the actors trained to hold suitable poses and expressions, was notably clever.

But . . .

'The Devil whispered among the leaves
It's clever but is it Art?'

The vexed questions, 'What is truth?', 'What is art?', have bedevilled photography throughout its history. Its critics claimed that the faults of photography undermined its pretensions to truth: the very accuracies of photography damaged its claim to art.

In 1857 the art critic, Lady Eastlake, looking at the improved collodion and albumen processes which were faster, clearer and more detailed than the early calotype process, concluded:

> 'Far from holding the mirror up to nature, which is an assumption usually as triumphant as it is erroneous, it holds up that which, however beautiful, ingenious, and valuable in powers of reflection, is yet subject to certain distortions and deficiencies for which there is no remedy. The science therefore which has developed the resources of photography, has but more glaringly betrayed its defects. For the more perfect you render an imperfect machine the more must its imperfections come to light: it is superfluous therefore to ask whether Art has benefited, where Nature, its only source and model, has been but more accurately falsified. If the photograph in its early and imperfect state was more consonant to our feelings for art, it is because, as far as it went, it was more true to our experience of Nature. Mere broad light and shade, with the correctness of general forms and absence of all convention, which are the beautiful conditions of photography, will, when nothing further is attempted, give artistic pleasure of a very high kind; it is only when greater precision and detail are superadded that the eye misses the further truths which should accompany the further finish.'[27]

Lady Eastlake's 1857 article is famous. It is less well known that ten years earlier she wrote an adverse review of the realistic modern school of painting in Germany (painters like Overbeck, Schadow and Sohn), which contained a wholesale endorsement of photography:

> 'One standard, however, there does exist, and one from which there is no appeal, for it rests upon demonstration, and not upon opinion. This is to be found in that wonderful source recently discovered—the only sure test for those artists who, professing to reflect Nature in their works, can by Nature herself only be judged: we mean the beautiful and wonderful Calotype drawings—so precious in every artist's sight, not only for their matchless truth of Nature, but as the triumphant proof of all to be most revered as truth in art . . . Every truth that art and genius has yet succeeded in seizing here finds its prototype.'[28]

Lady Eastlake was talking specifically about the photographs taken by David Octavius Hill and Robert Adamson in the calotype process, which was the first negative/positive process and produced a coarse, generalised print. The tempered enthusiasm of the 1857 article is, however, not *just* due to the shiny, precise effects of collodion. It must be remembered that the calotype was not the only form of early photography. The daguerreotype, a unique image printed on a shiny silver surface had all the same characteristics of precise, miniature detail that the albumen and collodion processes later achieved. In 1846, Lady Eastlake dismissed the daguerreotype in a footnote—'so different in every respect'—without explaining her dislike of it. By 1857, the paper calotype process had been usurped by the albumen and collodion processes which took photography as a whole in the direction of the daguerreotype, that is to say towards high finish and exaggerated realism.

Lady Eastlake preferred the coarser process which she had seen in the hands of the brilliant photographic partnership of David Octavius Hill and Robert Adamson. Hill himself said of the calotype:

> 'The rough and unequal texture throughout the paper is the main cause of the calotype failing in details before the Daguerreotype . . . and this is the very life of it. They look like the imperfect work of man . . . and not the much diminished perfect work of God.'[29]

Henry Peach Robinson, who was an authoritative and prolific writer on the art of photography, expressed the problem of photography in much the same way at the end of the century: 'Every other kind of artist but the photographer knows that there is little fear of his coming too near to nature; the photographer has to fear his work becoming too easily a thoughtless mirror.'[30]

If the way we see involved only a straightforward need for literal truth, the more realistic waxwork would have replaced portrait painting. Three-dimensional photography, whether the nineteenth-century photo-sculpture or the twentieth-century hologram, would have taken over from two-dimensional. Our mantlepieces would be loaded with little standing figures of our families and friends. The fact that we are not seeking realism alone, but qualities such as liveliness, means that we are looking for pictures which appeal to the mind in photography as in painting.

It is in searching for this direct appeal to the mind that art is called in, and it is this kind of search which makes the idea of a generalised, unfocused photograph acceptable. It does not of course follow that an unfocused photograph will automatically be more artistic, but lack of focus can help to evade the photographic problem of too much reality.

The problem was not however purely a photographic one. The painters had already identified the same danger well before the invention of photography and had drawn up their defences. As an example, the Royal Scottish Academy of the day specifically excluded 'mere transcripts of the objects of natural history'. Certain kinds of painting were simply mechanically accurate products serving to provide direct information about the object depicted.

There is no distinction between painting or drawing and photography that can say that photography tells the truth in a mechanical way while the painters use the skill of their hands. Painters require manipulative skill to achieve their results—a knowledge of paint, of brushes, of basic techniques—just as the photographer needs to know how to use his camera. Without expertise in the mechanical side of their work, neither the painter nor the photographer could produce anything at all.

The painters knew one kind of camera before it became the province of photography. The *camera obscura* was a drawing machine, projecting a picture through the lens onto a piece of paper where the painter could draw around the outlines of the landscape or buildings before him. This camera drawing was a mechanical substitute for the reality, which could be carried back to the studio and worked on.

The hostility to photography as an art was based on the argument that the camera was a mechanical aid when the painters used it. Extend its use so that the chemically-impregnated paper takes its own picture and even the artist's drawing skill is made redundant. So where was the art?

The definition of art, which influential painters like Sir Joshua Reynolds laid down before the invention of photography, was that art involved the ideal. It was based on the natural truths of accurate delineation but was then worked up by the artist towards an ideal *poetic* truth. That is to say, the artists were using the intelligence and the emotions to filter the information which came directly to the eye, and were translating the truth into paintings which would appeal to the intelligence and emotions of their audience.

The theoretical objection to photography, that it had no involvement with the ideal, was reinforced by a simple practical fact. Vast numbers of poor photographs were taken between the 1850s and the end of the century. The first excitement and enthusiasm for photography was substantially undermined by the weight of inferior photographs which enabled the painters to dismiss photography cheerfully. In 1896 H P Robinson remarked:

> 'The one intolerable defect in modern art is dullness. Now this is the prevailing feature of photography, and it has been unfortunate—let us hope an aberration of the past—that any attempt at originality in our art has been perhaps not a little snubbed by some of those who have acted as its foster-nurses but were perhaps afraid of finding forward children "grow out of their knowledge". I say it with many apologies for the discovery and much regret, that in a thousand photographs, nine hundred are all alike except in subject, and all are dull . . . As Sydney Smith said of a volume of sermons, "Their characteristic is decent debility."'[31]

The photographers defended their art in several ways. Clearly enough the camera did not take the photograph unaided, however inept the photographer. Moreover, photography was not as easy as it looked. Naturalism was not the same thing as the bald truth and the most 'natural' effects required an artist's skill in creating nature. Considering, as an example, the conditions of studio photography throughout the century, with the nervous sitter clamped into position, the majority of portrait photographs are true only in the sense that they show the position of the ears or the shape of the nose; the familiar vivid person escapes the camera. The impressive and relaxed portraits were taken by photographers capable of posing and keeping a sitter interested during the uncomfortable operation. In 1845 David Octavius Hill said, of composing such photographs, 'the arrangement of the picture is as much an effort of the artist as if he was in reality going to paint it.'[32] Nor was the landscape photographer pointing his camera at random at the view. He could choose his viewpoint, he could cut down trees, he could wait until the subject changed naturally.

H P Robinson advocated another kind of naturalism. He was famous for his composite groups (made up from several negatives) of 'natural' country scenes—happy girls bringing home the may or gossiping in a lane. He found that real-life models turned wooden when asked to pose, so Robinson chose models who could *look* natural. He went to considerable and sometimes startling lengths to achieve the right results:

> 'It is almost as difficult to get variety in dresses as in persons. I always endeavour to secure a picturesque dress when I see it. It is not always easy to explain what you really mean when you meet a girl in a lonely country lane, and you offer to buy her clothes, but a little perseverance and a good offer usually succeed. A country girl's dress is not often worth more than eighteen pence, and if you turn the pence into shillings, and look business-like all the time, you may make pretty sure of walking off with the property, or, at all events, getting it sent to you the next day.'[33]

In Robinson's terms, his models looked more truly natural in the unnatural conditions of photography than real country girls would have done. A second method of achieving this 'ideal' naturalism was to select the subject matter with such care as to exclude the inartistic.

Peter Henry Emerson, who was one of H P Robinson's most acid opponents, took the view that selection and long consideration were essential. His recommendations include:

> 'For a tennis picture, fine girls, physically well-formed, should be chosen . . . The model's dress should be very simple and well-fitting, such dresses as were worn by Botticelli's women. . . The best material for dresses for pictures is a coarse, limp, self-coloured muslin (butter-cloth is excellent for the purpose). All jewelry should be eschewed.' When it came to landscape, Emerson was yet more exclusive: 'All nature near towns is tinged with artificiality, it may not be very patent but the close observer detects it. Among fisher-folk this may be seen in the sealskin cap, in the rustic it shows itself in the hard, billycock hat, in landscape pure it may be seen in some artificial forms of the river-banks, or in artificial undergrowths; the work of the beast, the stamp of vulgarity, that hydra-headed monster which always appears whenever a few men are gathered together, is sure to be found somewhere. For this reason then the would-be landscape photographer should pack up his things and go to some locality with which he is in sympathy, just as a painter does.'[34]

Emerson's dictates sound distressingly exclusive and archaic but he was expressing opinions held by contemporary painters and, more interesting, he was expressing the attitudes most modern amateur (and many professional) photographers still hold to. No more than Emerson do we take photographs of factories and we would always prefer to photograph a Highlander in full Highland dress rather than one in an anorak and gumboots. We, like Emerson, photograph the beautiful and the picturesque with the idea that this will make our photographs beautiful and picturesque.

An alternative way of making photography more acceptably artistic was to make alterations to the negative and the print during processing. This idea was the source of a bitter quarrel in the photography camp.

After 1857, the generous enthusiasm of the small numbers who pioneered photography was swamped by thousands of new photographers all with their own ideas on the subject. The photographic societies and journals were dominated by discussions of chemistry and equipment. Photographic exhibitions raised the terrible question of judging excellence in a photograph. One side said technical perfection should be judged first, the other said, no, art is more important. Technical perfection was dismissed on the opinion of the miniature painter, Sir William Newton, that an out-of-focus photograph could be better than a focused one: 'their appearance ought not to be so *chemically,* as *artistically* beautiful.'[35] The most important photographer in the deliberately out-of-focus fashion was Julia Margaret Cameron whose excellent large-scale portraits taken in the 1860s and 1870s were commonly marred by chemical stains and imperfections. The embarrassing corollary of this was a cheerful assumption that a messy or out-of-focus print would *necessarily* be more artistic.

The cavalier approach to chemistry and technique was not calculated to endear the artists to the technicians, but Julia Margaret Cameron's art was at least photographic. She boasted of never touching up or improving her negatives and prints.

Others boasted of the opposite. Paint on top of a photograph, they said, and *that* will make it art. Touch up the negative to remove the spots and wrinkles and a portrait will become ideal. At the end of the century, a further group of photographers decided that art-photography might be divorced from its dubious mechanical background if the prints were not merely touched up but actually manipulated. One of the principal photographers of this kind was Robert Demachy who wrote in *Camera Work* in 1907:

> 'The photographic character is, and always has been, an anti-artistic character and the mechanically produced print from an unretouched negative will always have in the eyes of a true artist faults in values and absences of accents against which the special qualities so loudly proclaimed will not count for much.'[36]

Demachy favoured the gum-bichromate and the oil-pigment processes both of which were comparatively easy to manipulate and both of which bore a physical resemblance to oil-painting.

Photography spent much of the nineteenth century dogging the heels of the painters and engravers, and many of its failures can be attributed to its attempts to imitate the other media. Held up against a painting, the photograph lacked the impact of colour and scale and where it was attempting to follow the painting tradition it was bound to lose out. It was also misguided.

George Bernard Shaw, one of the most vigorous defenders of photography, attacked photography's attempts to follow painting in response to Demachy's views:

> 'I say that a photographer imitating the work of a draughtsman is like a man imitating the noises of a barnyard: he may do it very cleverly, but it is an unpardonable condescension all the same. Also, he is substituting an easy, limited, and exhausted process for a difficult one which has never yet been pushed to the limit of its possibilities. He fails in respect for his art. He is a

traitor in the photographic camp. If he really prefers the old methods, let him practise them in the old way, and leave the genuine old-fashioned mark of the human finger and thumb on his copies of Nature; for the camera will never catch the true flavour of that quaint bungling; and even if it could, humanity would rightly refuse to concede to it that allowance which we make so willingly for the infirmity of the painter's hand, and the clumsiness of his medium. We can stand things from Corot that we would not stand for a moment from Demachy.'[37]

Art is an uncertain and changing concept. Lady Eastlake remarked, 'of all the delusions which possess the human breast, few are so intractable as those about art.'[38] Attempts to draw lines and barriers around the subject and to define it in some neat verbal fashion are doomed to failure, partly because of the historical process. The art of one generation is not the art of the next and what has been condemned as outside the pale of art can be brought into the fold at a later date.

This puts us in a happy position with regard to nineteenth-century photography. We may ignore the limiting strictures of Robinson and Emerson and look directly at the material. Certainly photography was a limited, constrained art form, but by a convenient paradox it is often when art is most constrained that it may flourish; there are greater works scribbled in pencil on the backs of envelopes than there may be on canvas in full technicolour. Photography was a comparatively cheap and easy art-form which attracted none of the weighty respect reserved for painting, but painting bore also the weight of convention and public expectation. Photographers could take risks, break with convention and experiment with far greater ease. Where photography has led, painting has followed.

The vast quantities of poor photographs taken during the last one hundred and fifty years might oppress photography, dull the eye and depress the mind: 'Photographs possessing all the desirable points are as scarce and valuable as the gems of India or Brazil, and thousands of multiplied copies of the one are as common and worthless as the counterfeit glass imitations of the other.'[39] The passing of time gives an antiquarian interest and charm to much of the commonplace of the past and many of the images will be redeemed in that way. The fact remains that after rejecting hundreds of thousands of run-of-the-mill photographs, there are still hundreds of thousands of photographic pictures left which light up the eye and mind, which take us beyond academic criticism into simple pleasure. Moreover, photography is so big a subject that it is substantially unresearched. We are at liberty to enjoy that rare experience of choosing our own aesthetic pleasures from the work of nameless photographers and unidentified subjects.

The photographs in this book have been chosen with this idea in mind. Mr Riddell's collection was made with a generous, wide-reaching enthusiasm for nineteenth-century photography which is still well in advance of the textbooks on the history of the subject. The choice is intended to show the collection, not as a neatly-defined package fitting within the established canons of photographic history, but as an untapped source of knowledge and aesthetic pleasure: a real photographic goldmine.

1 The note on Mr Riddell's life was kindly supplied by his family

2 George Mason, 'Joe', *Pictures in Black and White,* no date

3 Albert Sands Southworth, 'The Early History of Photography in the United States', 1871, reprinted in *Photography: Essays and Images,* ed Beaumont Newhall, 1980, p 41

4 Lady Eastlake, untitled review, *The Quarterly Review,* 1857, p 457

5 John Werge, *The Evolution of Photography*, 1890, p 102

6 Henry Mayhew, *London Labour and the London Poor,* vol III 1861, pp 206–7

7 *The Art Journal,* 1857

8 'A Head Rest Fifteen Years Ago', *The Photographic News,* vol X 1866, p 516, quoted from *The Magazine of Science,* vol I 1841, p 272

9 William Lake Price, *A Manual of Photographic Manipulation,* 1858, p 152

10 *ibid,* p 154

11 Review of the Photographic Society of Scotland's exhibition, *Caledonian Mercury,* 24 December 1864

12 Dr John Brown, 'Mr Hill's Calotypes', *Scotsman,* 10 February 1862. Despite the title of the review, John Brown is not referring to D O Hill's photographs in this passage

13 W Ingles Roger, 'Incidental Experiences', *The British Journal Photographic Almanac,* ed J Traill Taylor, 1888, p 397

14 Advertisements in *The British Journal of Photography,* 7 March and 1 April 1890, pp 159 and 255

15 Samuel Bourne, 'A Photographic Journey through the Higher Himalayas', *The British Journal of Photography,* 24 December 1869, p 614

16 *ibid*

17 John Werge, *op cit* pp 141–2

18 I am grateful to Joan Schwartz for providing me with the full, hair-raising account of this photographer's career

19 'Our leaders No 38 Valentine Blanchard', *The Practical Photographer,* vol IX October 1898, p 289

20 Joseph Ellis, quoted in 'The Progress of Photography', *Illustrated London News,* 27 September 1856, p 321

21 Dr John Brown, *op cit*

22 Robert Hunt, 'Photography', *The Art Journal,* April 1852

23 Lady Eastlake, *op cit*

24 Lady Eastlake, untitled review of books on modern German painting, *The Quarterly Review,* March 1846, p 338

25 Oliver Wendell Holmes, 'The Stereoscope and the Stereograph', *Soundings from the Atlantic,* 1864, p 161

26 M S Emery, *Mont Blanc,* 1902, pp 32 and 34

27 Lady Eastlake, *op cit* note 4

28 Lady Eastlake, *op cit* note 25. This review is anonymous, like the 1857 review, but bears all the hallmarks of Lady Eastlake's style and opinions

29 Letter from David Octavius Hill to Mr Bicknell, 17 January 1848, quoted in Colin Ford and Roy Strong, *An Early Victorian Album. The photographic masterpieces (1843-1847) of David Octavius Hill and Robert Adamson,* 1976, p 30

30 Henry Peach Robinson, *The Elements of a Pictorial Photograph,* 1896, p 26

31 *ibid,* p 37

32 Letter from David Octavius Hill to David Roberts, 12 March 1845, in a private collection, quoted in Sara Stevenson 'Cold buckets of ignorant criticism: Qualified success in the partnership of David Octavius Hill and Robert Adamson', *The Photographic Collector,* vol IV Winter 1983, p 337

33 Henry Peach Robinson, *Picture-making by Photography,* 1897, 5th edition, pp 53–4

34 Peter Henry Emerson, *Naturalistic Photography,* 1899, book 3, pp 20–23

35 Sir William Newton, 'Upon Photography in an Artistic View, and its Relation to the Arts', 1853, reprinted in *Photography: Essays and Images,* ed Beaumont Newhall, 1980, p 79

36 Robert Demachy, 'Monsieur Demachy and English Photographic Art', *Camera Work,* April 1907, no 18, p 44

37 George Bernard Shaw, *Camera Work,* April 1907, no 18, p 45

38 Lady Eastlake, *op cit* note 4

39 Albert Sands Southworth, *op cit* p 41

The photographic chemists experimented with an enormous range of materials during the nineteenth century. The processes mentioned in the catalogue are as follows:

1 *The daguerreotype:* a single, positive photograph on a copper plate coated with silver giving a clear, detailed image, usually in a hinged leather case, popular between 1840 and 1855.

2 *The calotype:* a negative and positive process on good drawing or writing paper, brown or purplish in colour resulting in a coarse image, popular between 1840 and 1855. Photographers who liked the generalised effects of the calotype process used an equivalent of the calotype positive, which is also known as the 'salted paper print', in printing from later, improved kinds of photographic negative, specifically the waxed paper and the collodion negatives.

3 *The albumen print:* made from a negative and positive process which used a film of egg white or collodion on a glass plate for the negative and a film of egg white on smooth paper for the positive. The result was a clear, detailed image, brown in colour, popular between 1850 and 1890.

4 *The carbon print:* a positive made from a negative using a layer of gelatine on the print. The image was made in relief in the gelatine, the dense areas dark and the thin areas light. The colour was added to the photograph as a dye or pigment, rather than being a natural result of the process, so it could be any colour from brown to pink or pea-green. Popular between 1870 and 1910.

5 *The platinum process:* a negative and positive process using plain paper, usually dense black in colour, a comparatively coarse image. Popular between 1880 and 1910.

6 *Photogravure:* a printing process in which the image was photographically imprinted onto gelatine spread on a copper plate and then transferred in ink onto paper.

Note: for an efficient and comprehensible guide to nineteenth-century photographic processes see, Brian Coe and Mark Haworth-Booth, *A Guide to Early Photographic Processes,* 1983.

Measurements in the catalogue are in metres, height preceding width.

Plate 1 ANNAN & SONS
Glasgow Harbour Series No 1
1894

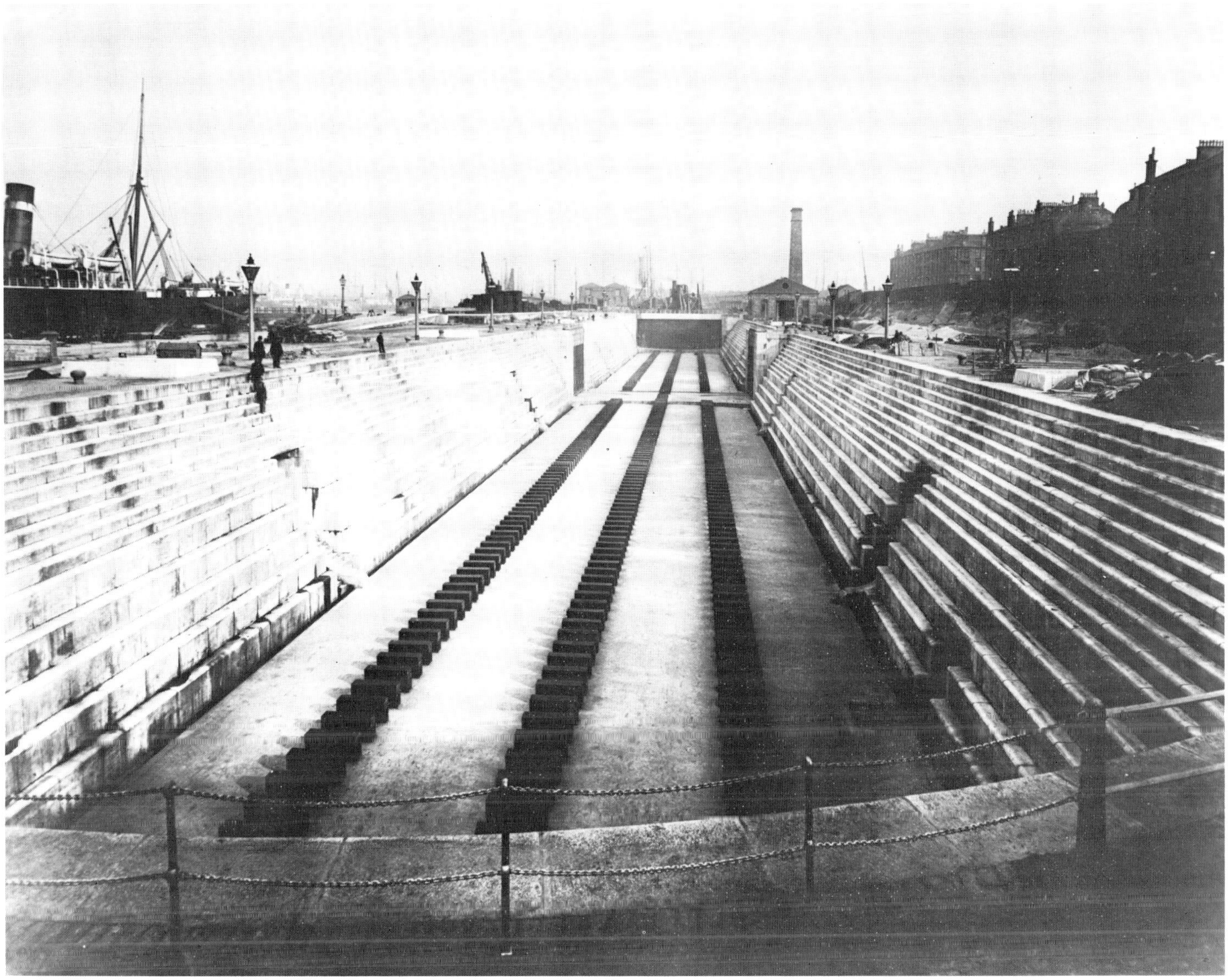

Plate 2 ANNAN & SONS
Glasgow Harbour Series No 3
1898

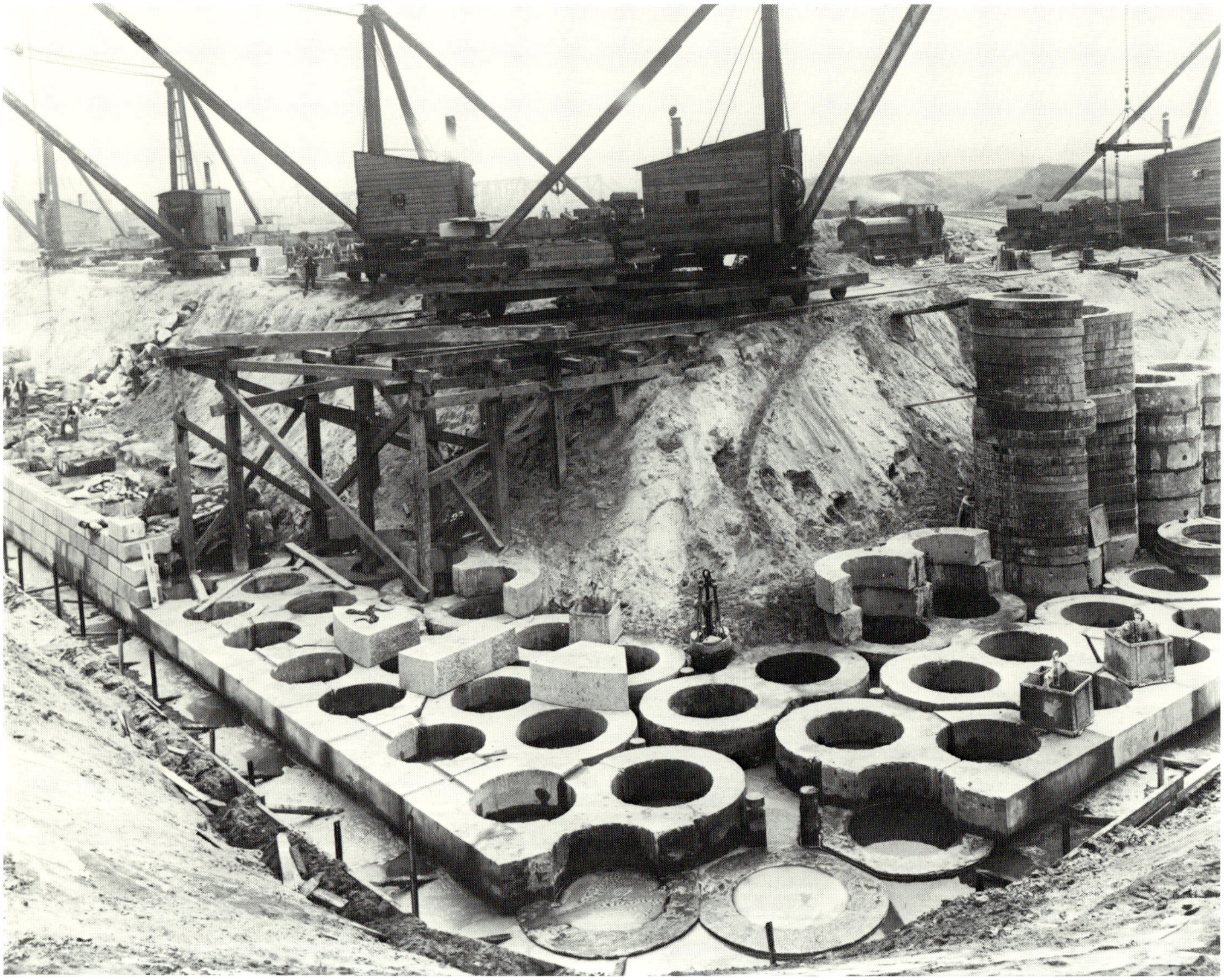

Plate 3 JAMES CRAIG ANNAN
A Utrecht Pastoral
1892

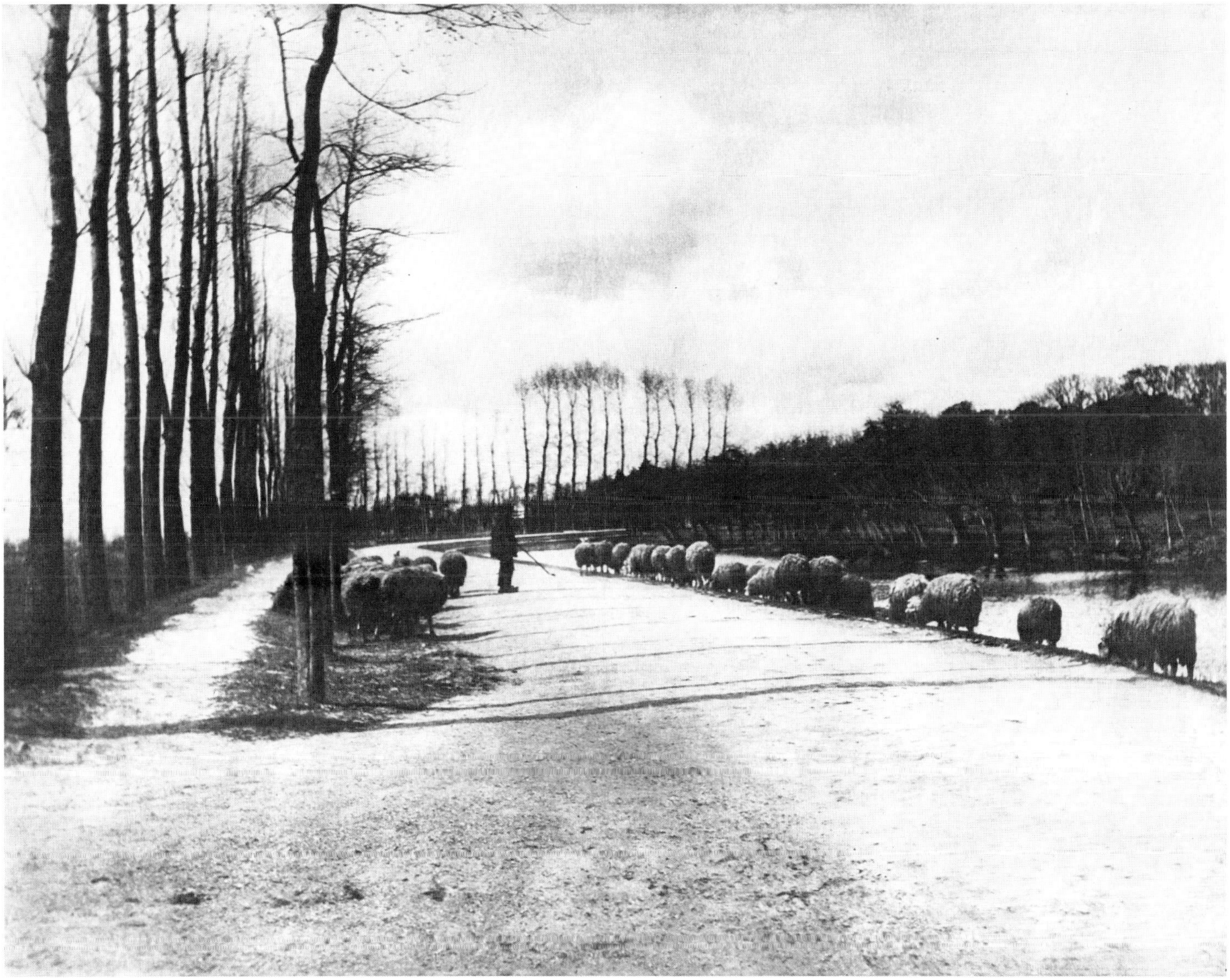

Plate 4 JAMES CRAIG ANNAN
A Genoa Harbour
1894

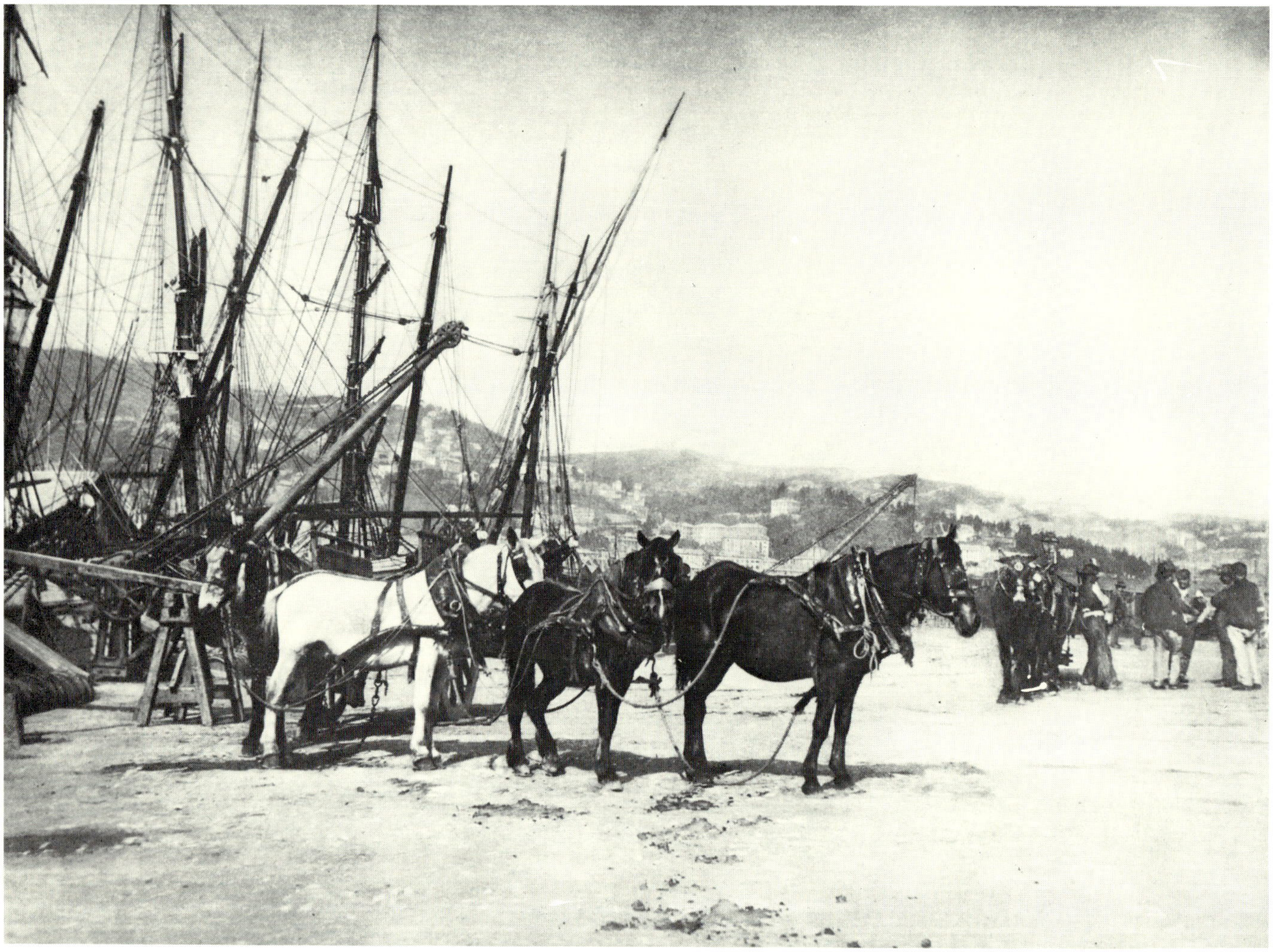

Plate 5 JAMES CRAIG ANNAN
Harlech Castle
about 1908–9

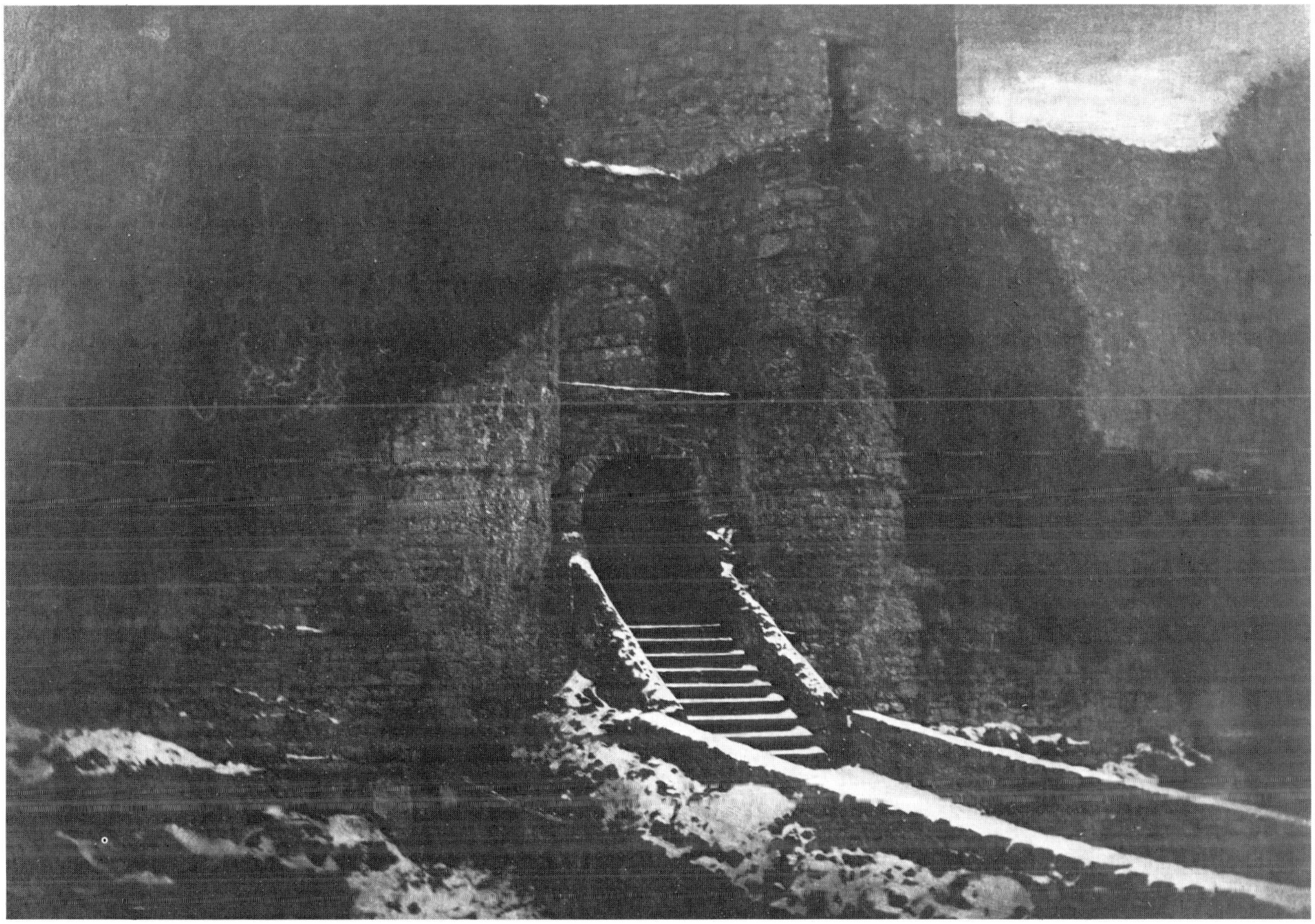

Plate 6 JAMES CRAIG ANNAN
Miss Dacre
1906

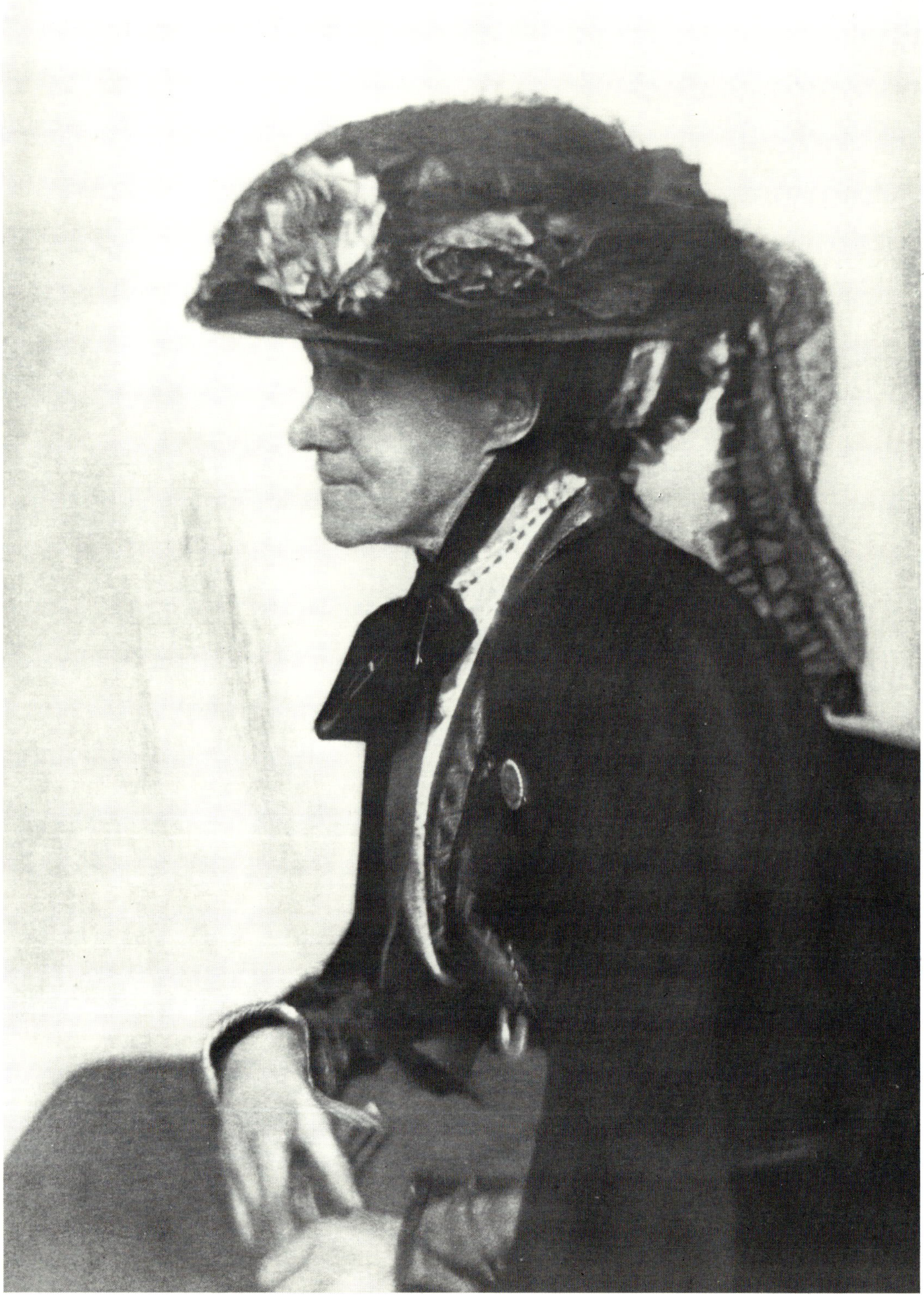

Plate 7 PLATT D BABBITT
Group at Niagara Falls
about 1855

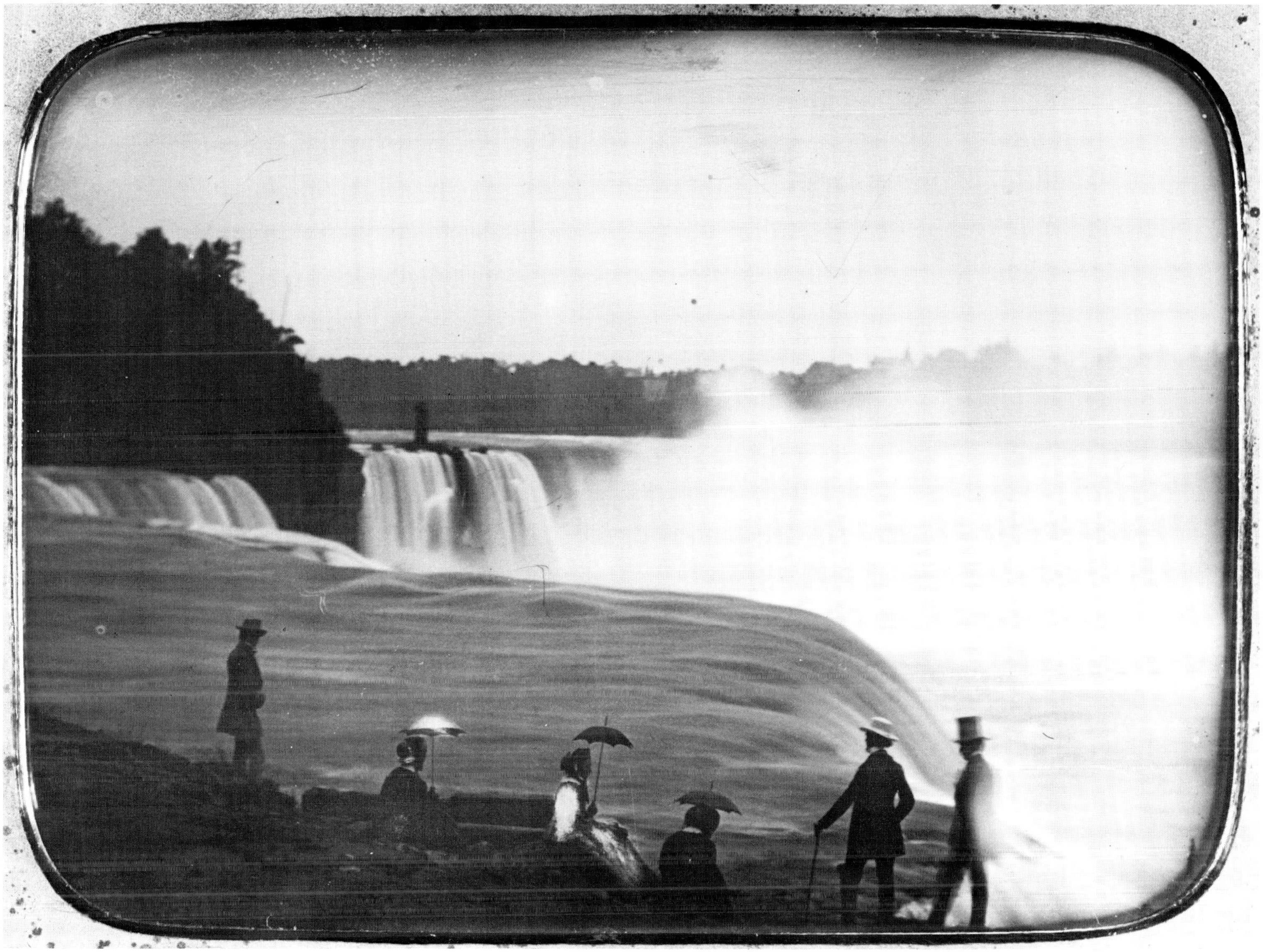

Plate 8 FRANCIS BEDFORD
Mer de Glace
undated

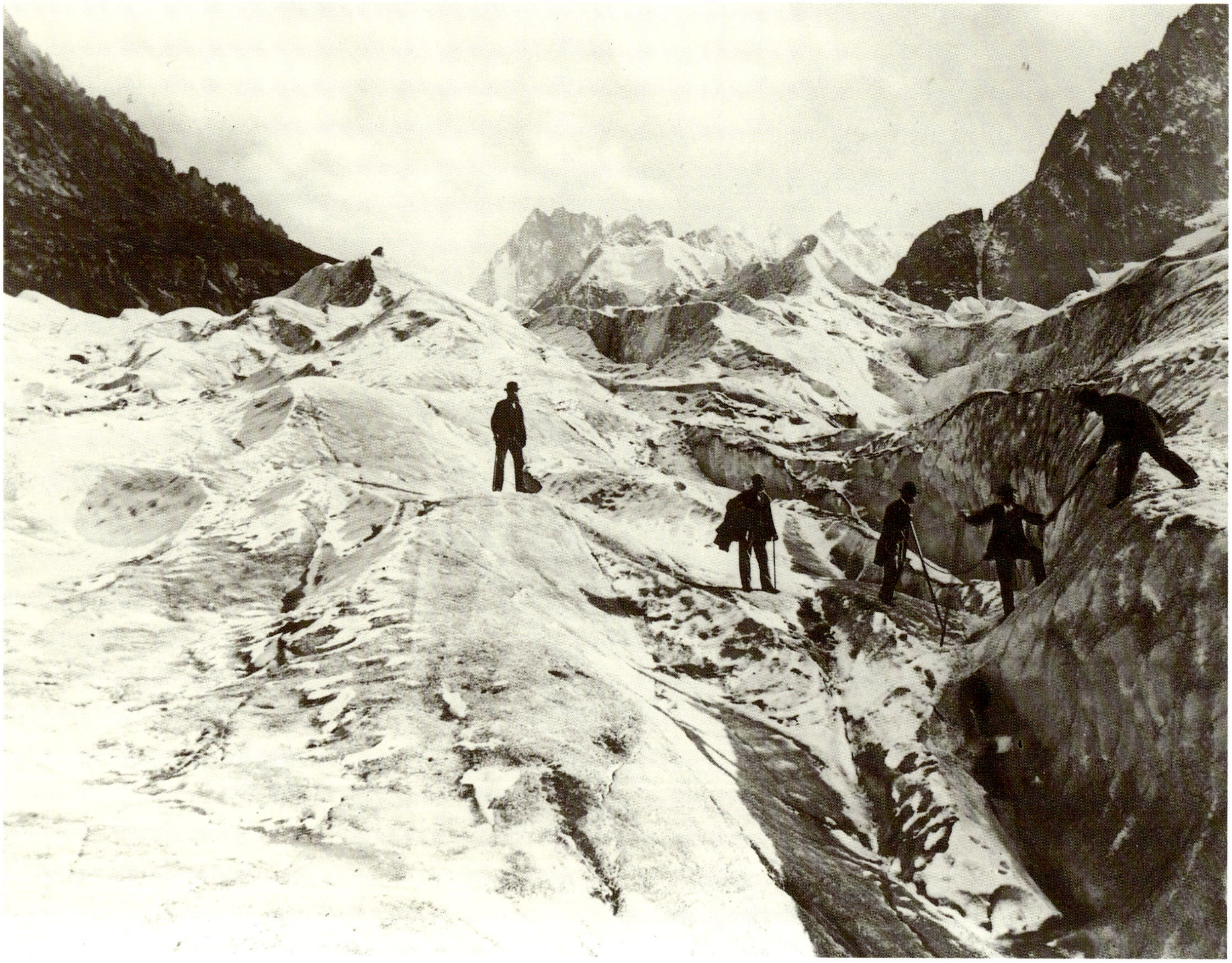

Plate 9 SAMUEL BOURNE
Mussucks for Crossing the Beas below Bajoura
1866

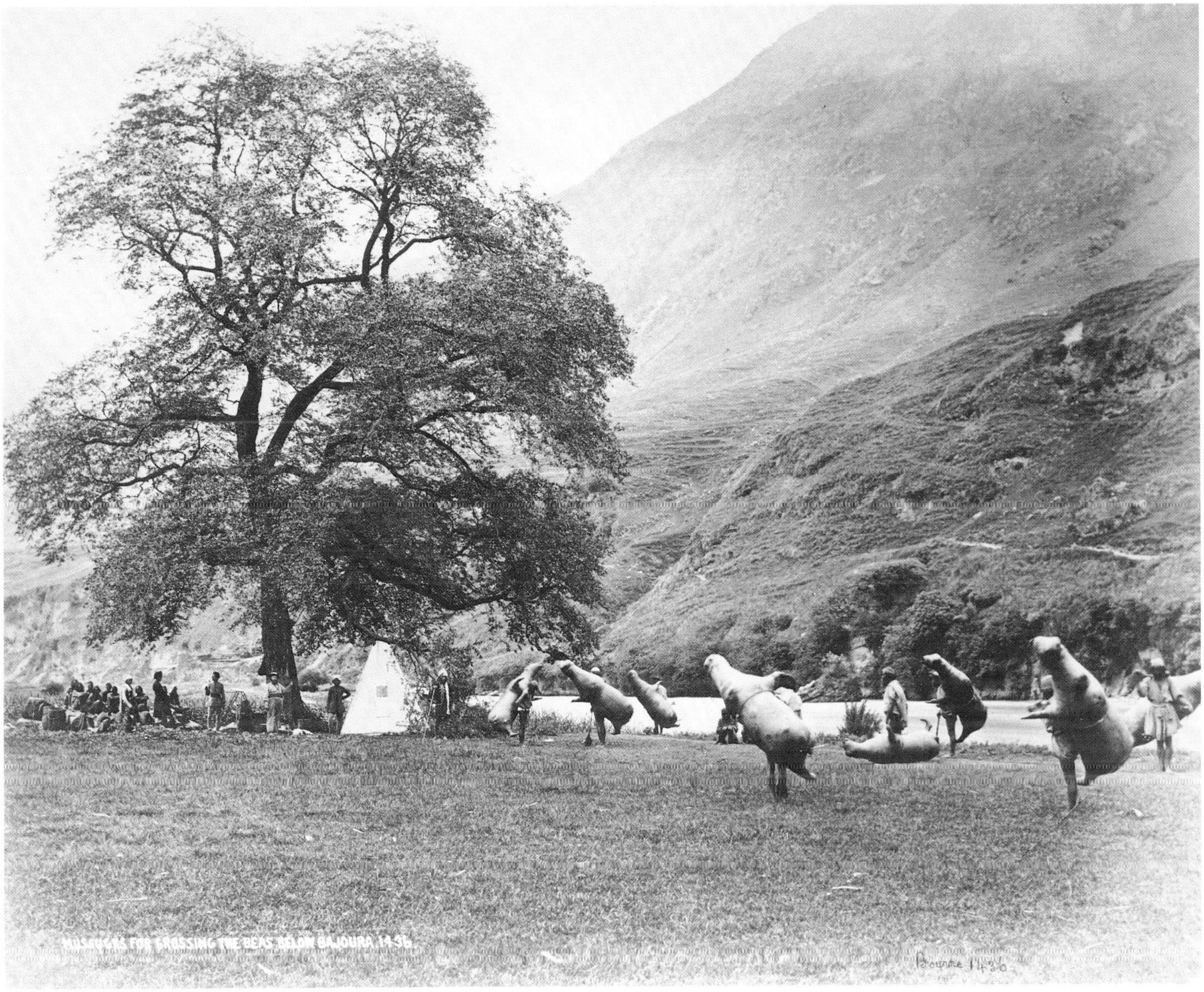

Plate 10 SAMUEL BOURNE
The Ki Monastery, Spitti
1866

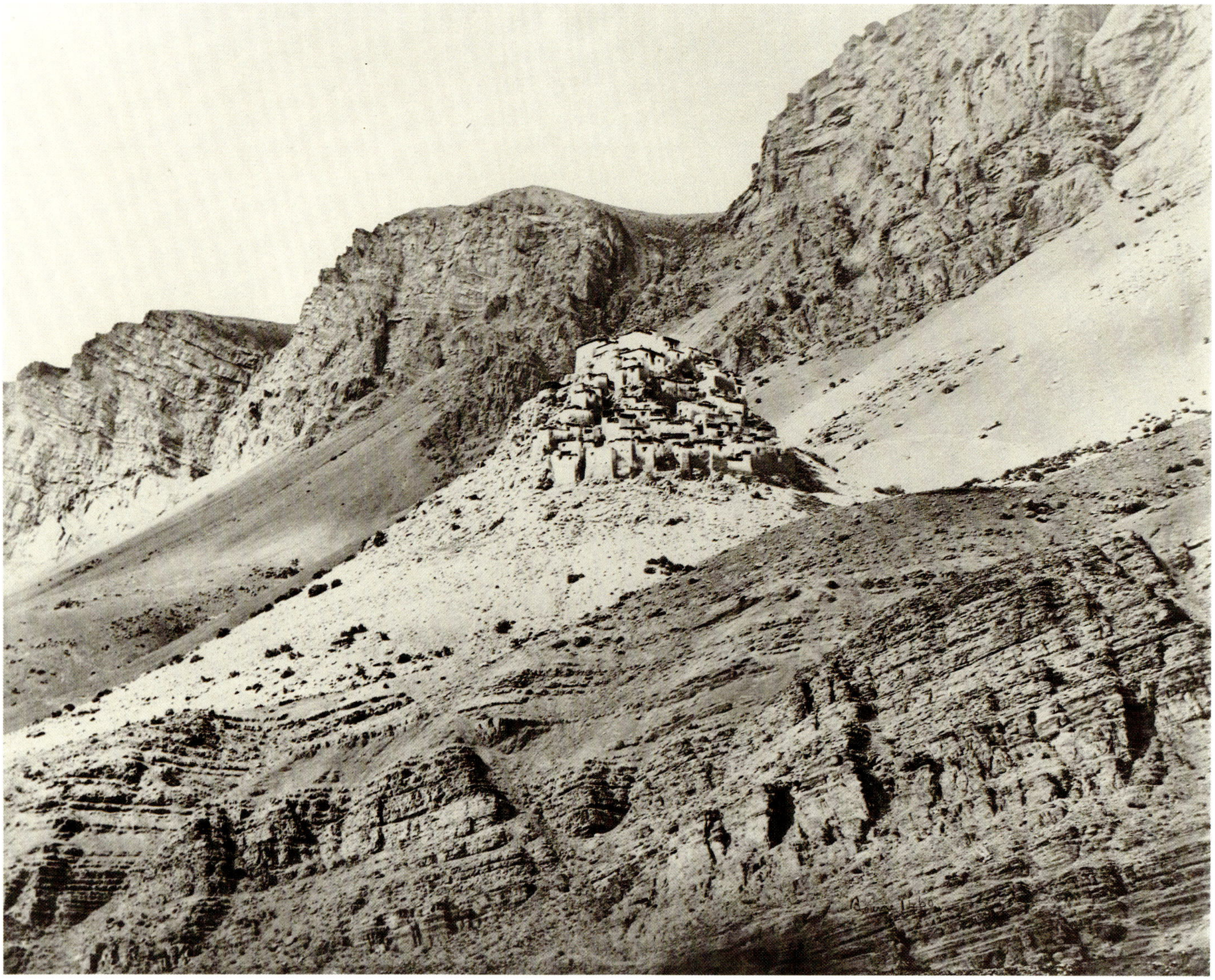

Plate 11 SAMUEL BOURNE
Twig Bridge over Spitti River
1866

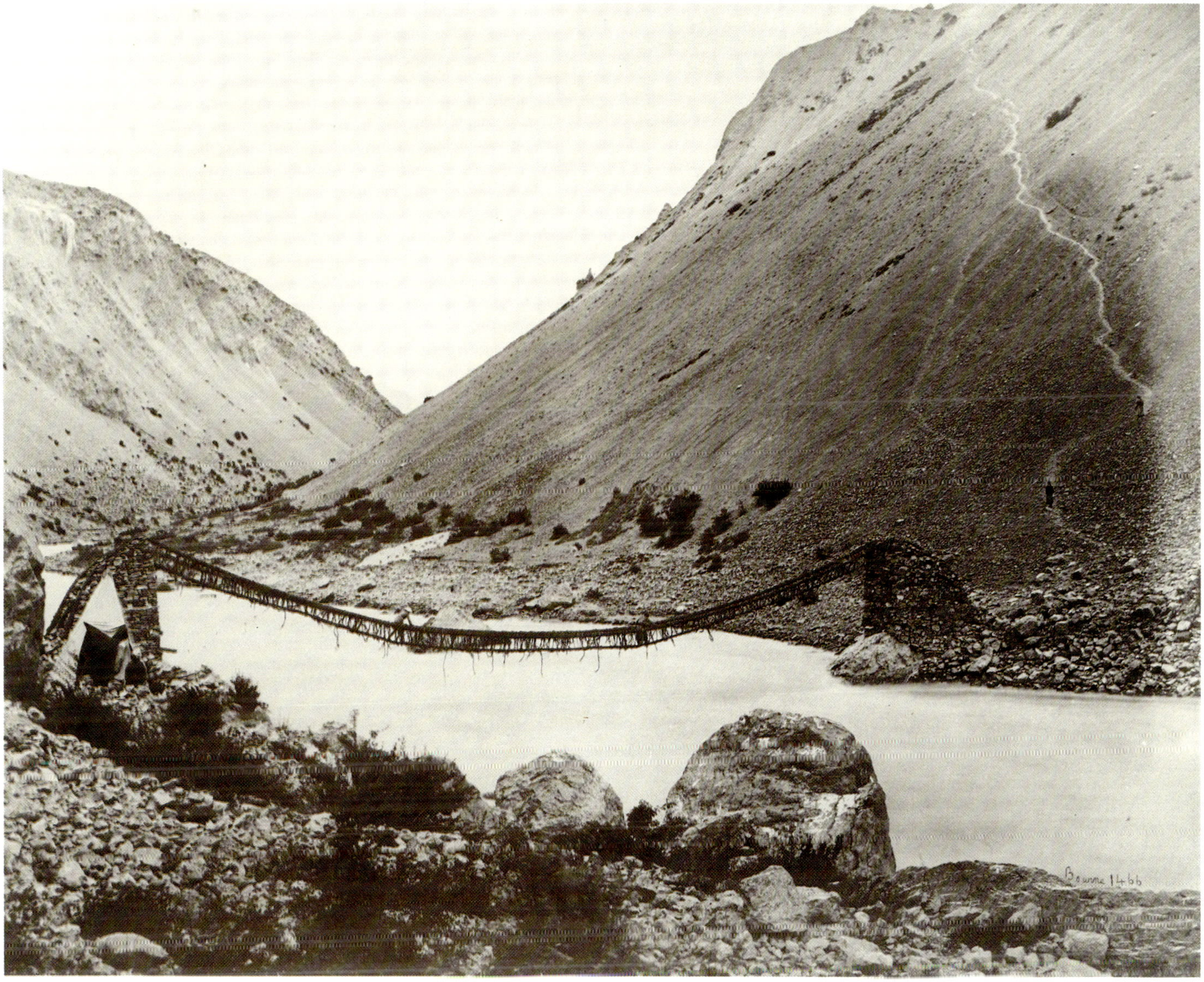

Plate 12 ARCHIBALD BURNS
The Horse Wynd, Edinburgh
1871

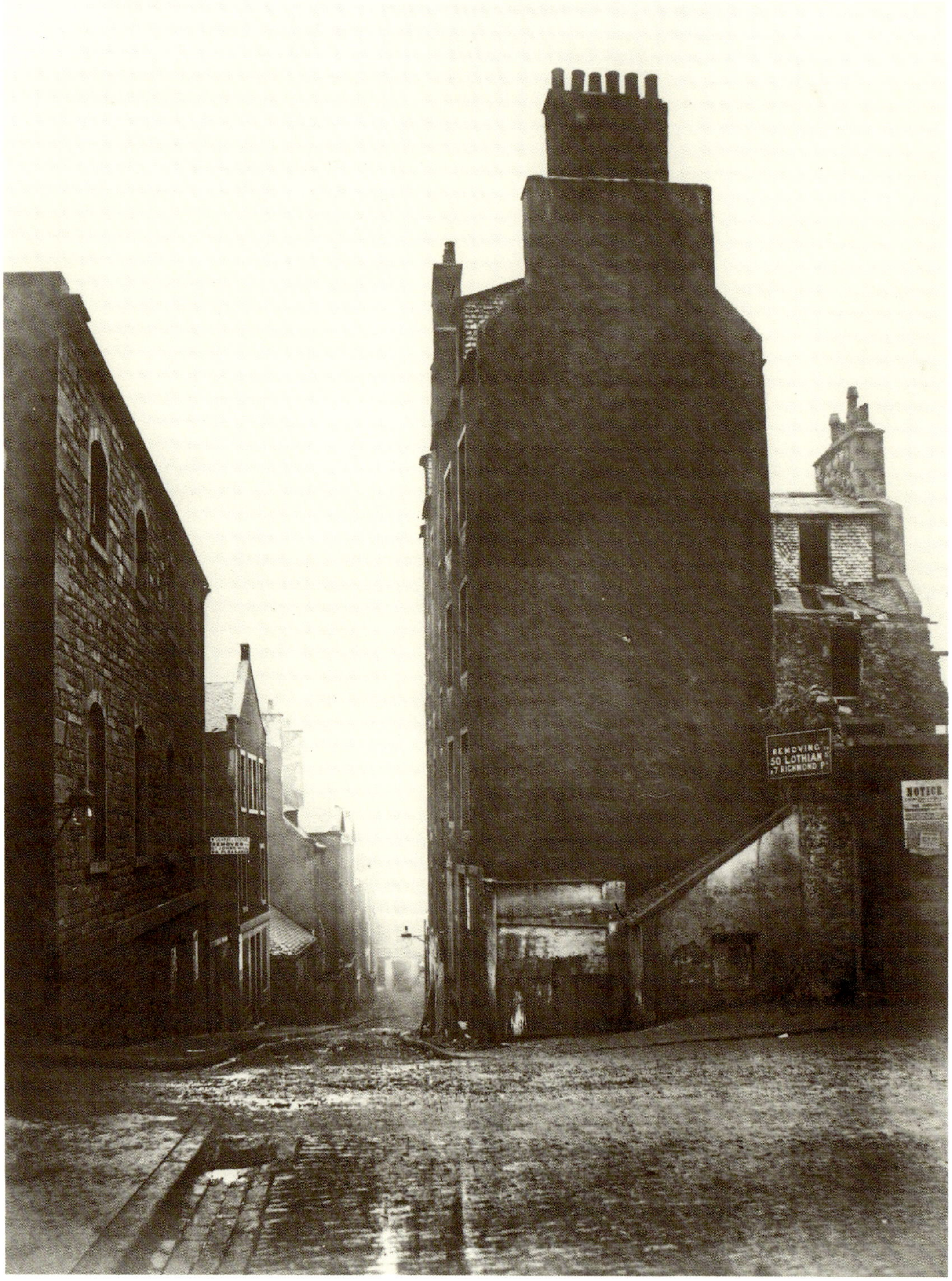

Plate 13 ARCHIBALD BURNS
East Side, Horse Wynd, Edinburgh
1871

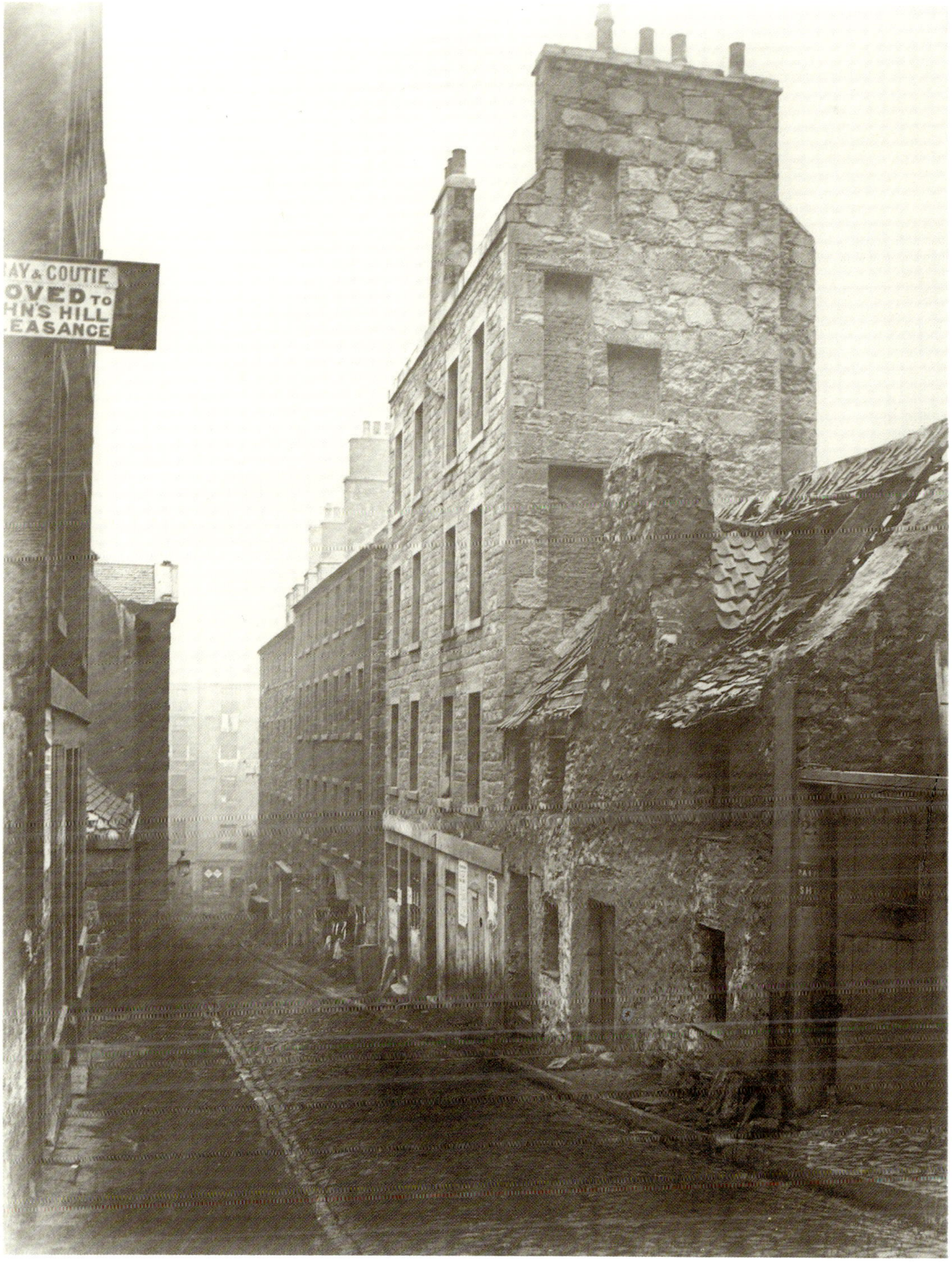

Plate 14 ARCHIBALD BURNS
The Cowgate, Edinburgh
1871

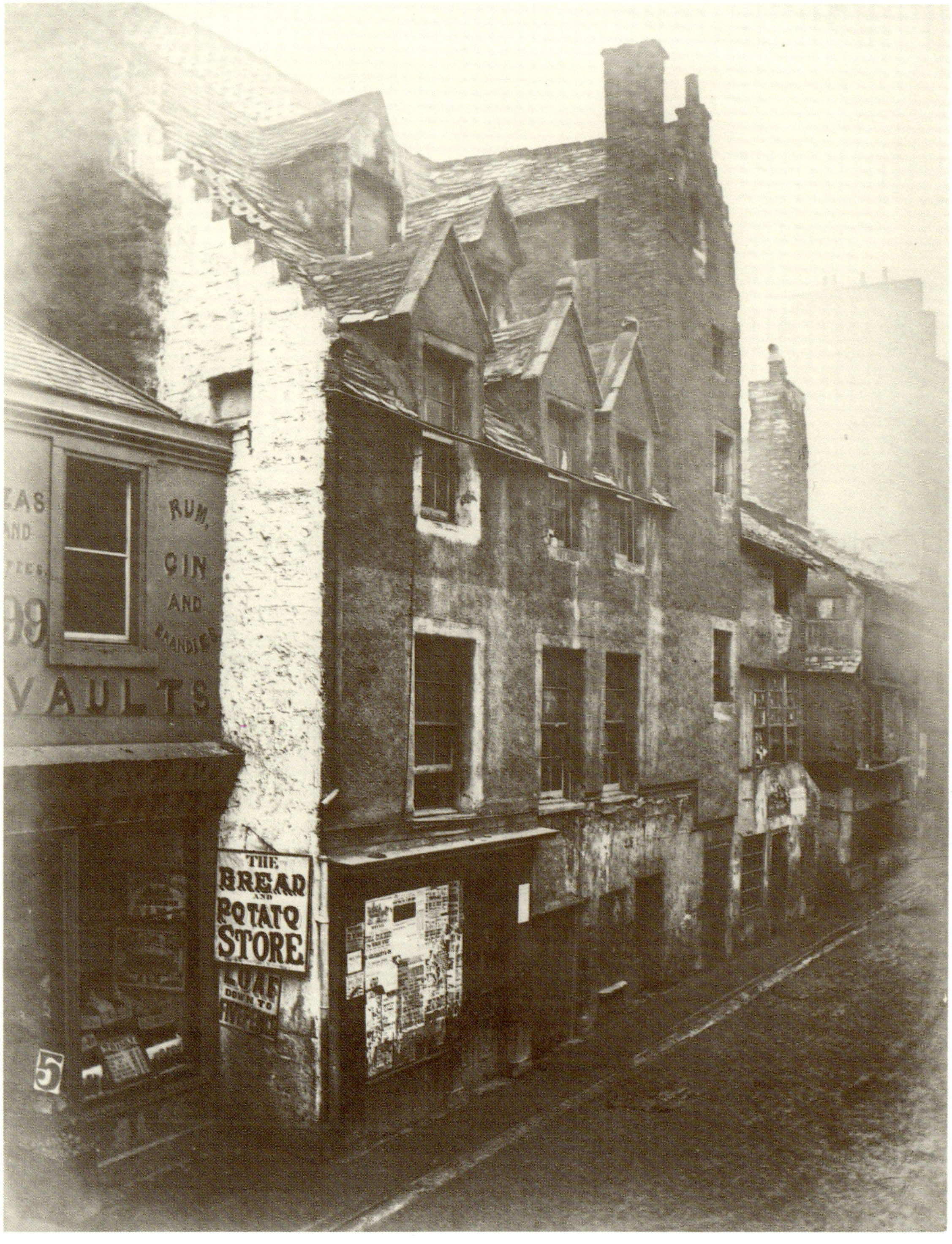

Plate 15 ARCHIBALD BURNS
Back of House in College Wynd, Edinburgh
1871

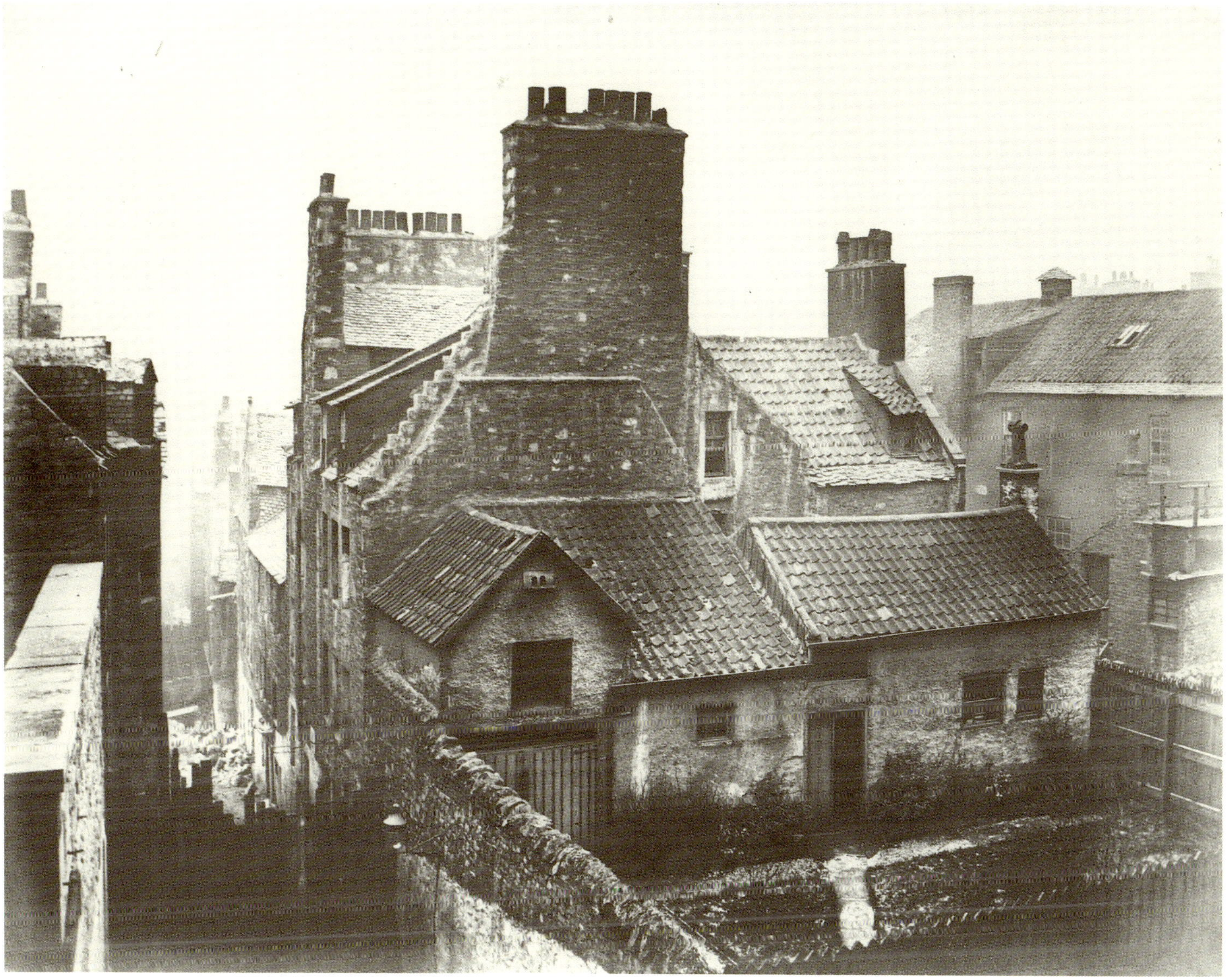

Plate 16 WILLIAM DONALDSON CLARK
The National Gallery and Royal Institution
(Royal Scottish Academy) Edinburgh
about 1858

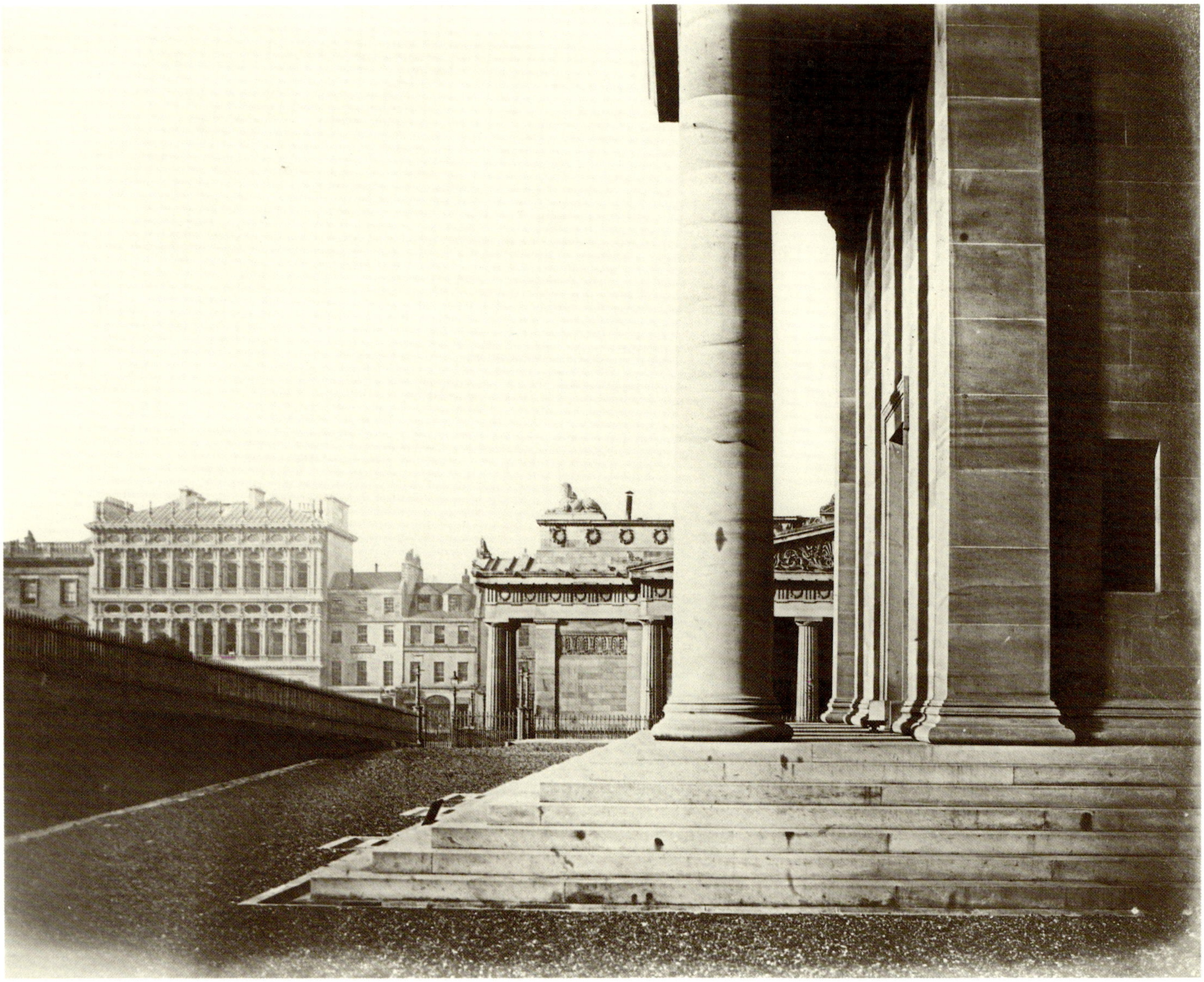

Plate 17 WILLIAM DONALDSON CLARK
Princes Street, Scott Monument and Royal Institution (Royal Scottish Academy) Edinburgh about 1858

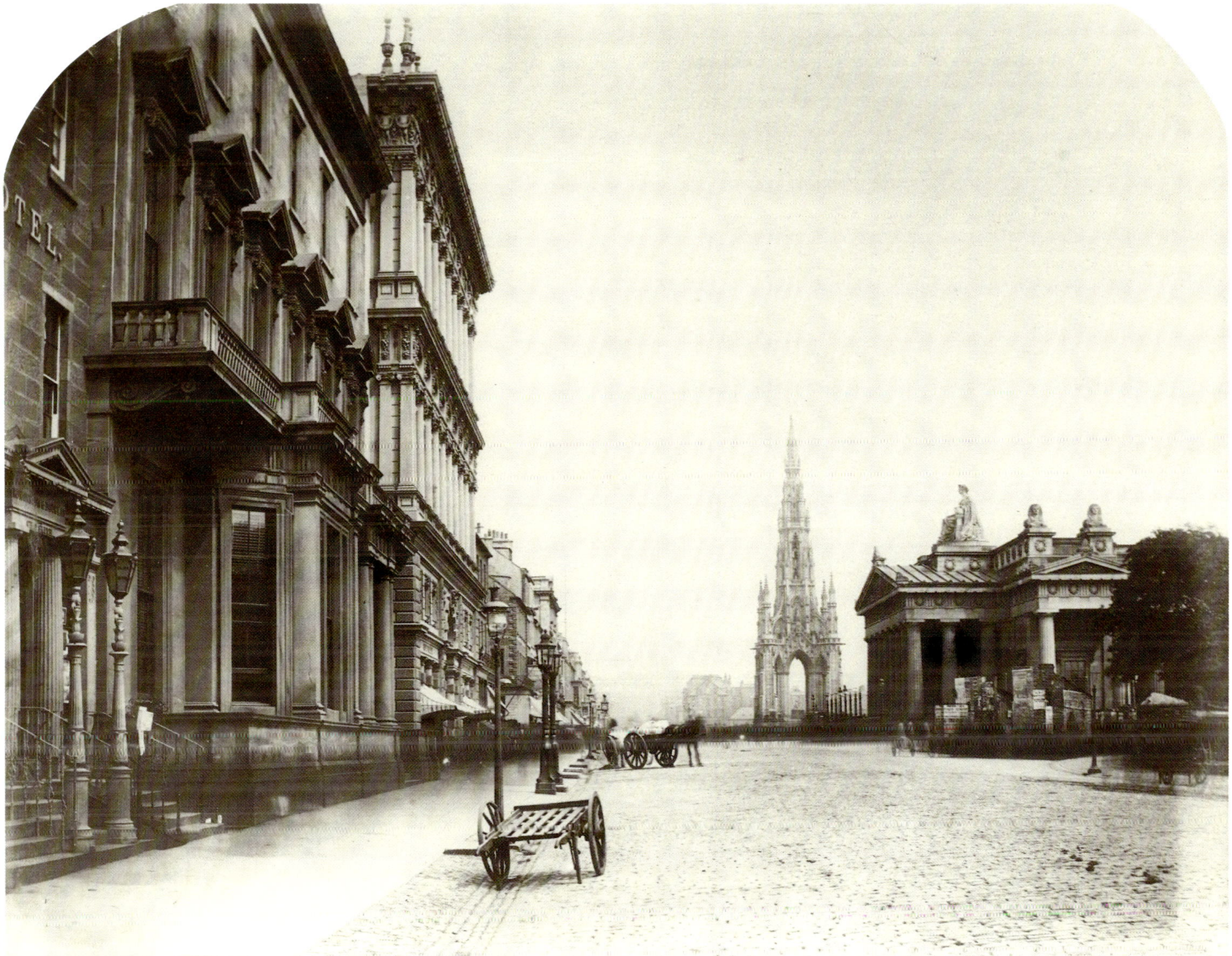

Plate 18 WILLIAM DONALDSON CLARK
The Bank of Scotland from Princes Street Gardens, Edinburgh
about 1858

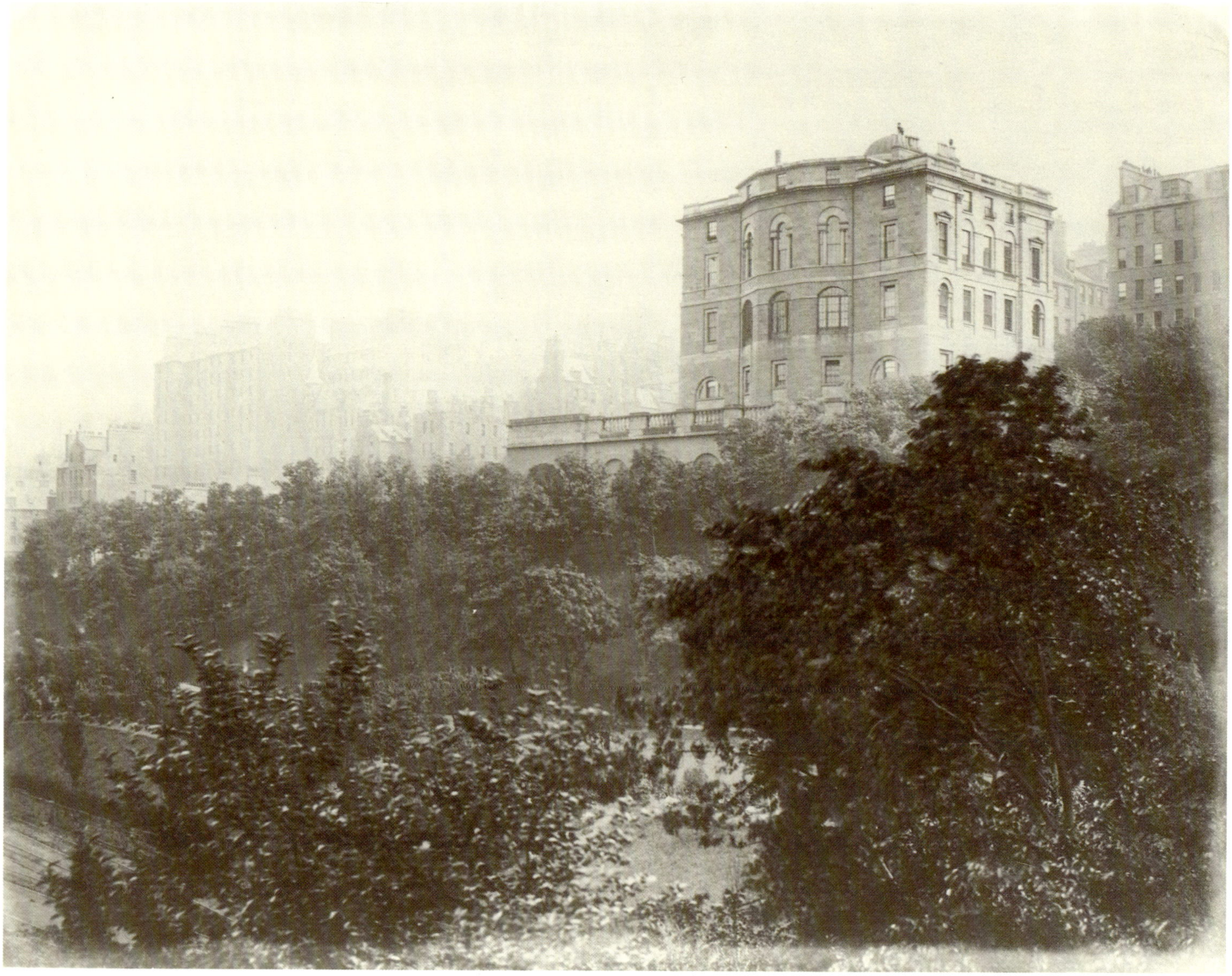

Plate 19 WILLIAM DONALDSON CLARK
The Lawnmarket, head of the West Bow,
Edinburgh
about 1860

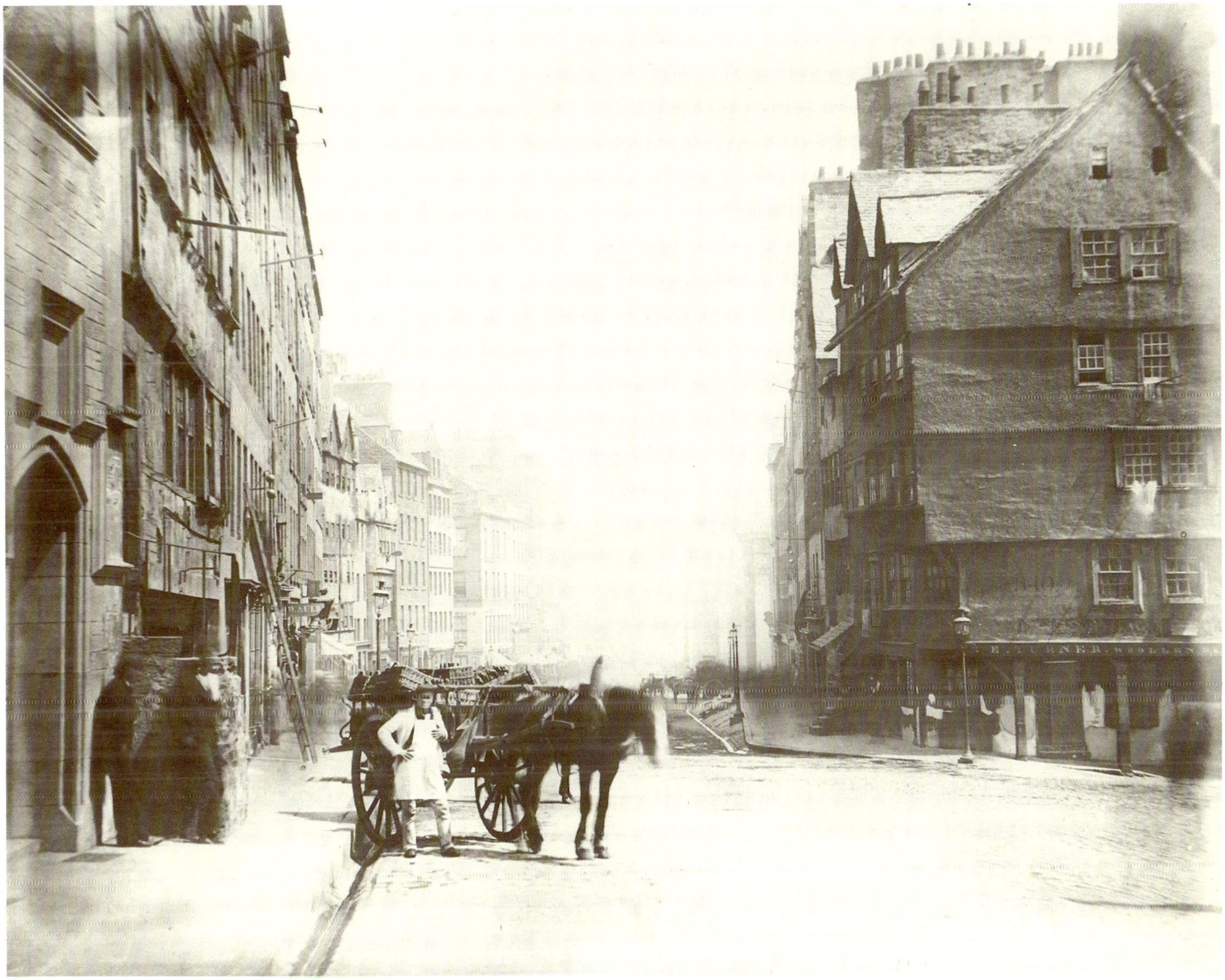

Plate 20 WILLIAM DONALDSON CLARK
The Cowgate Arch of George IV Bridge,
Edinburgh
about 1860

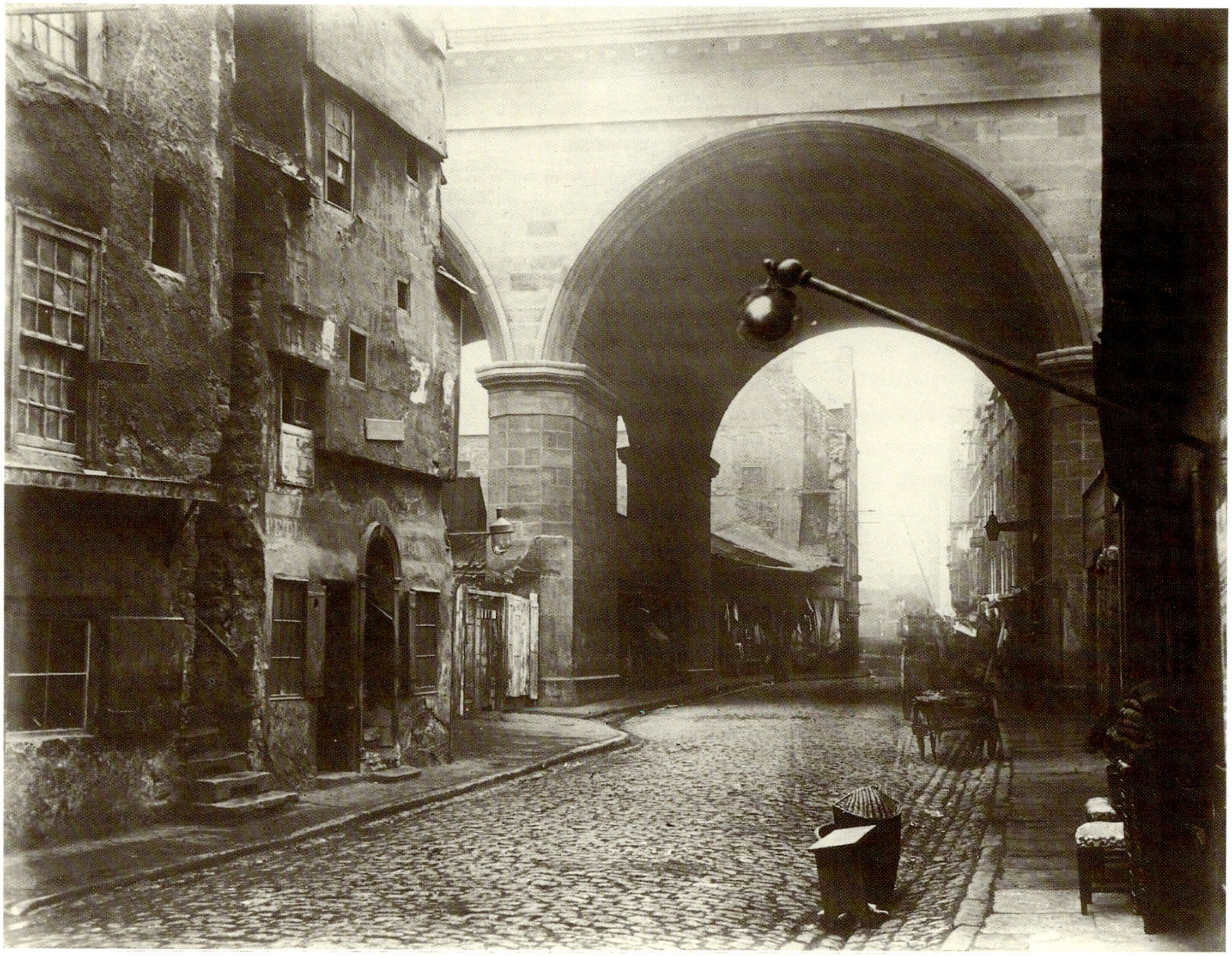

Plate 21 WILLIAM DONALDSON CLARK
Three figures in a tree-lined lane
about 1864

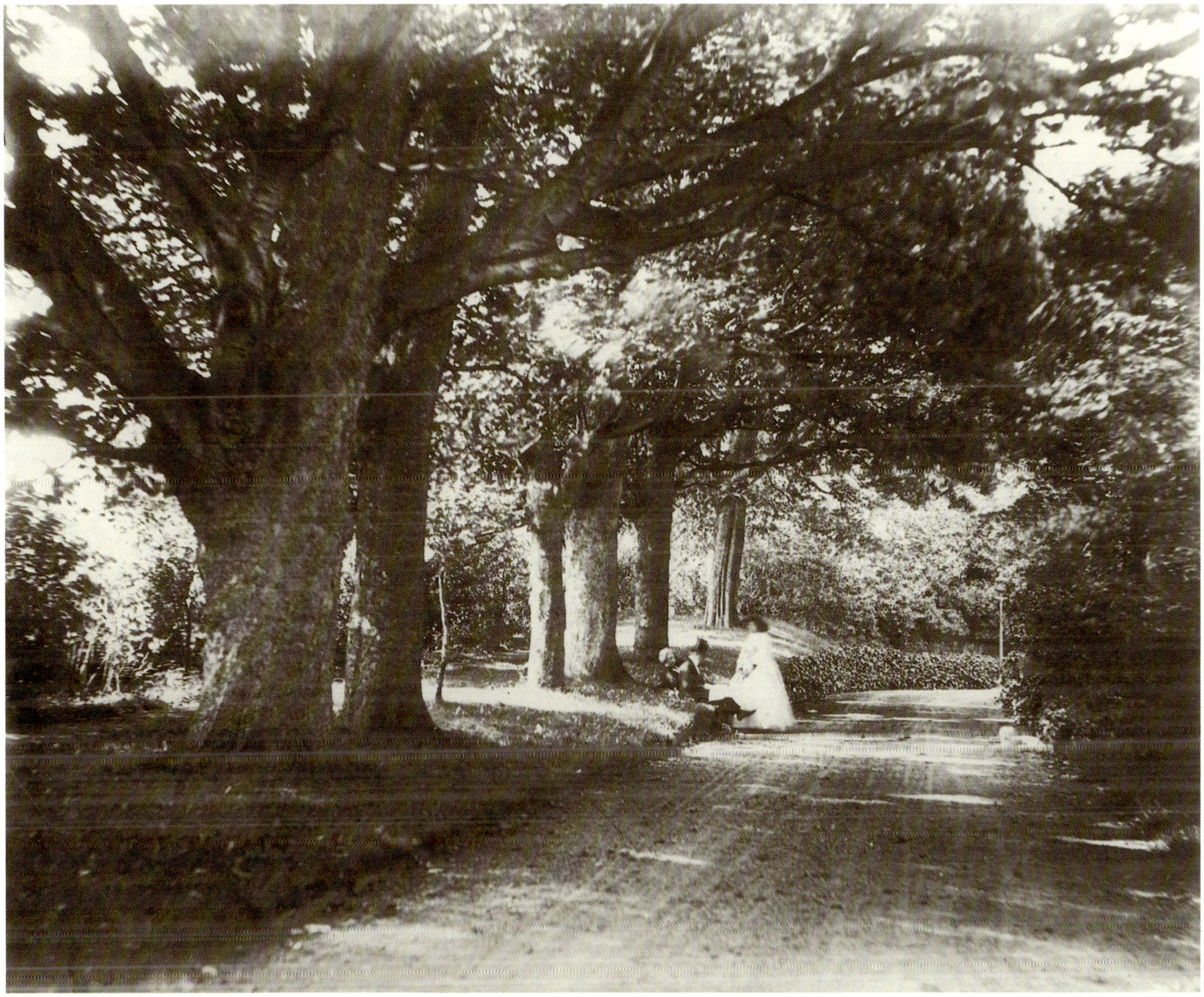

Plate 22 WILLIAM DONALDSON CLARK
Melrose Abbey, piers of the nave
1866

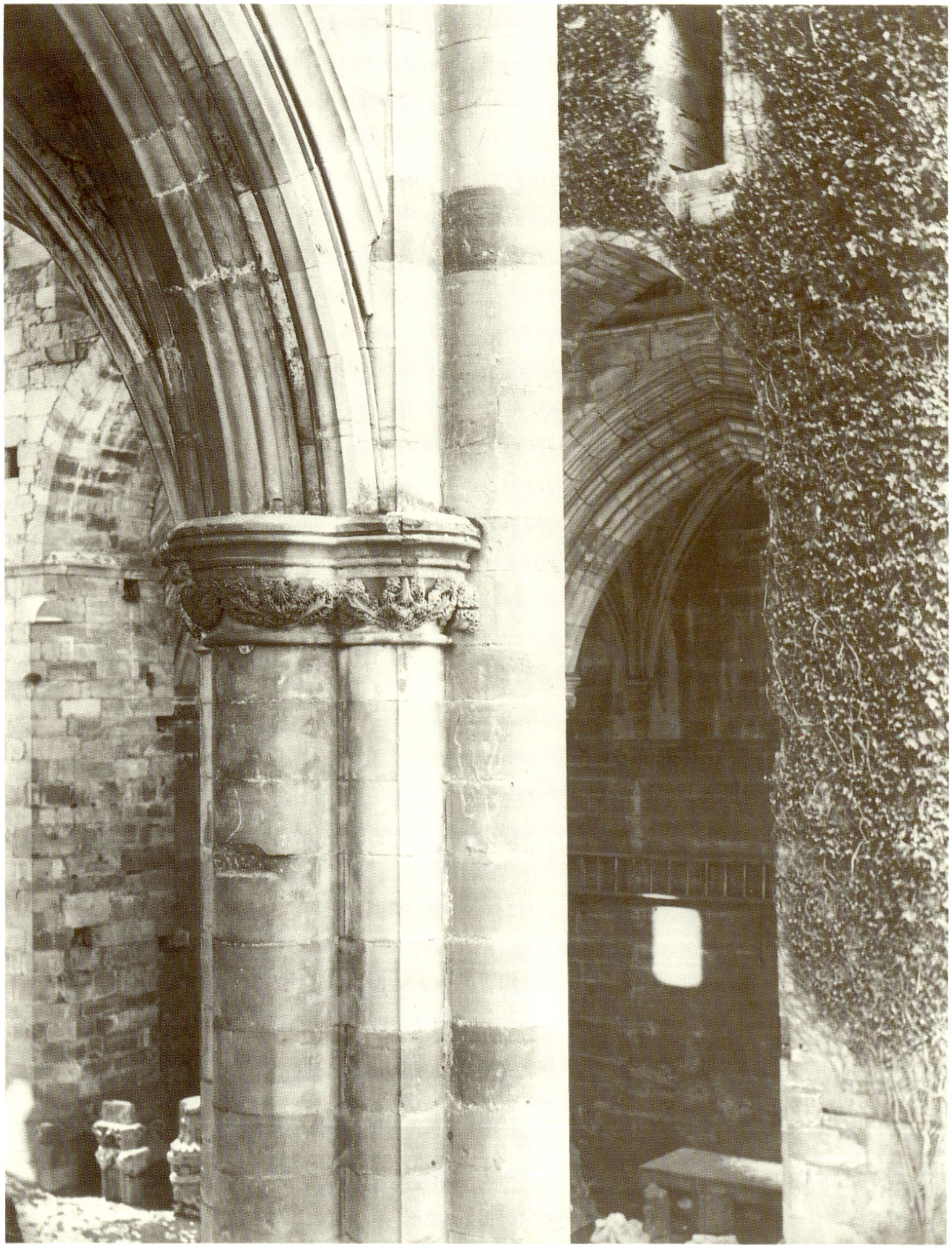

Plate 23 ALVIN LANGDON COBURN
G K Chesterton
published 1913

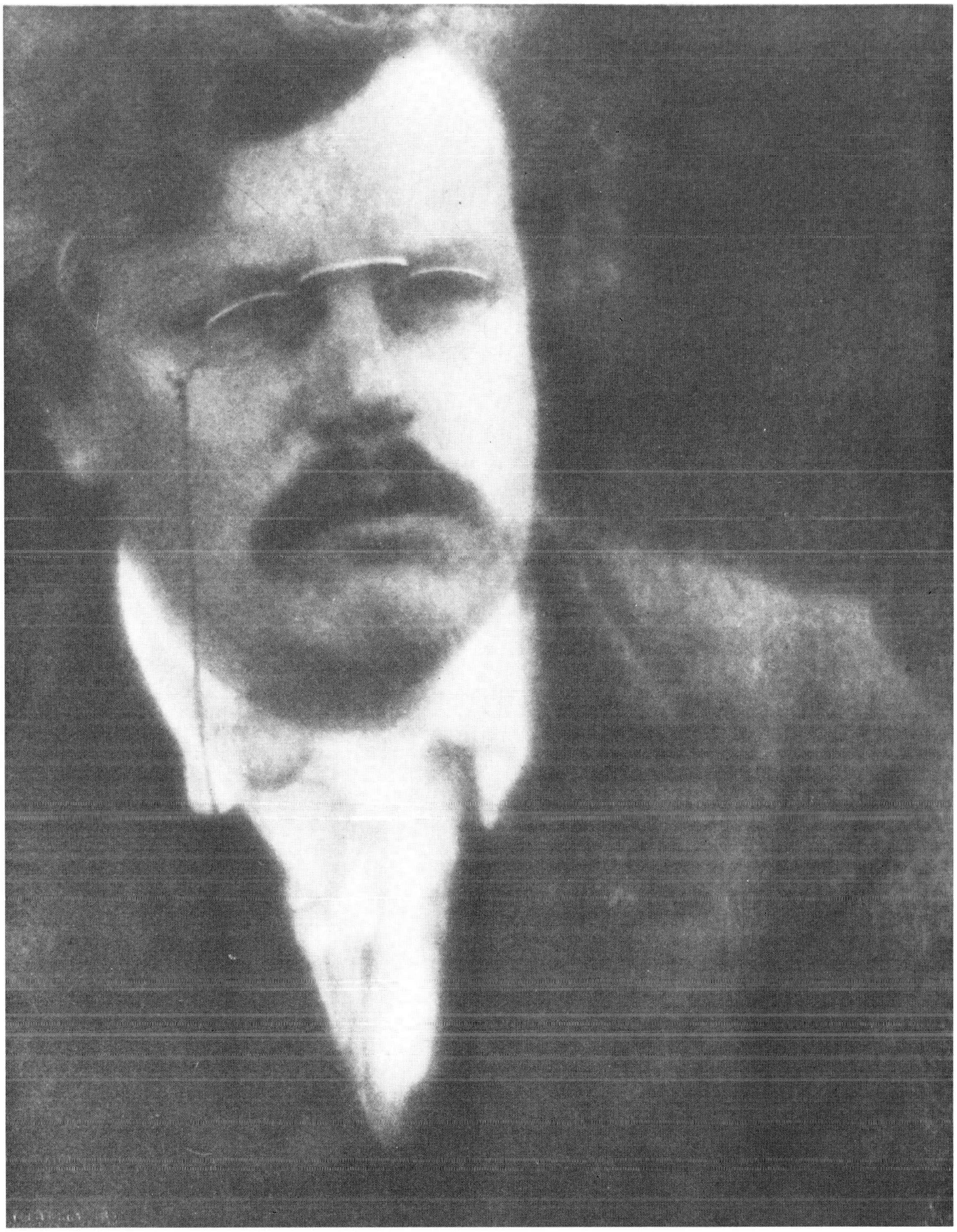

Plate 24 JAMES CRIGHTON
Washing-day, Newhaven
undated

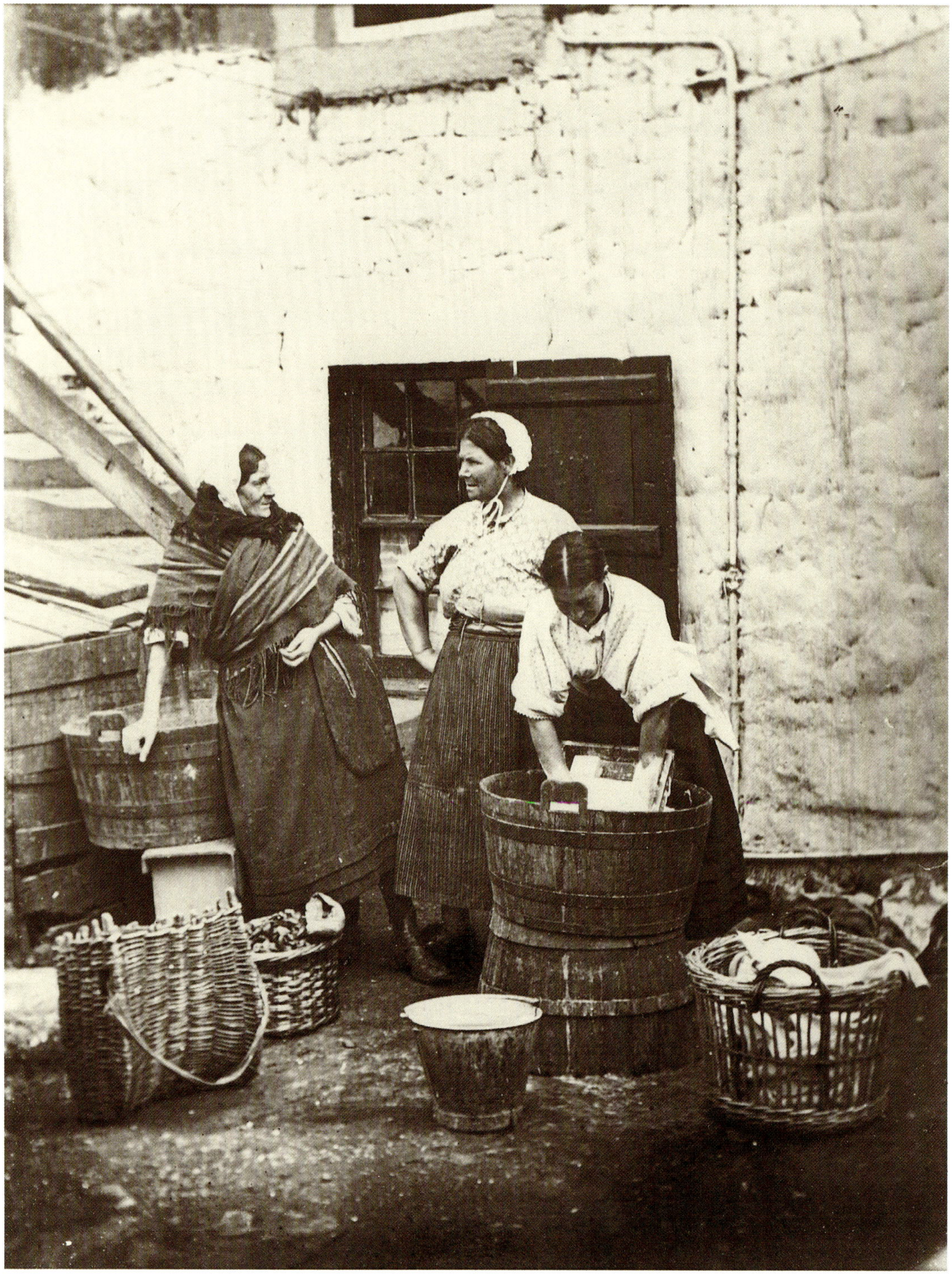

Plate 25 WILLIAM ELSMORE & CO
School Band
between 1897 and 1906

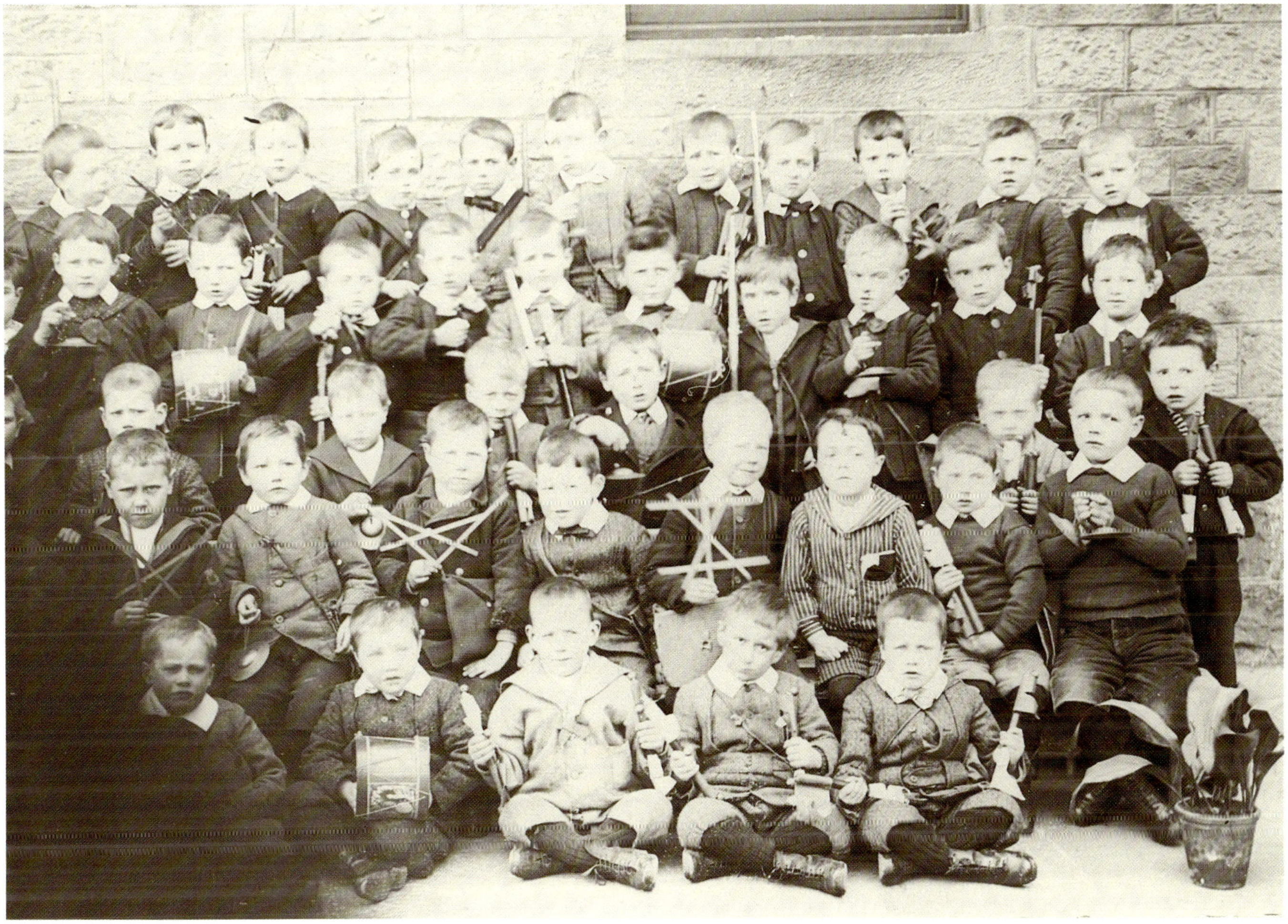

Plate 26 FREDERICK HENRY EVANS
Aubrey Beardsley
1893

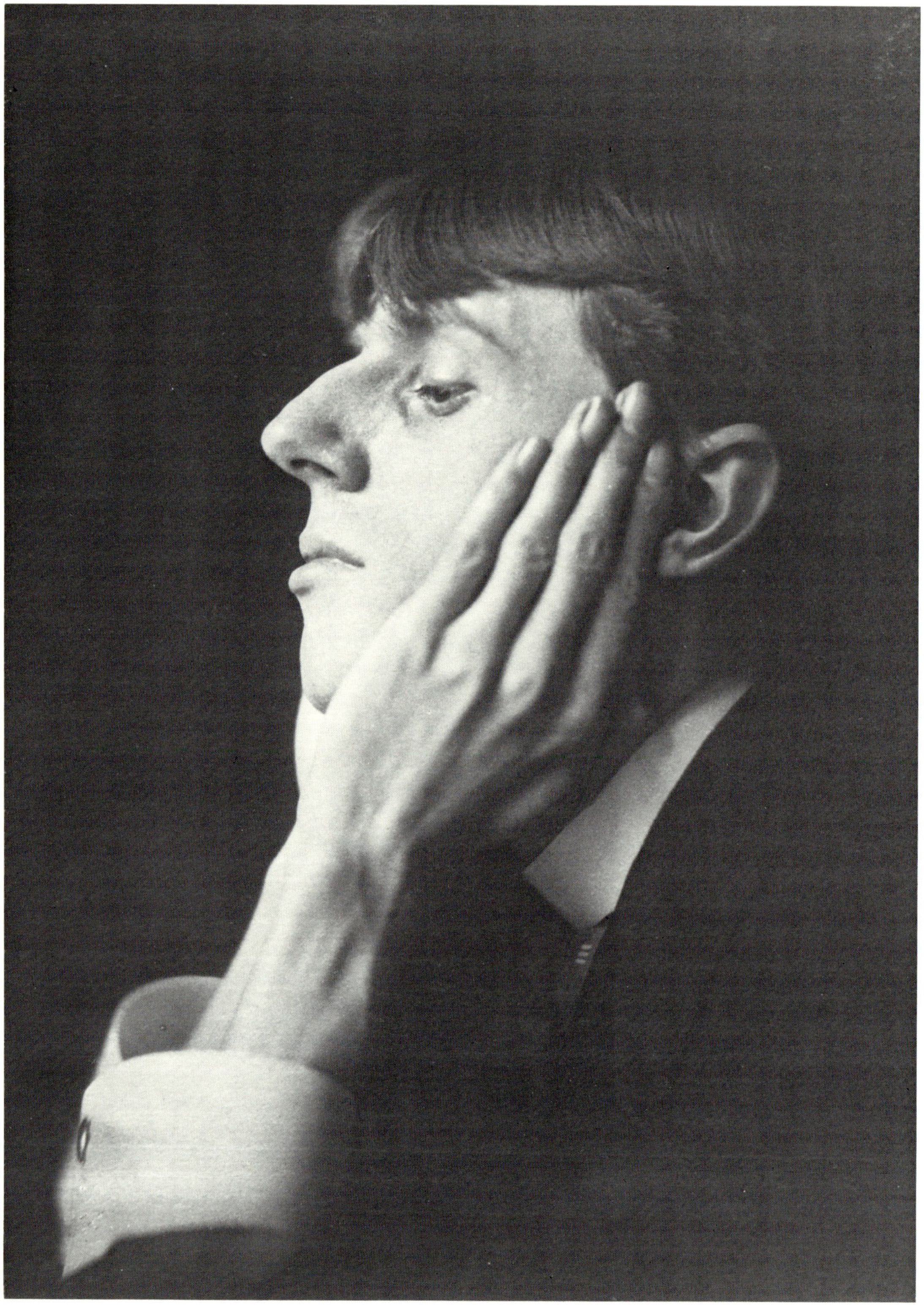

Plate 27 (?) FRANCIS FRITH
The Khasneh, Petra
between 1856 and 1860

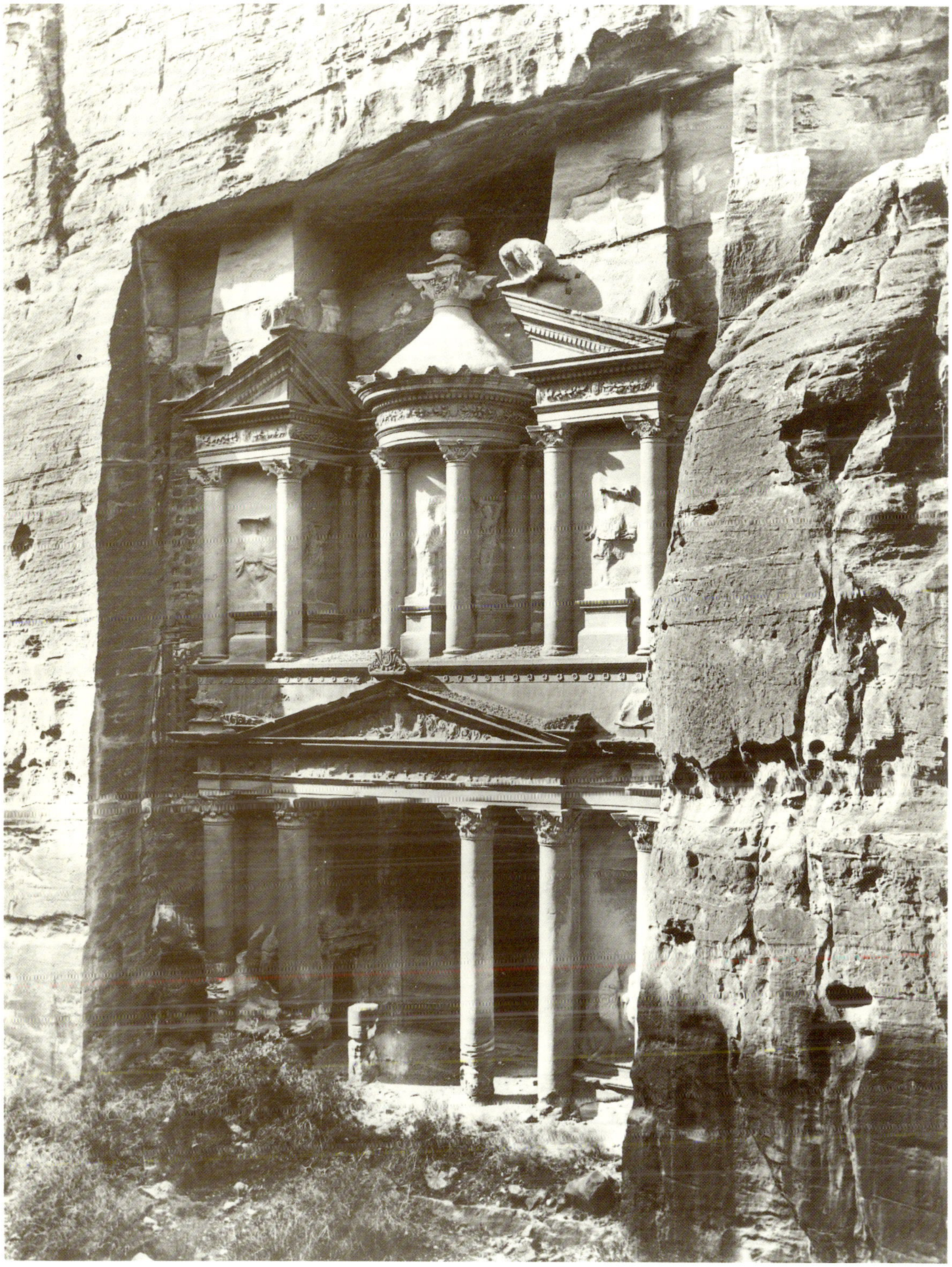

Plate 28 ALEXANDER HENDERSON
A Train in the Snow
undated

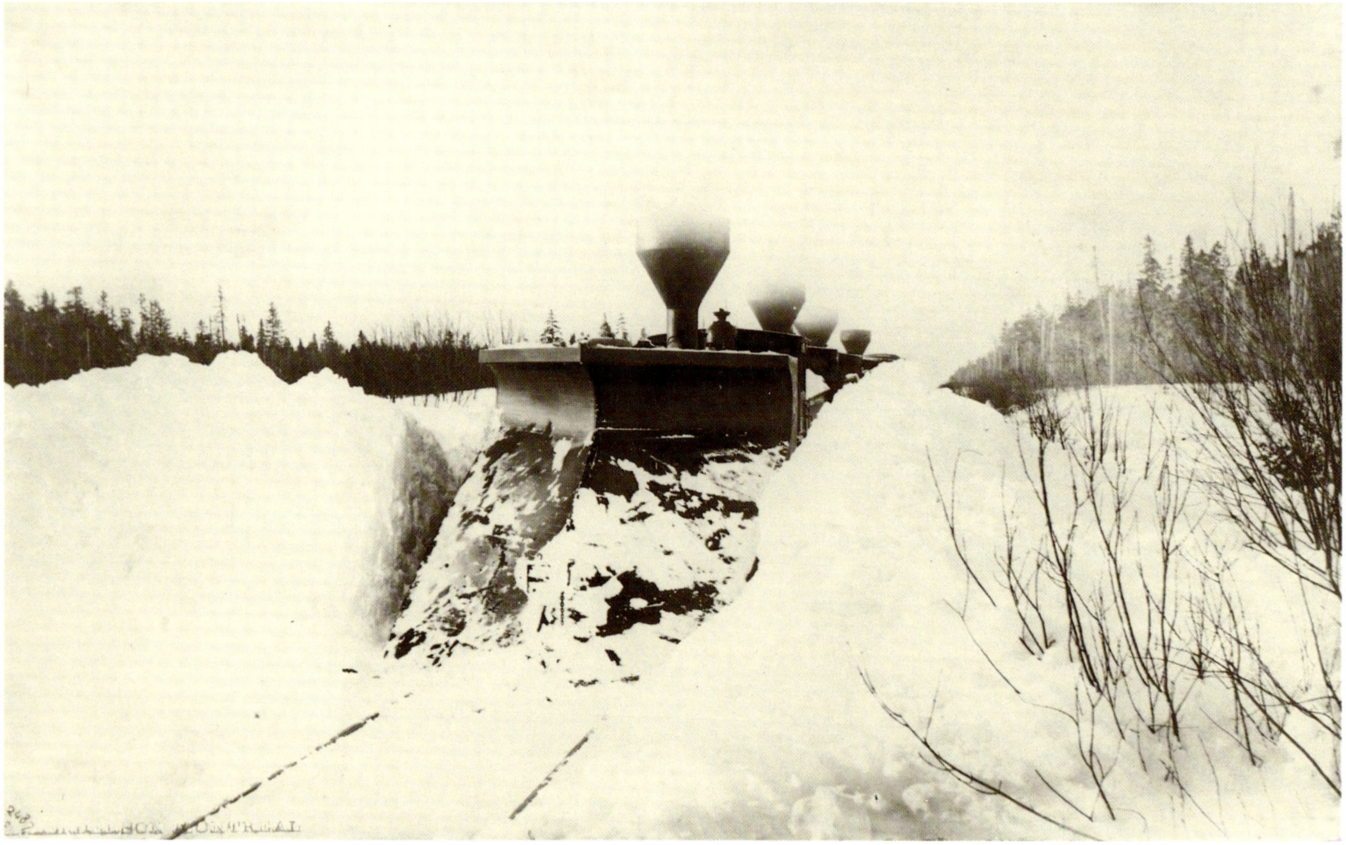

Plate 29 D O HILL and ROBERT ADAMSON
Lady Ruthven
about 1847

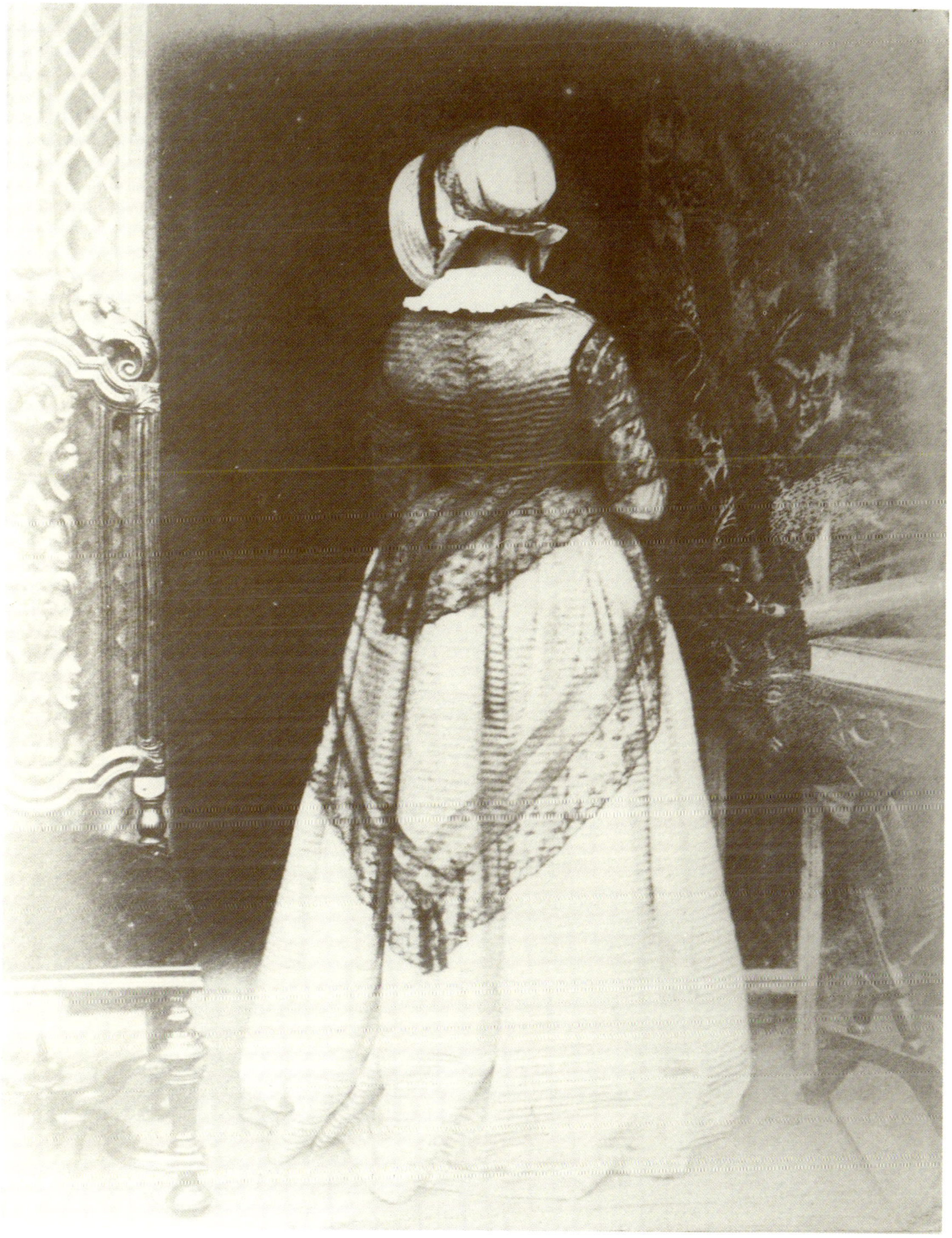

Plate 30 EUGENE CLUTTERBUCK IMPEY
The Kootub, near Delhi
between 1858 and 1865

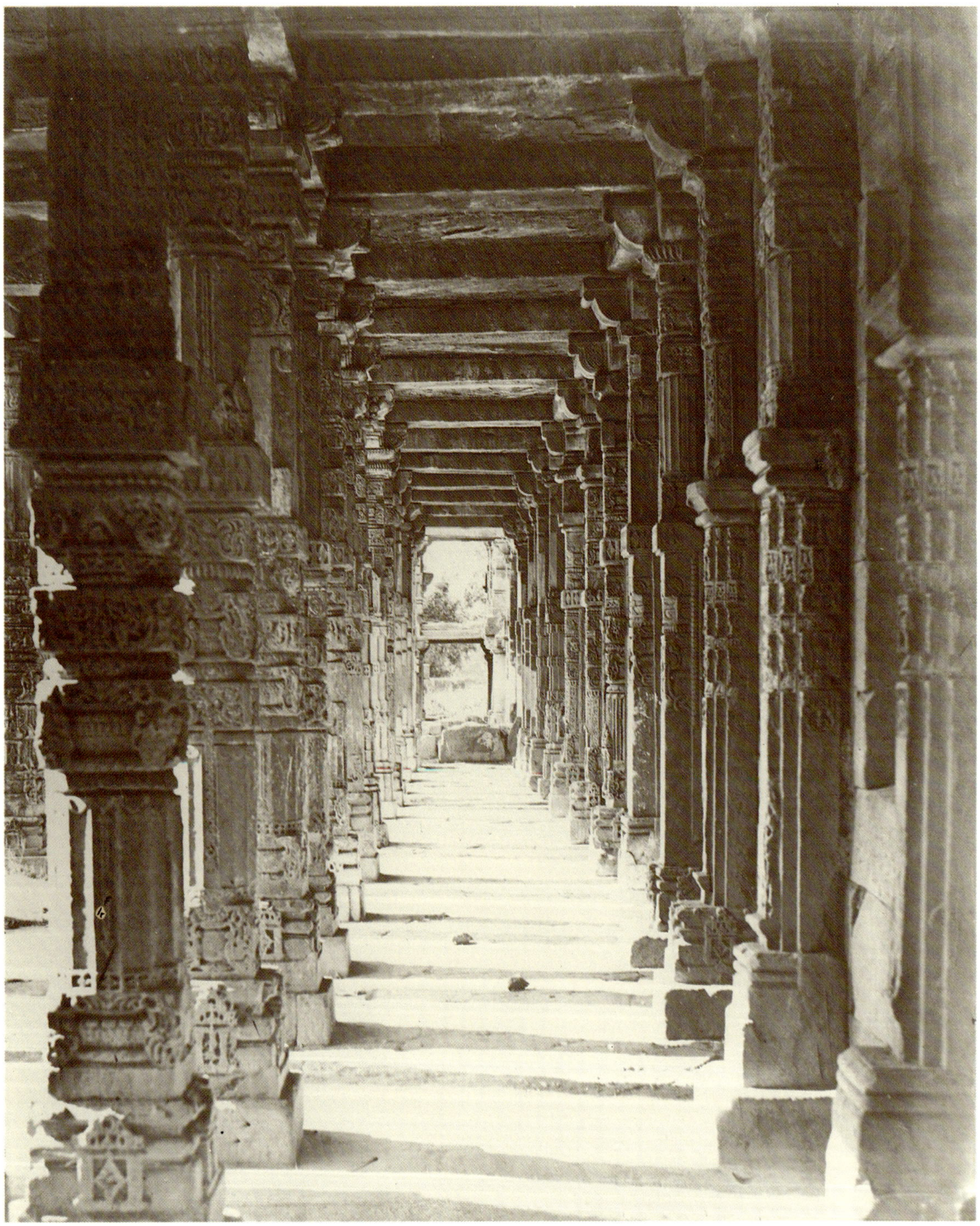

Plate 31 EUGENE CLUTTERBUCK IMPEY
Ulwur, The Cenotaph of Rao Raja Bukhtawur Singh
between 1858 and 1865

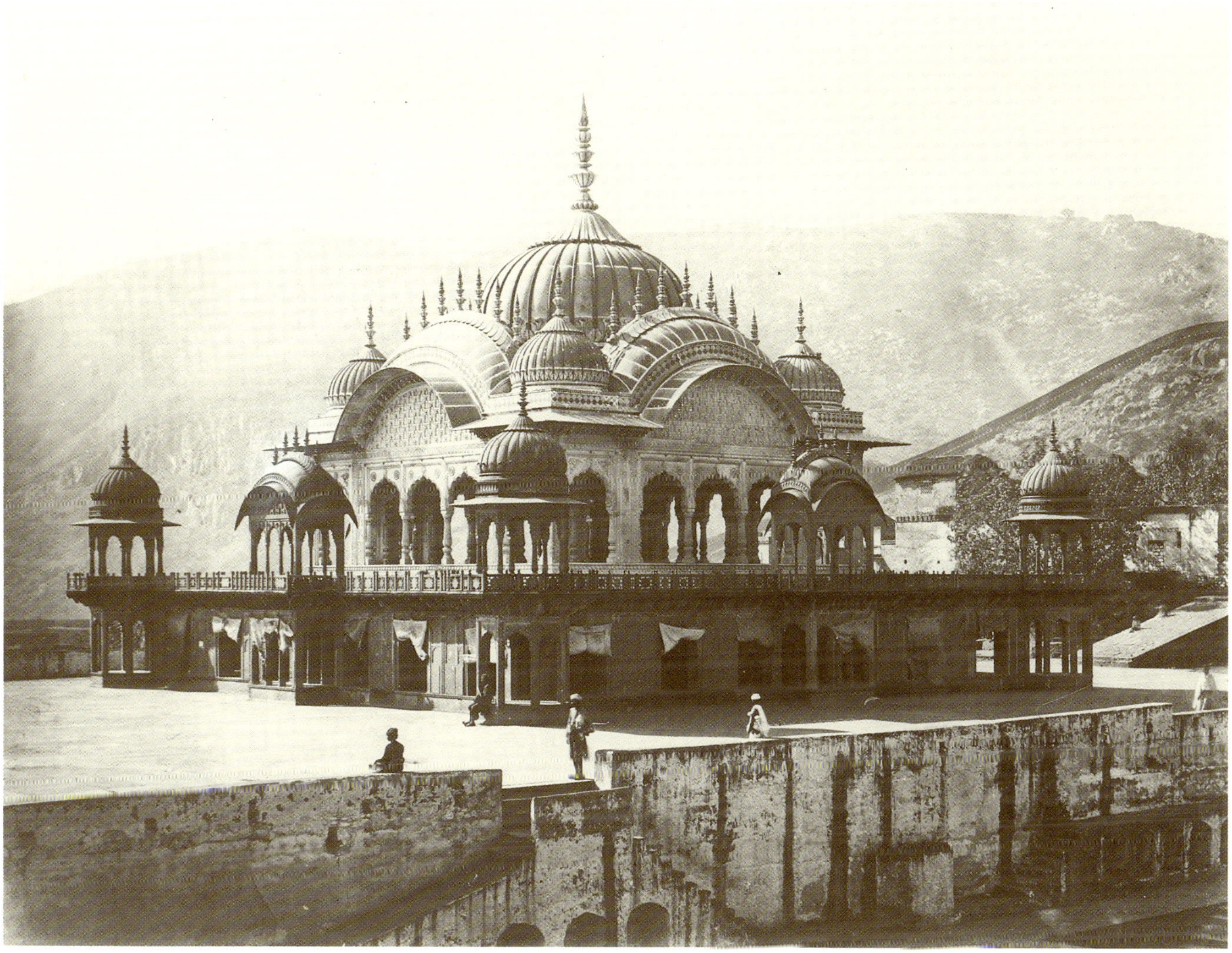

Plate 32 EUGENE CLUTTERBUCK IMPEY
A Bheestie or water-carrier with his Bullock
between 1858 and 1865

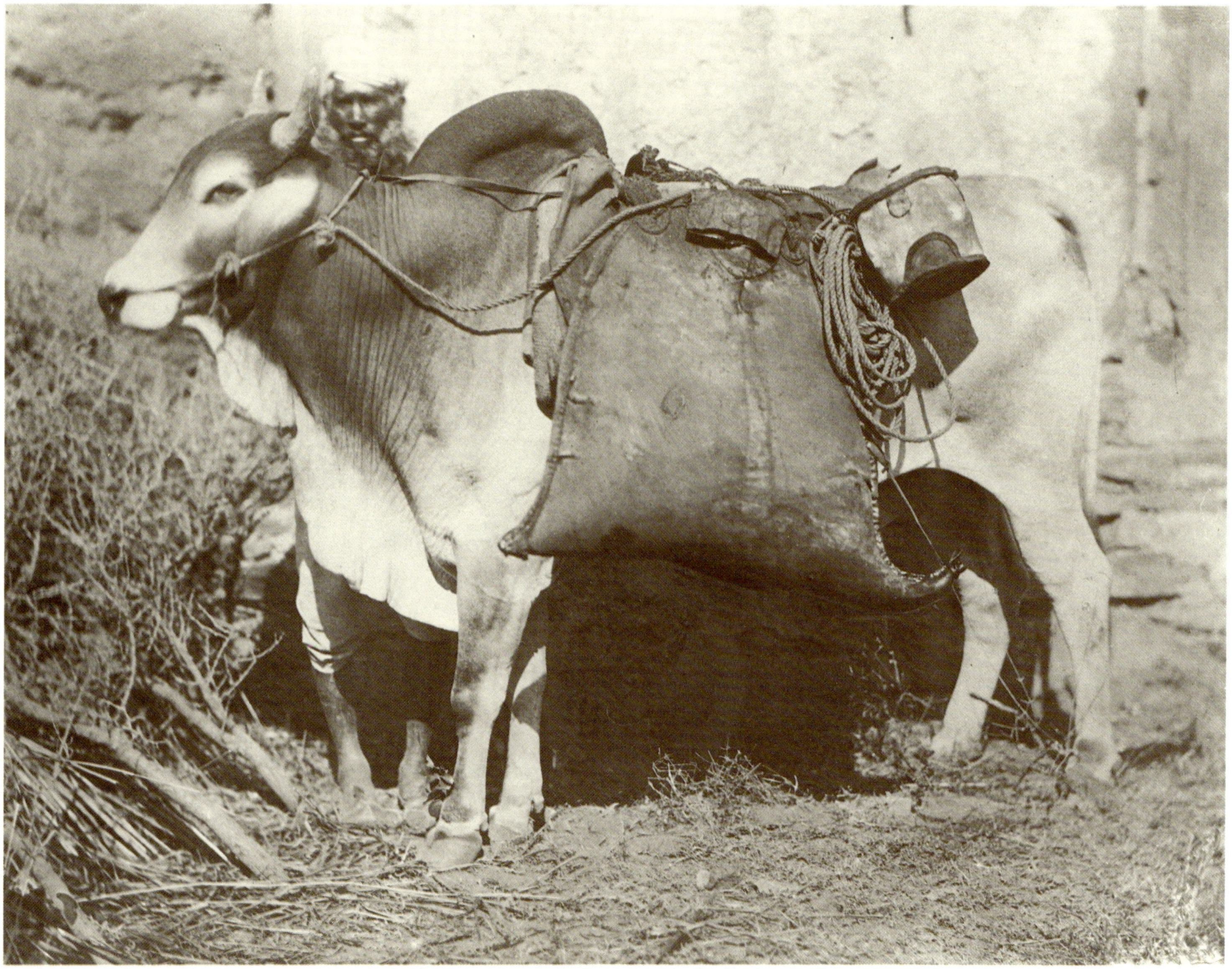

Plate 33 EUGENE CLUTTERBUCK IMPEY
Bullocks yoked to a Cart
between 1858 and 1865

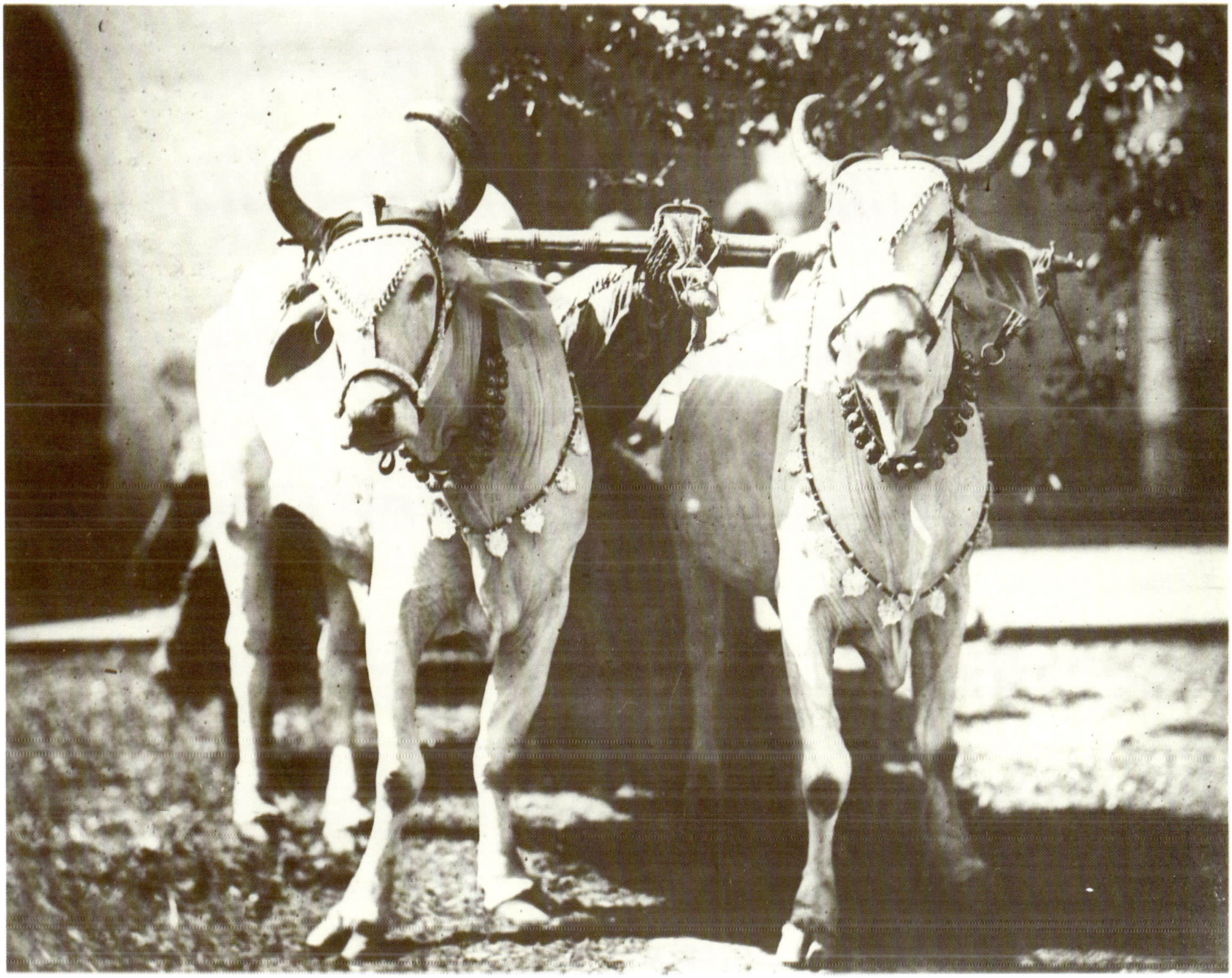

Plate 34 EUGENE CLUTTERBUCK IMPEY
Rajpoots playing Pucheesee
between 1858 and 1865

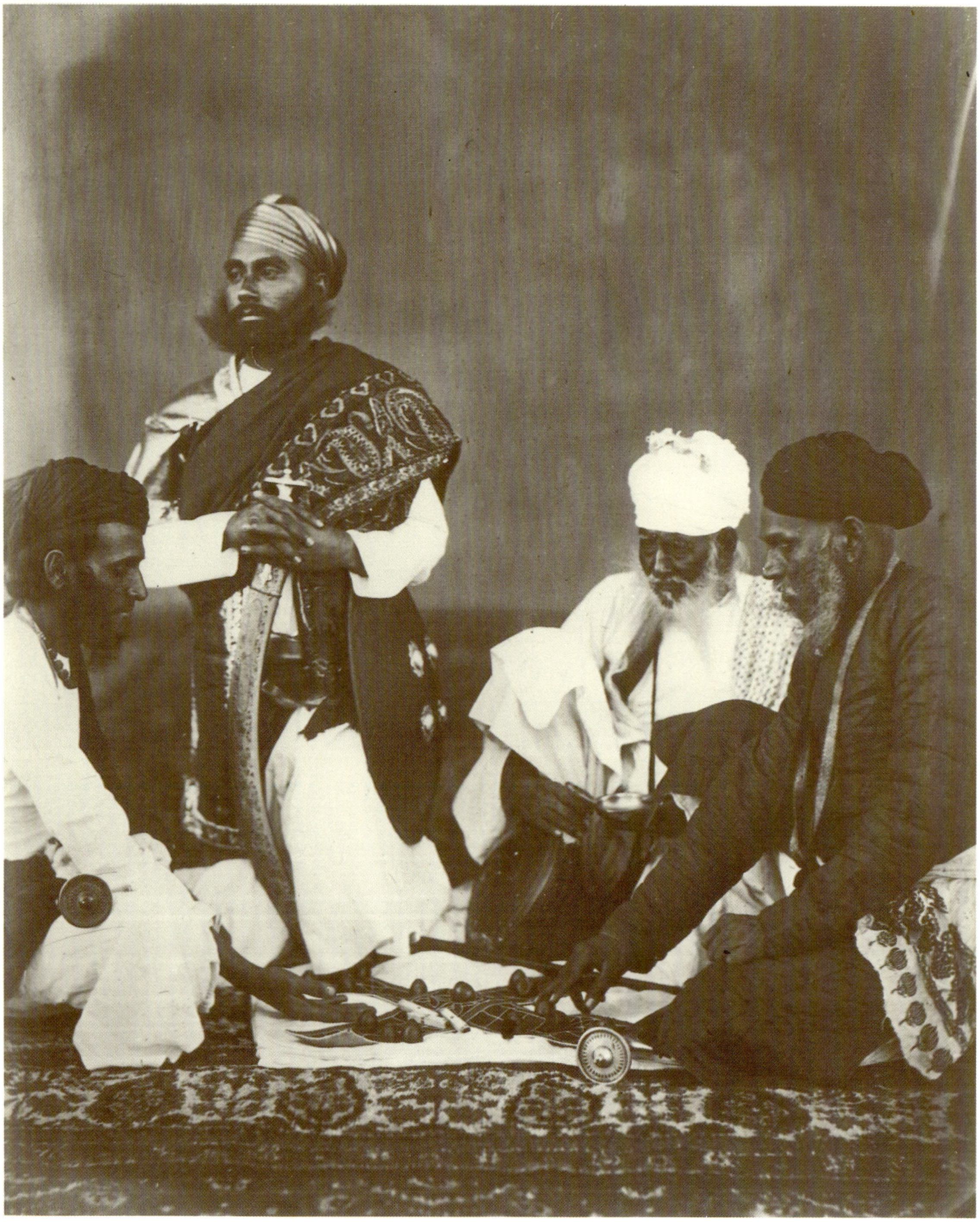

Plate 35 EUGENE CLUTTERBUCK IMPEY
Portrait of Thakoor Lukhdeer Singh, Rajpoot of Ulwur
between 1858 and 1865

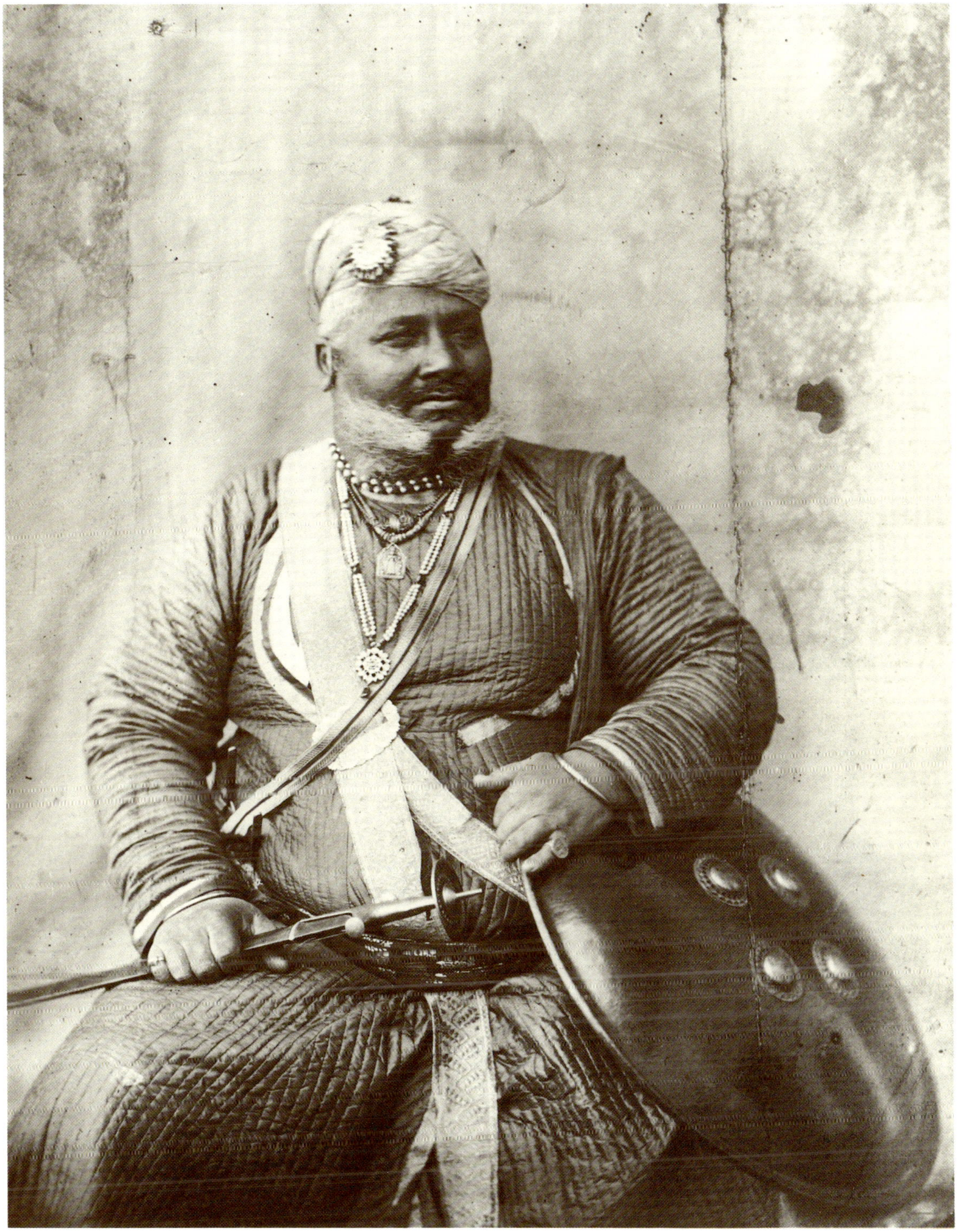

Plate 36 GERTRUDE KÄSEBIER
Miss Minnie Ashley
published 1905

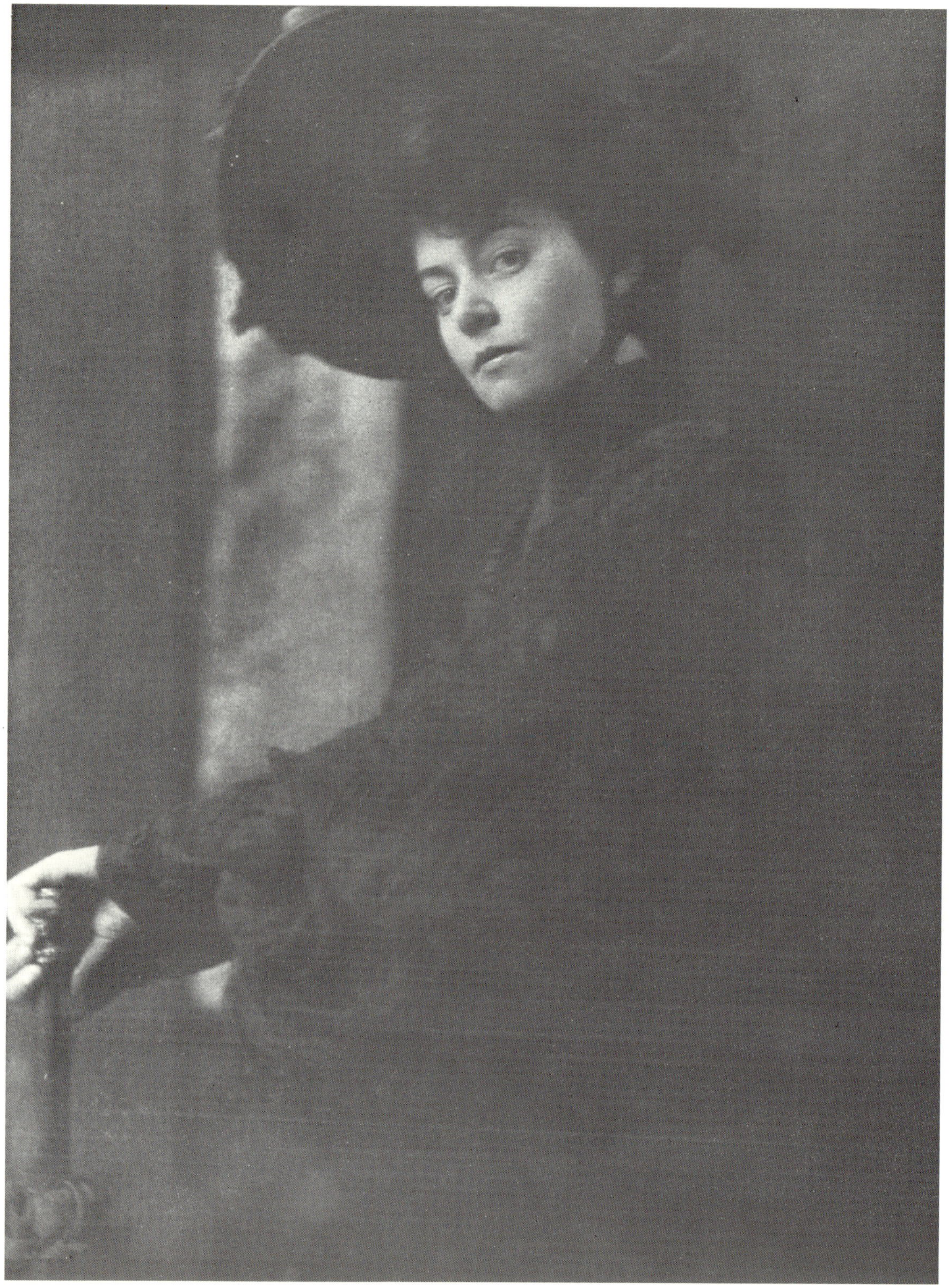

Plate 37 POW KEE
Hankow during Floods
1887

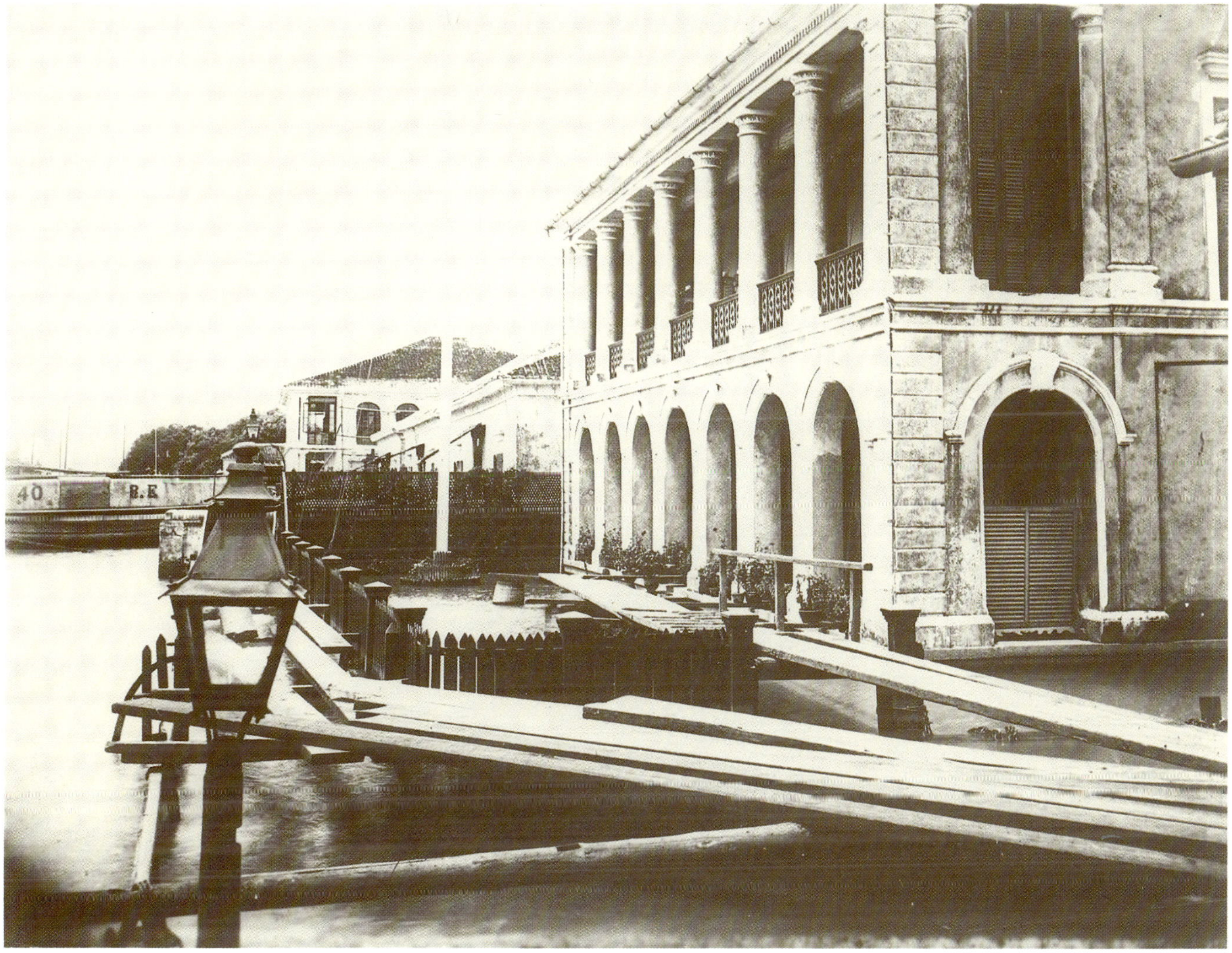

Plate 38 POW KEE
Fishing, Hankow
1884

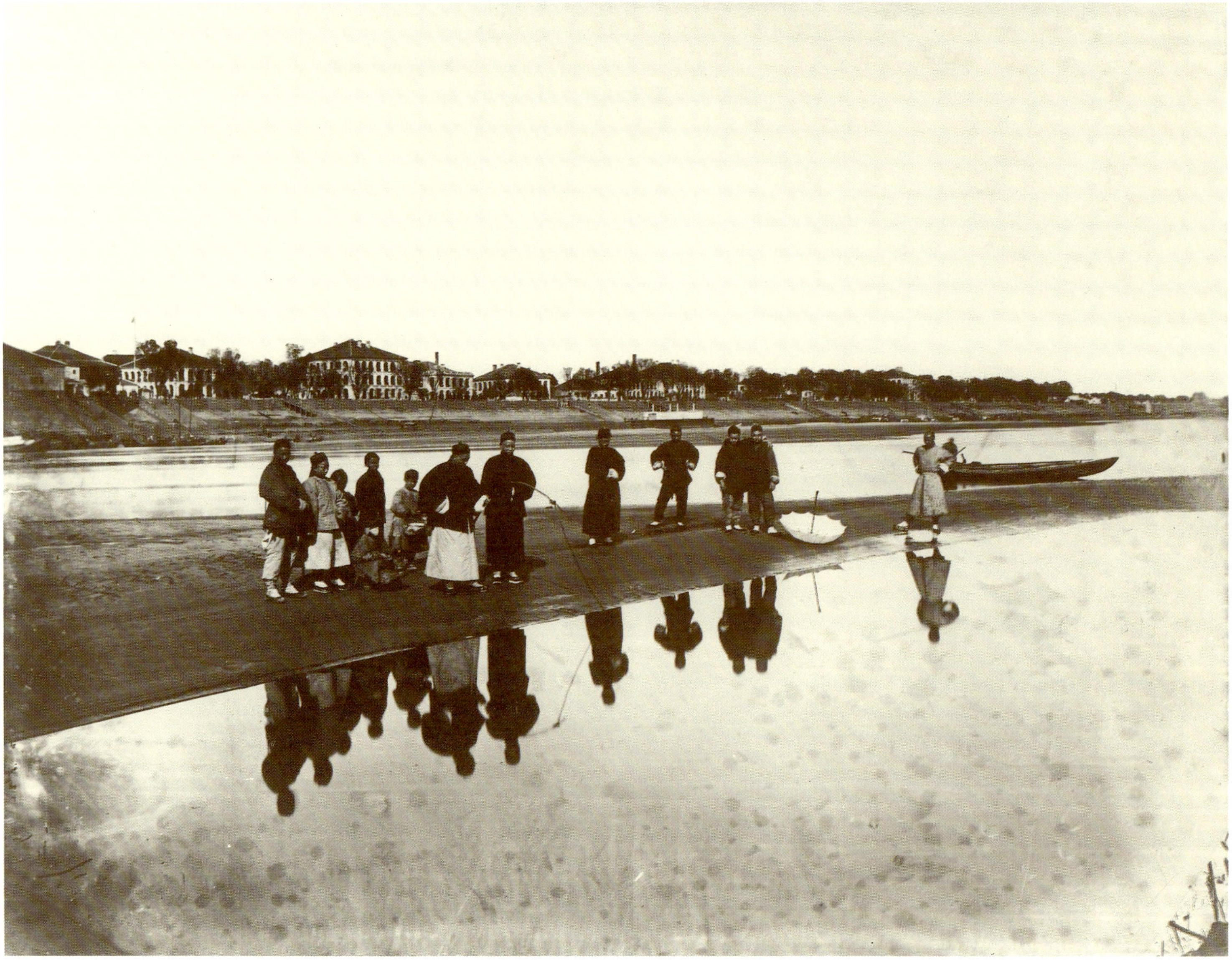

Plate 39 (?) A O KNOBLAUCH
Pitch and Toss
1909

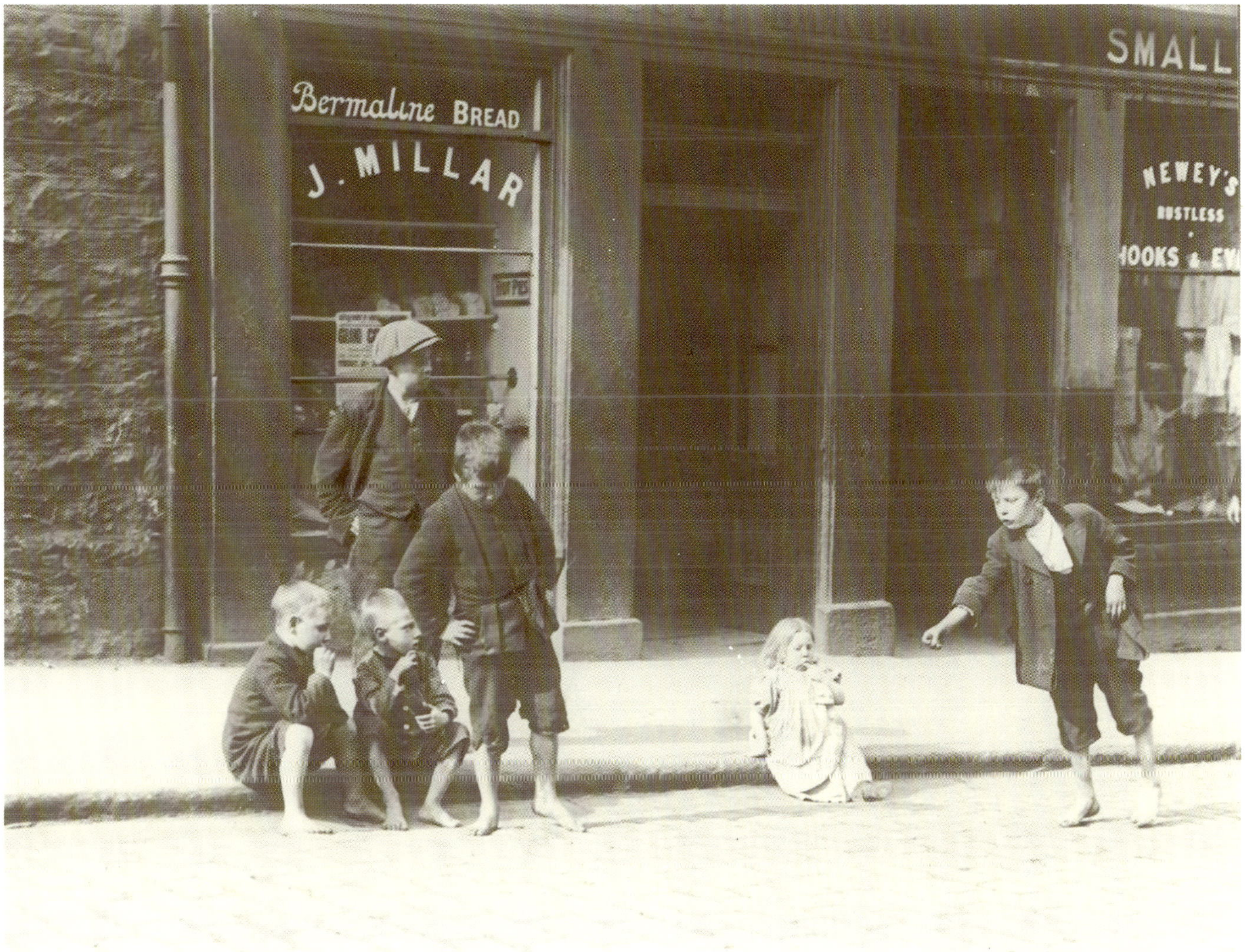

Plate 40 J LAWTON & CO
Waterfall with figures
about 1870–4

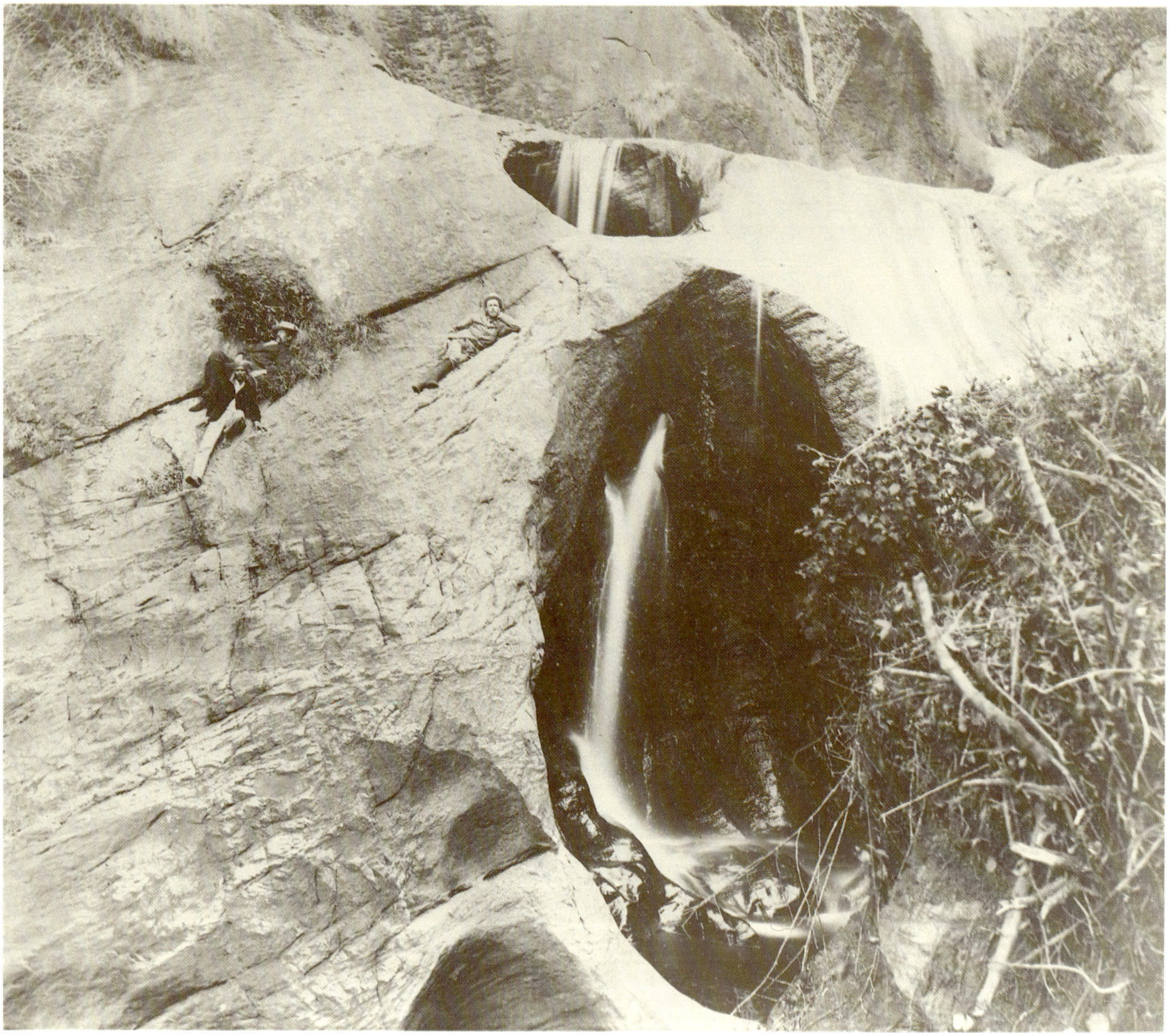

Plate 41 F-J MOULIN
A Game of Chess in Algeria
1856

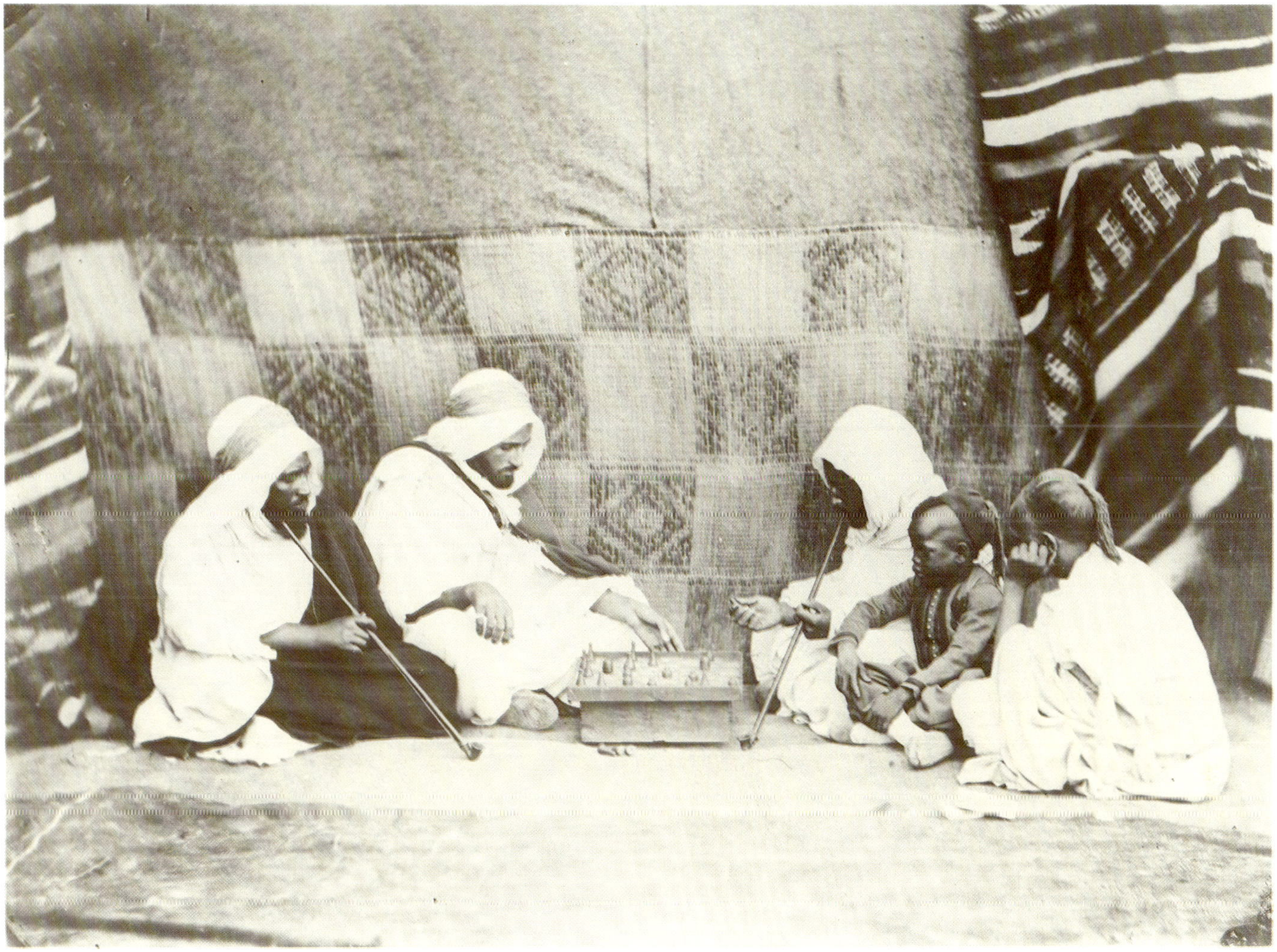

Plate 42 A NOACK
Boy with Cow
undated

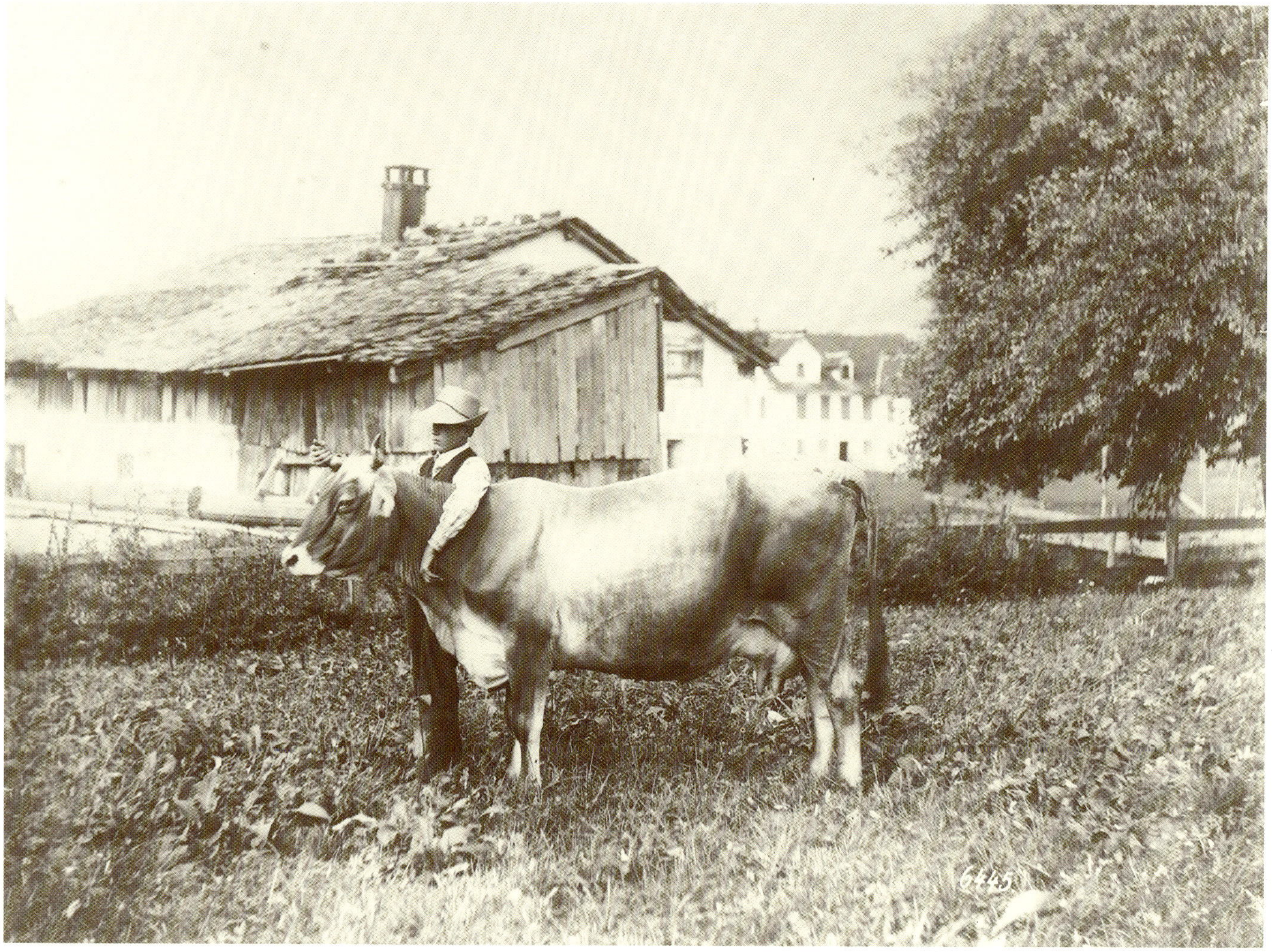

Plate 43 JOHN PATRICK
St Margaret's Loch, Edinburgh
undated

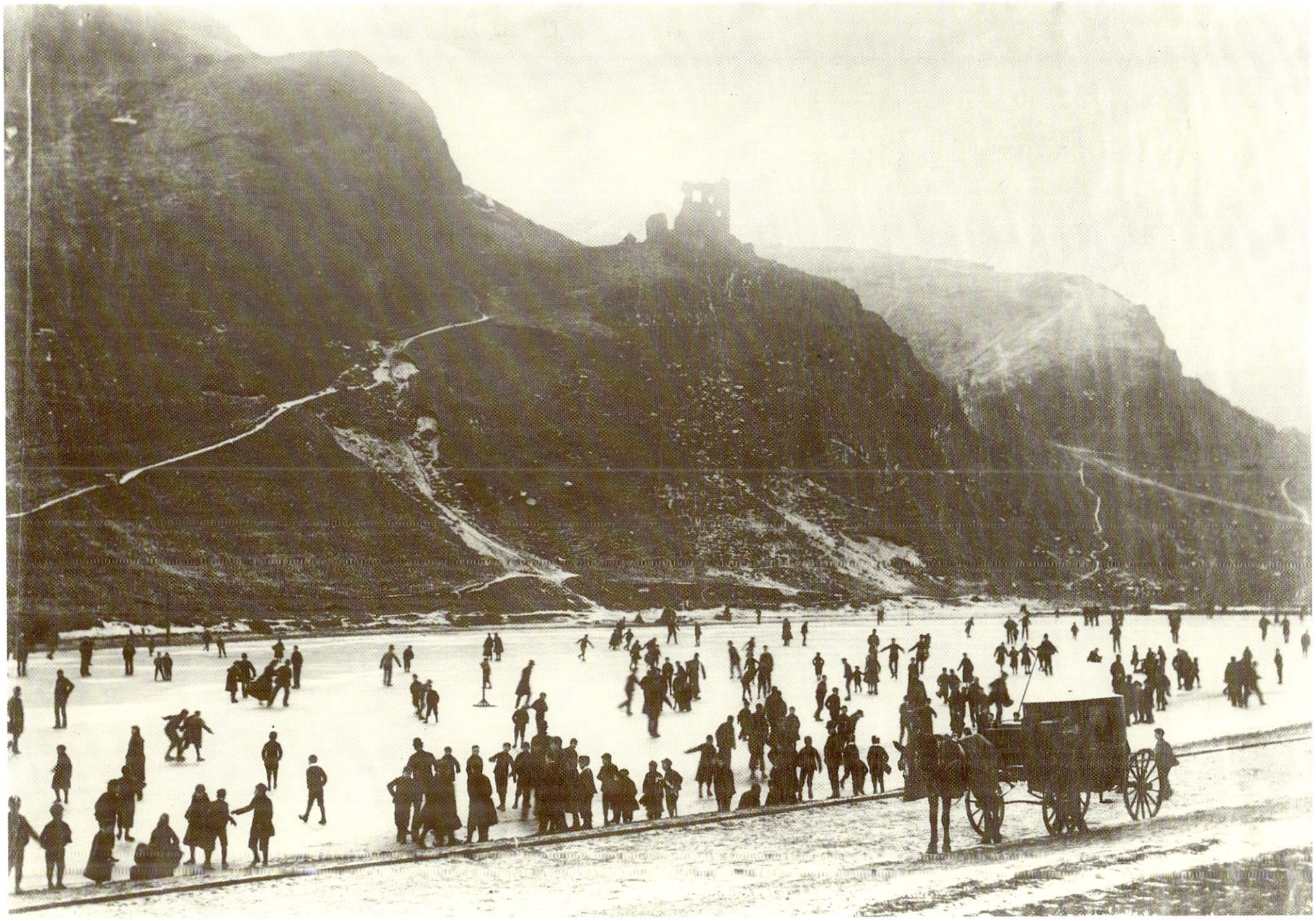

Plate 44 THOMAS RODGER
Walter Little Gilmour
about 1858

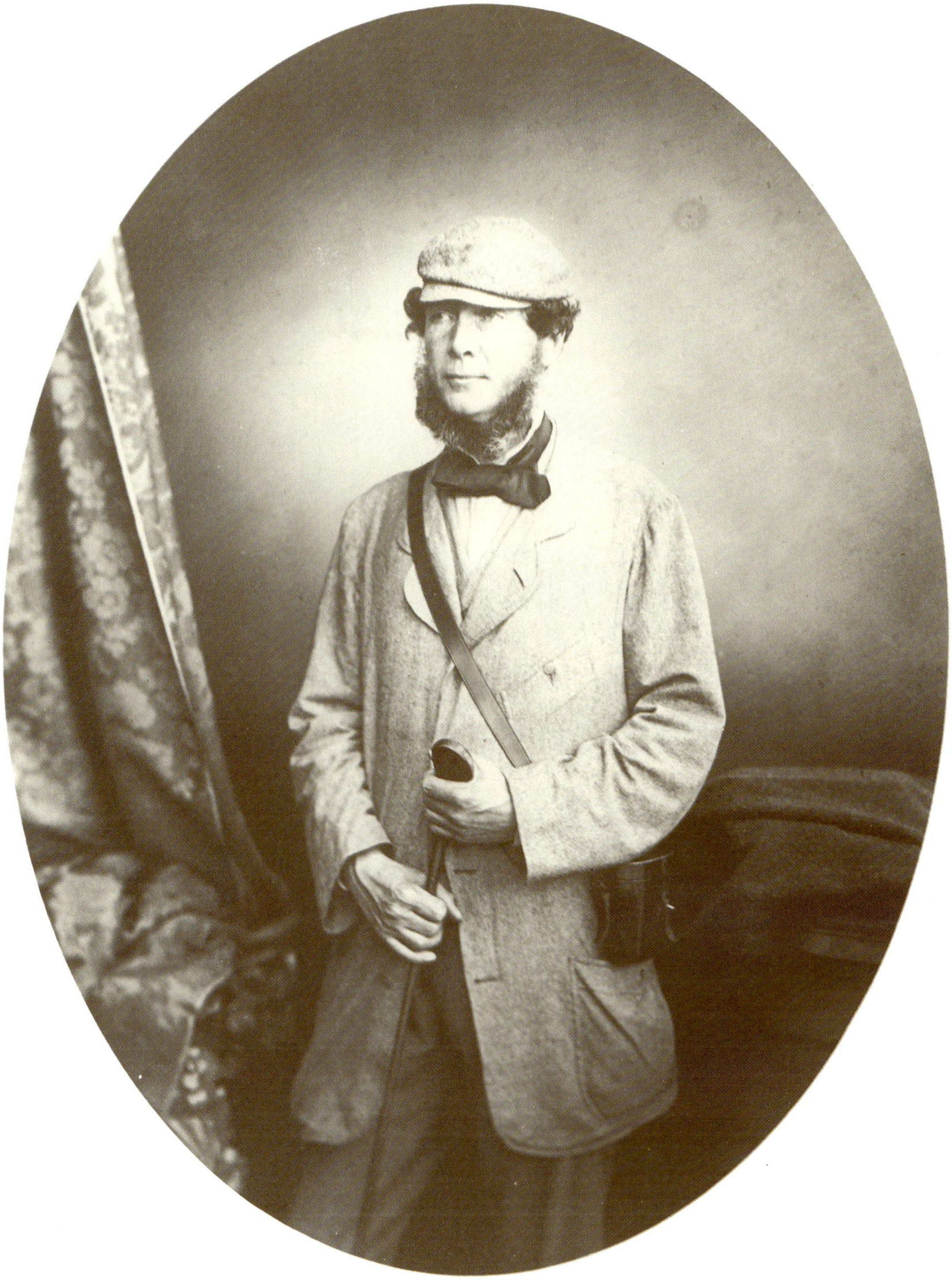

Plate 47 CHARLES SHEPHERD *and* ARTHUR ROBERTSON
Bheesties, Delhi
between 1862 and 1868

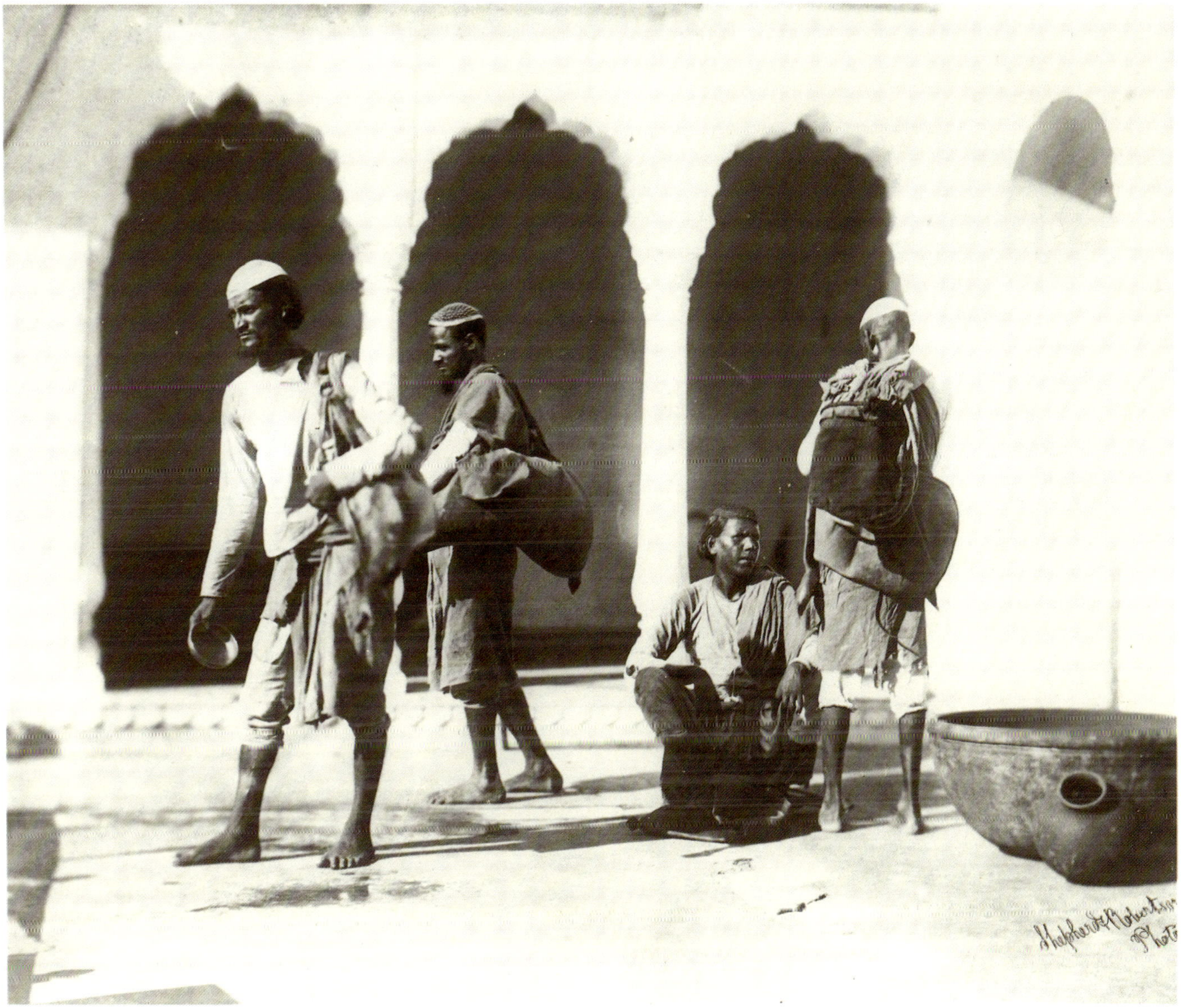

Plate 48 CHARLES SHEPHERD *and* ARTHUR ROBERTSON
Chohan Rajpoots, Delhi
between 1862 and 1868

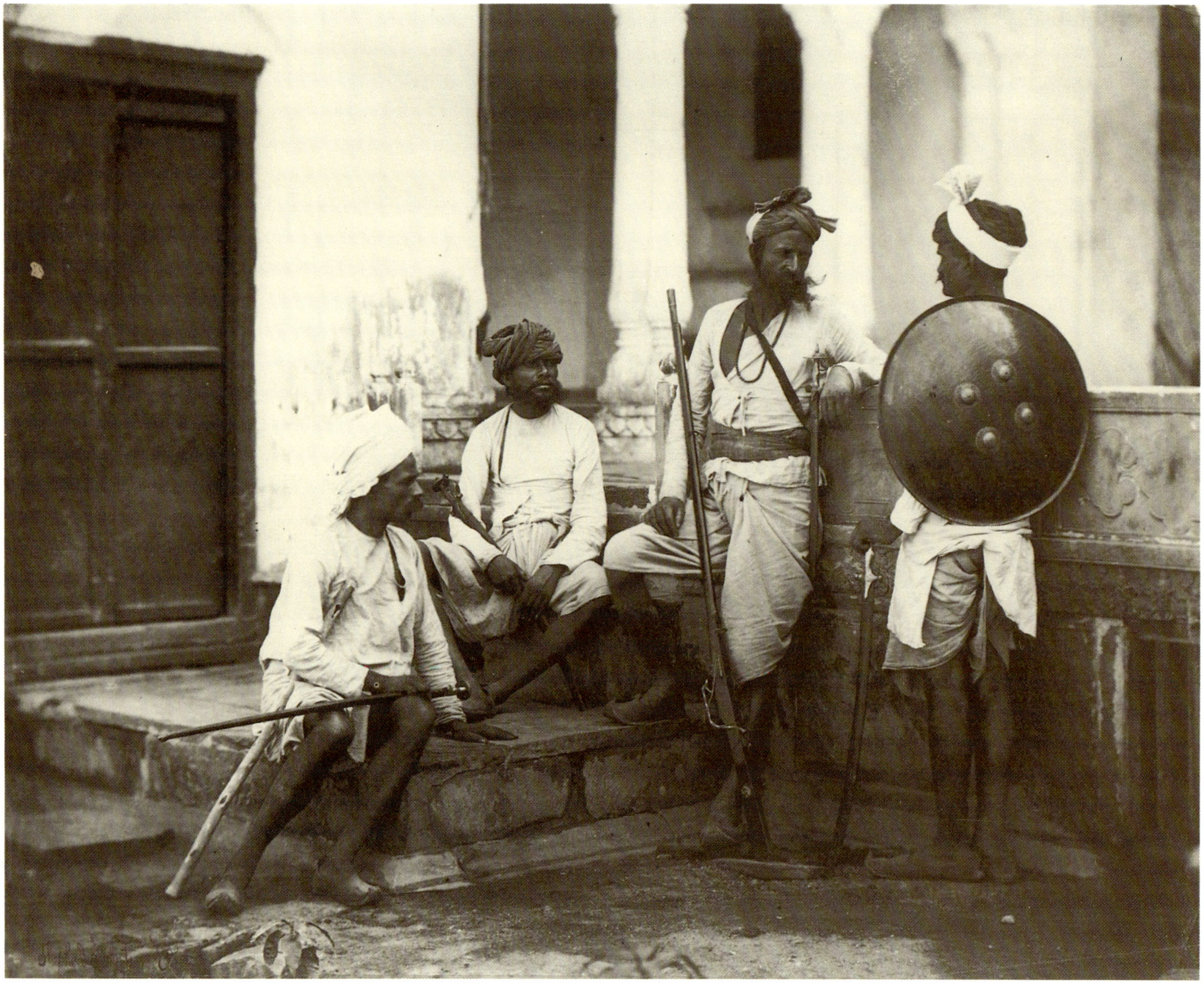

Plate 45 (?) CHARLES T SCOWEN
Singhalese Woman
undated

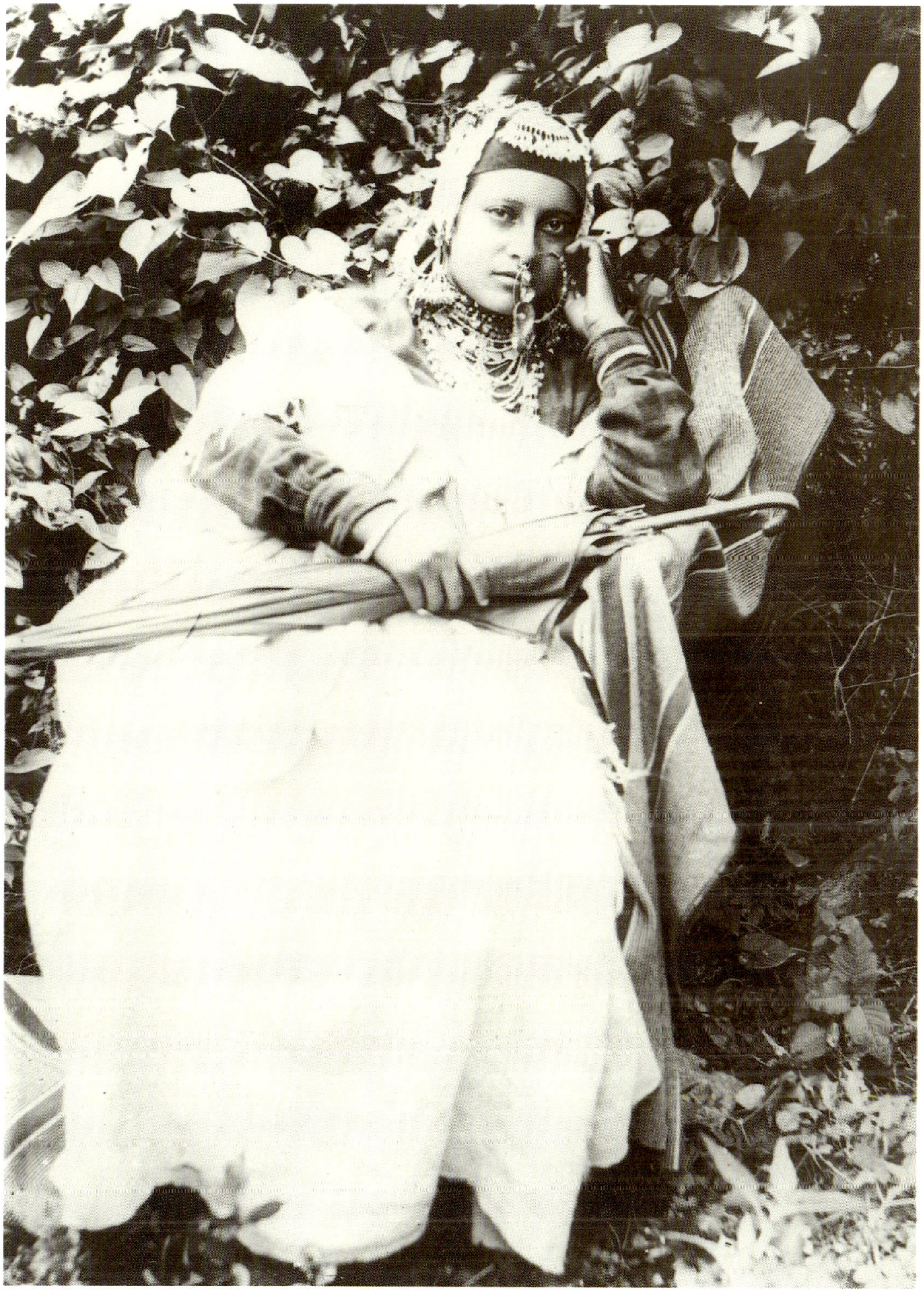

Plate 46 (?) CHARLES T SCOWEN
Singhalese Woman
undated

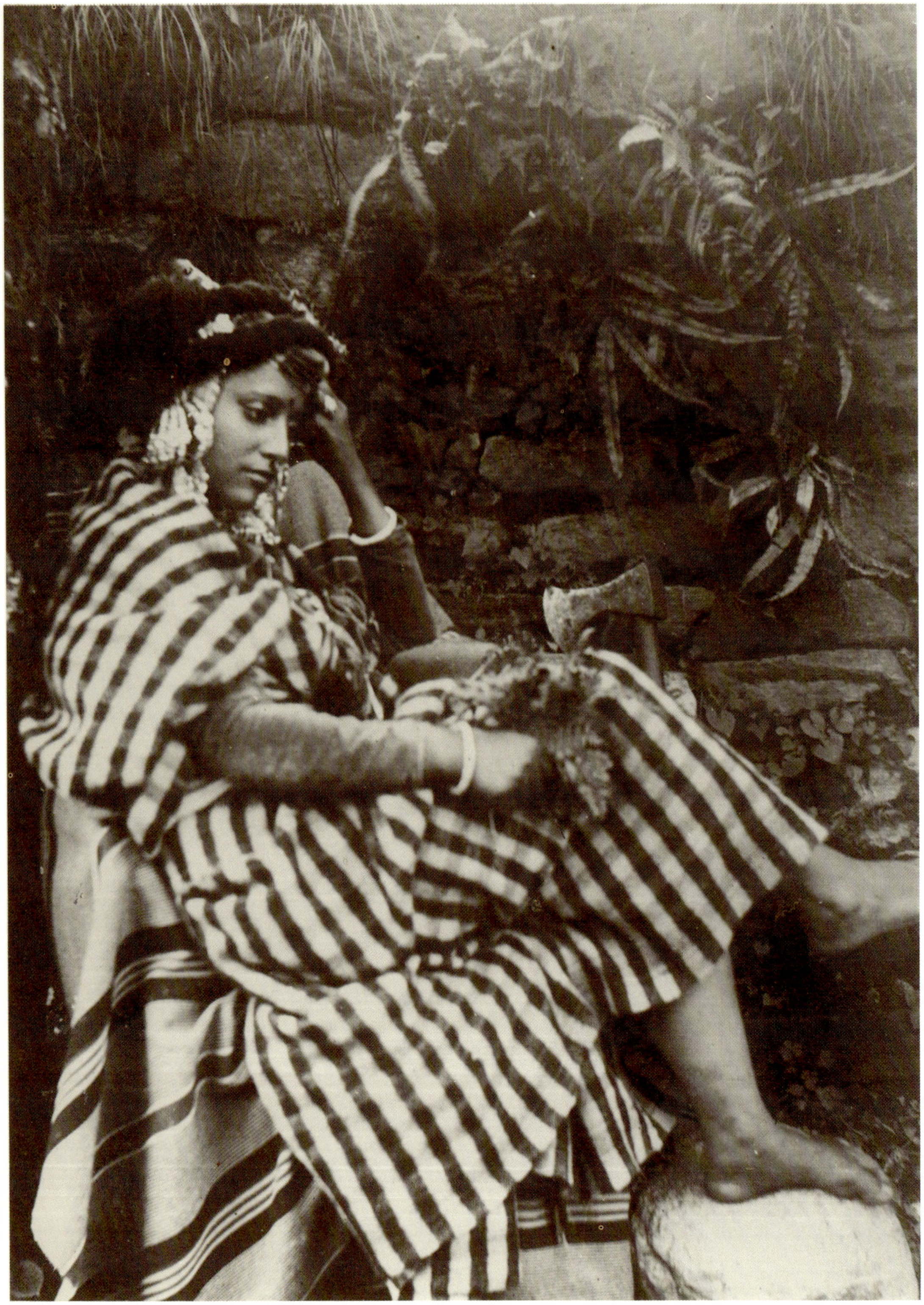

Plate 49 W L H SKEEN & CO
Two Singhalese Girls
undated

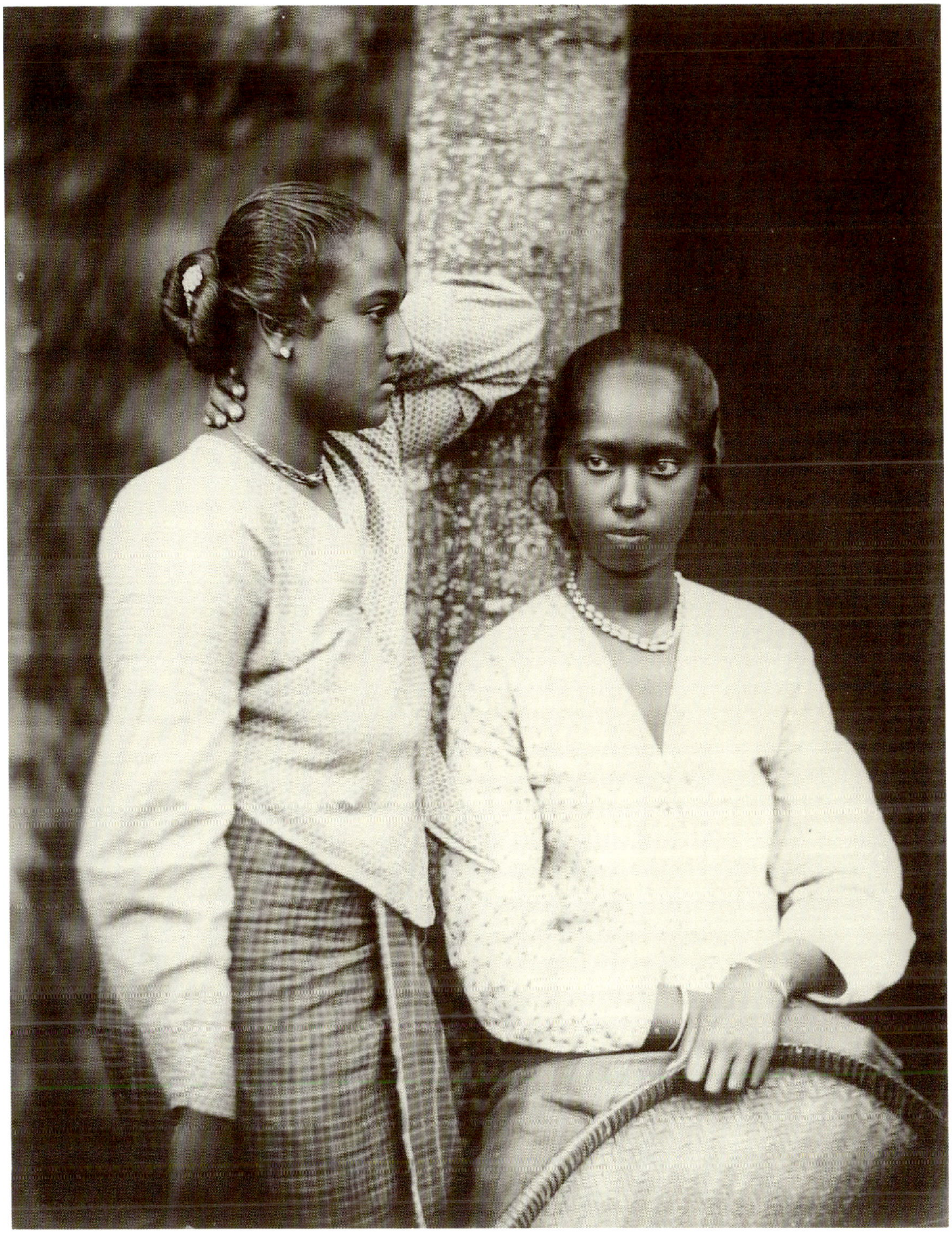

Plate 50 W L H SKEEN & CO
Bamboos
undated

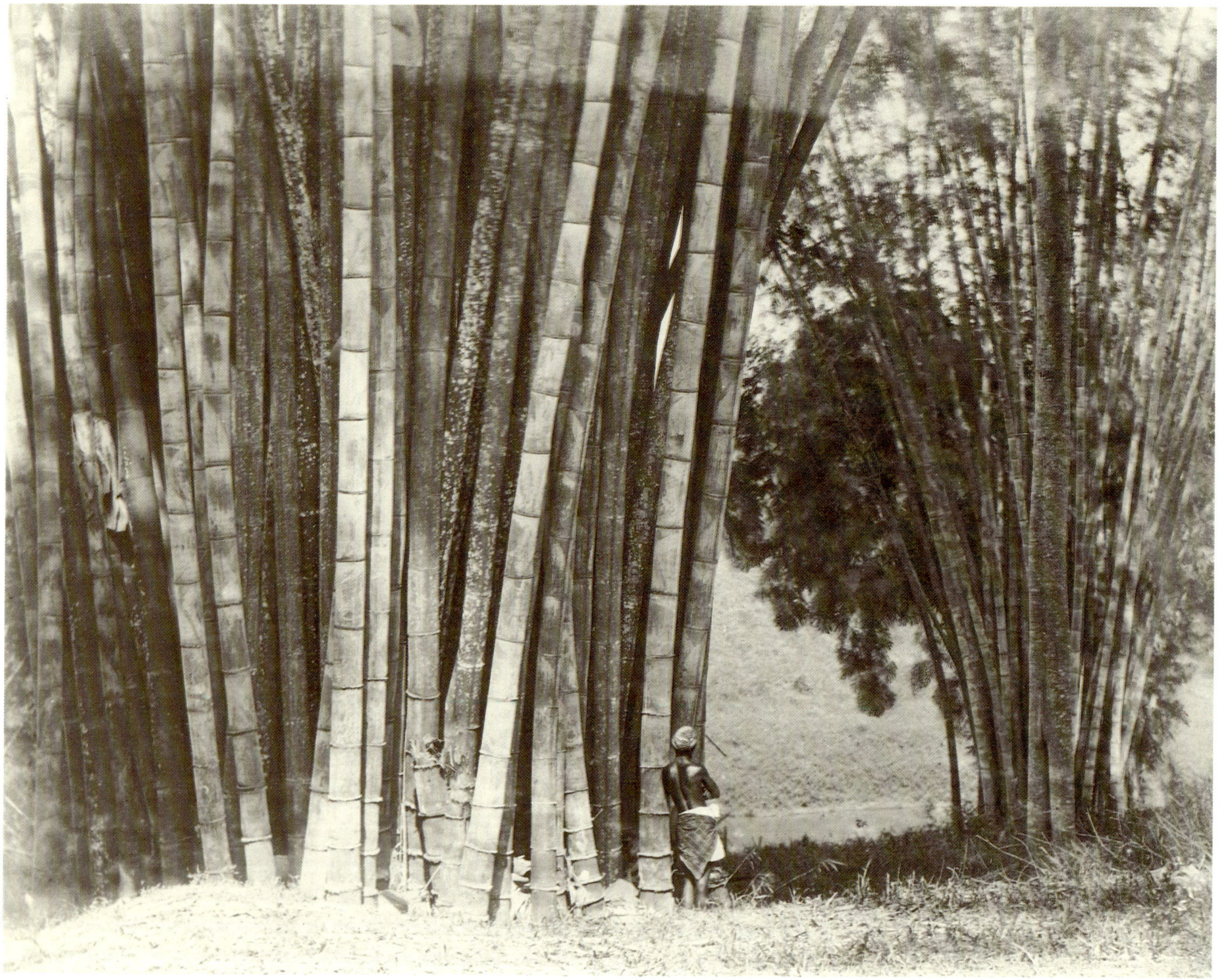

Plate 51 W L H SKEEN & CO
The Devil's Elbow, on the way to Kandy
undated

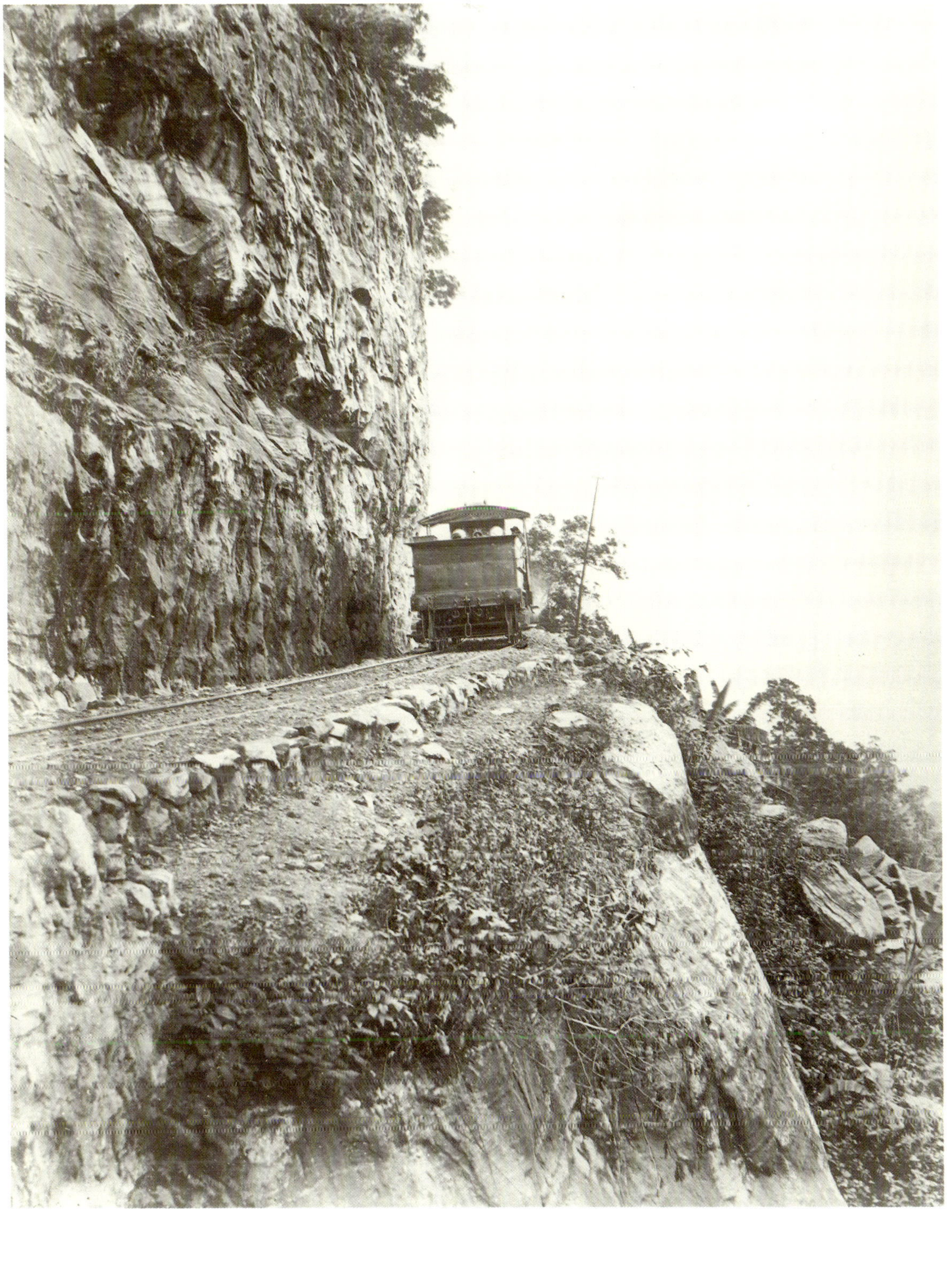

Plate 52 ISAAC WEST TABER
Chinese Butcher and Grocery Shop, Chinatown,
San Francisco
1887

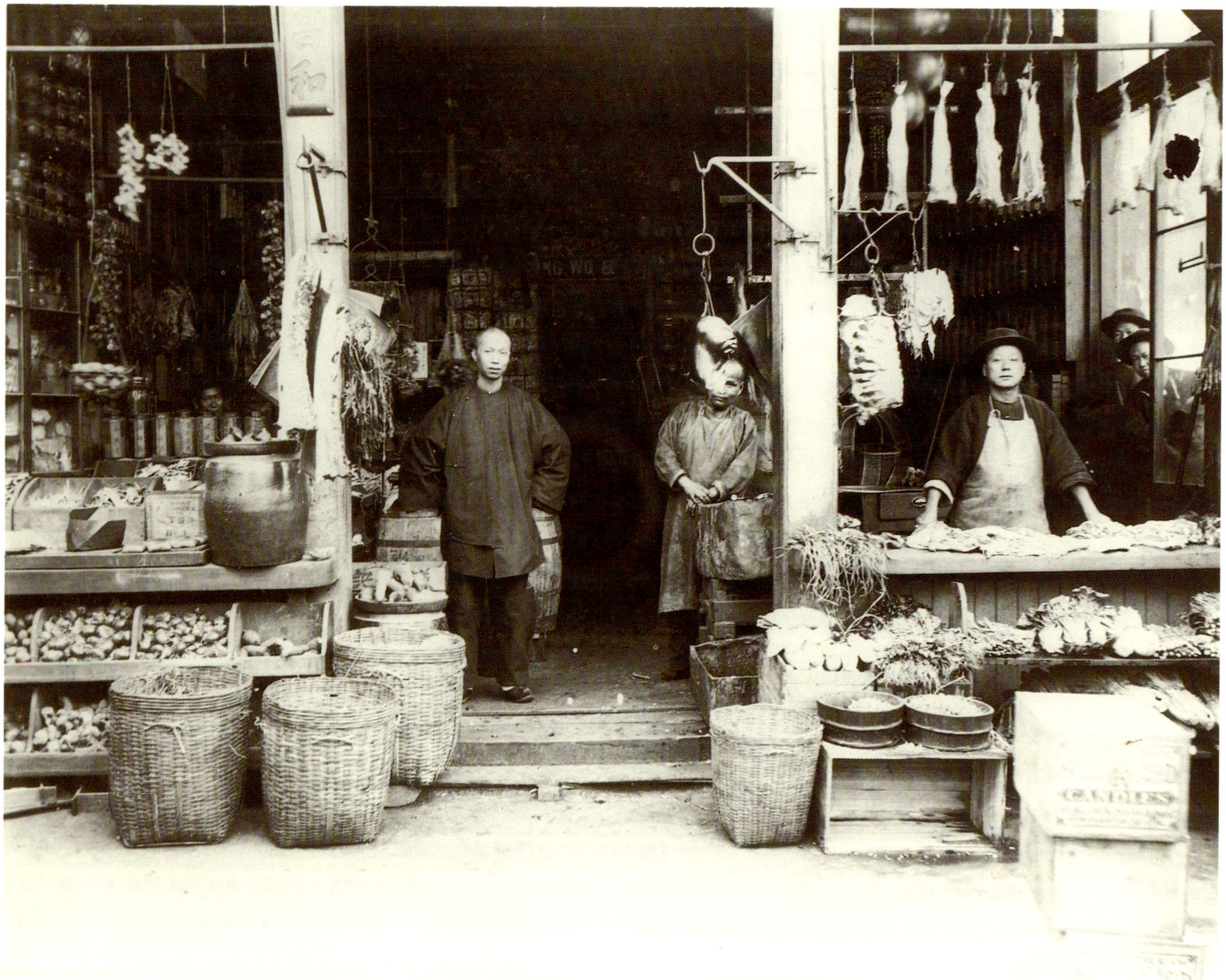

Plate 53 WILLIAM HENRY FOX TALBOT
The Scott Monument under Construction
1844

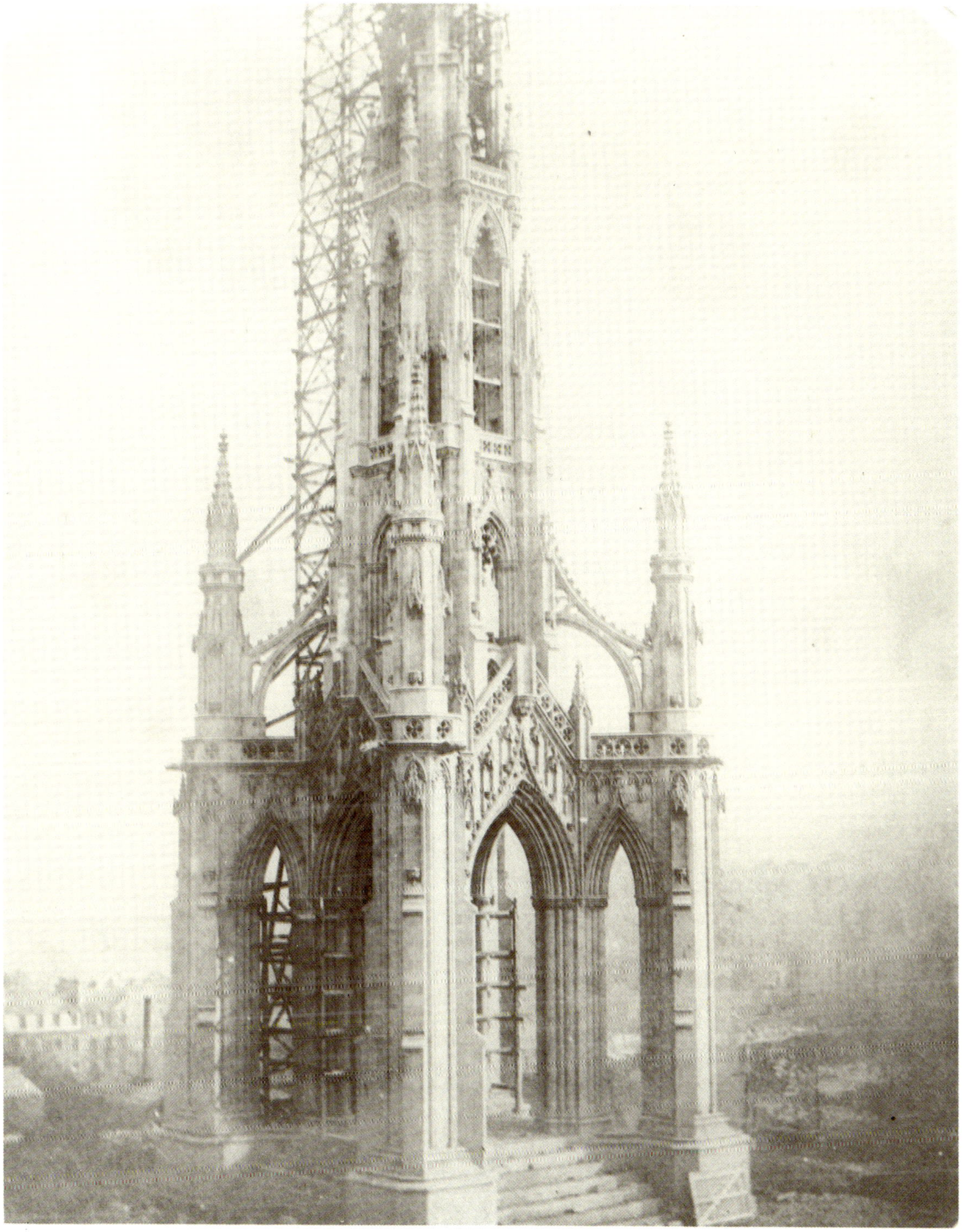

Plate 54 JAMES VALENTINE
Ben Lomond from Luss
undated

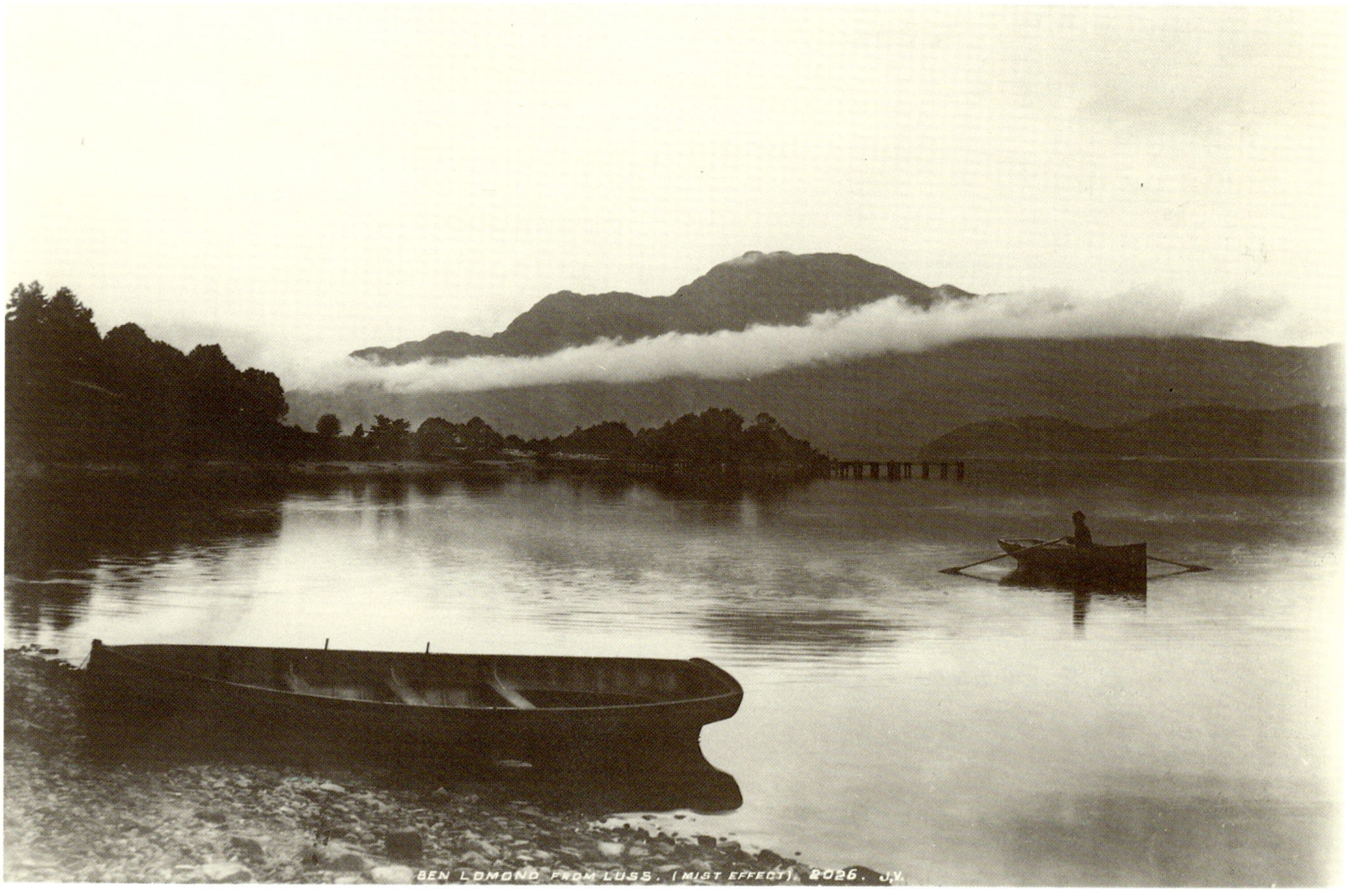

Plate 55 JAMES VALENTINE
Staffa, the Clam Shell Cave
undated

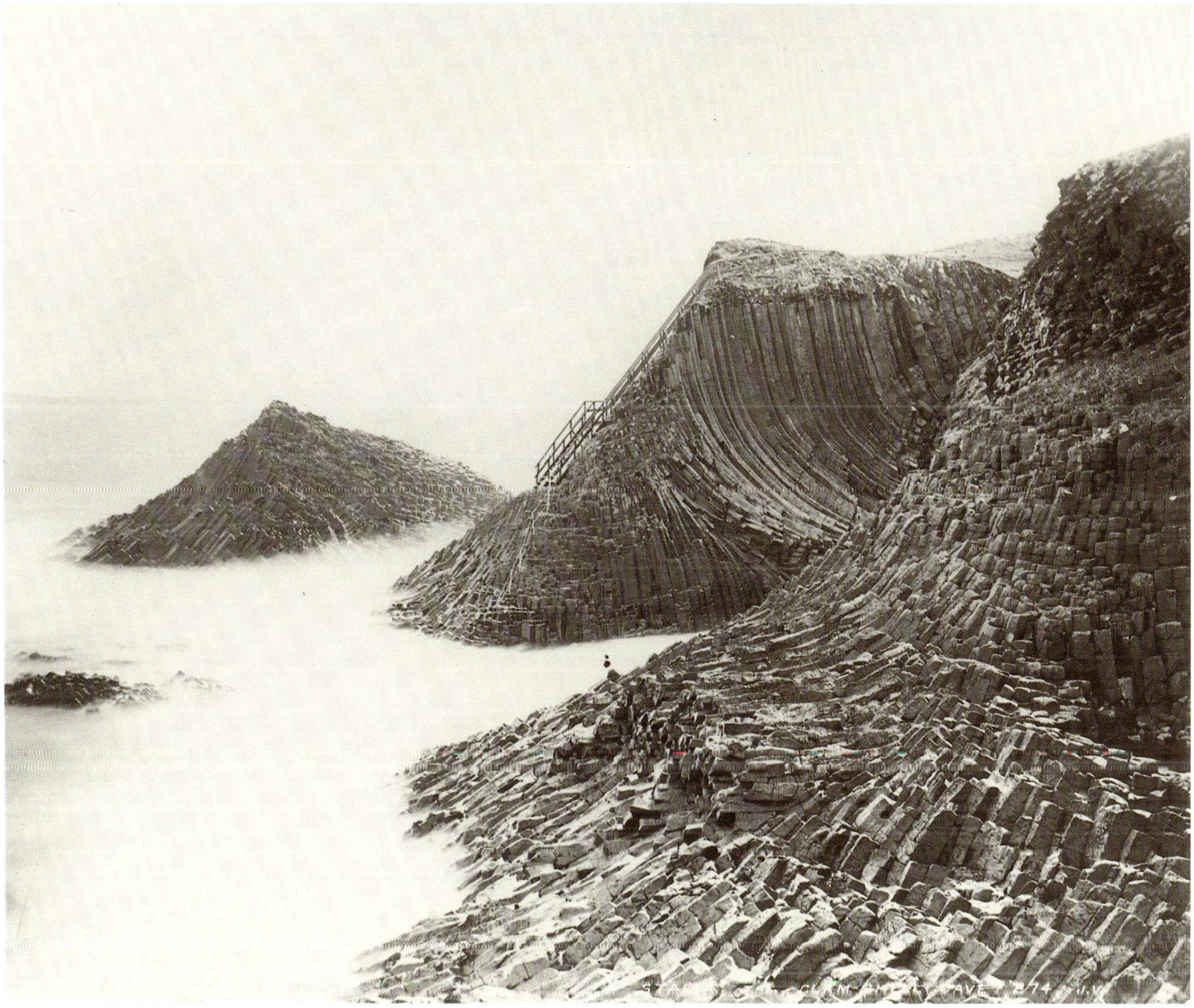

Plate 56 GEORGE WASHINGTON WILSON
View in Leith Docks
undated

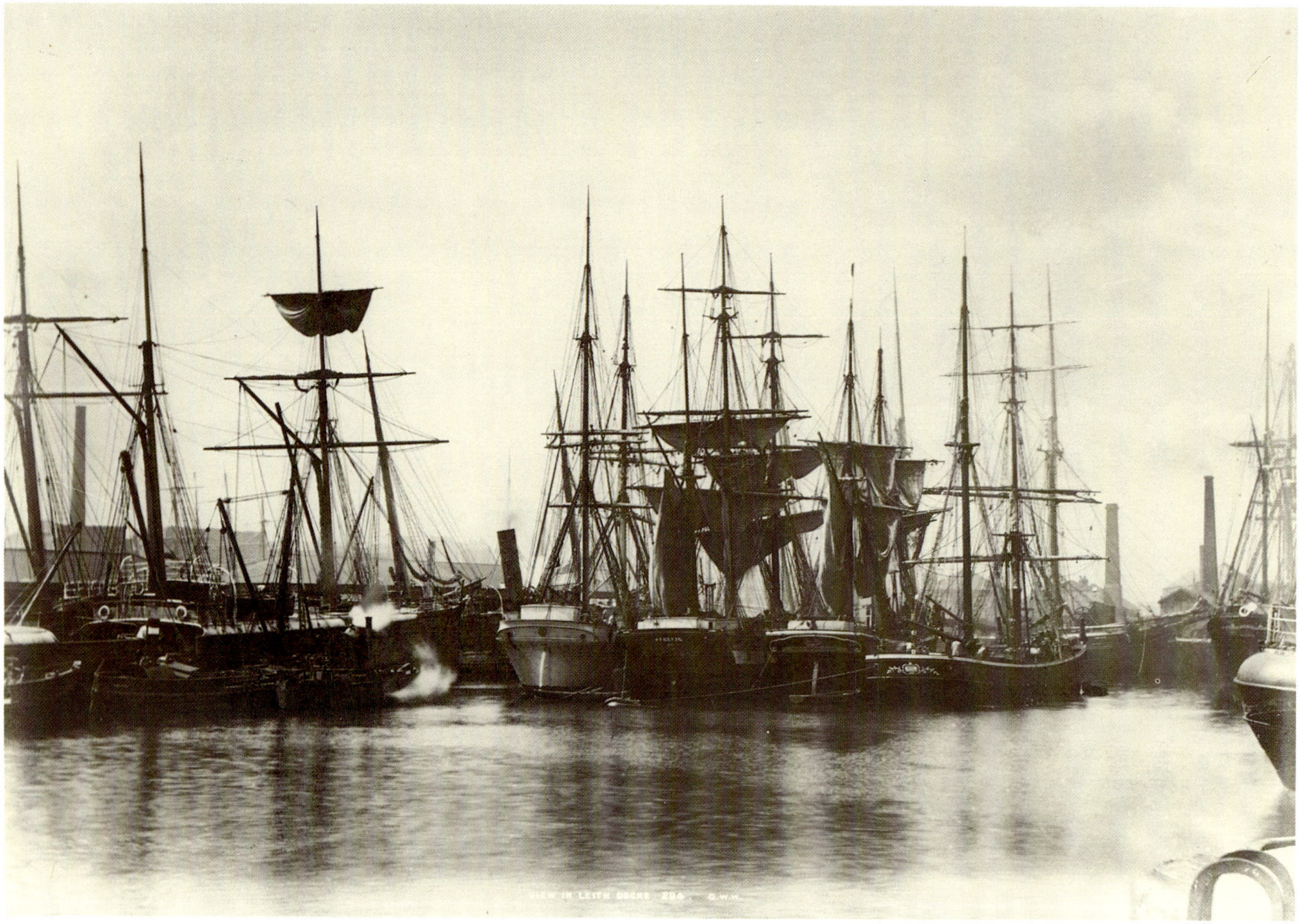

Plate 57 GEORGE WASHINGTON WILSON
Chancel, St Mary's Cathedral, Iona
undated

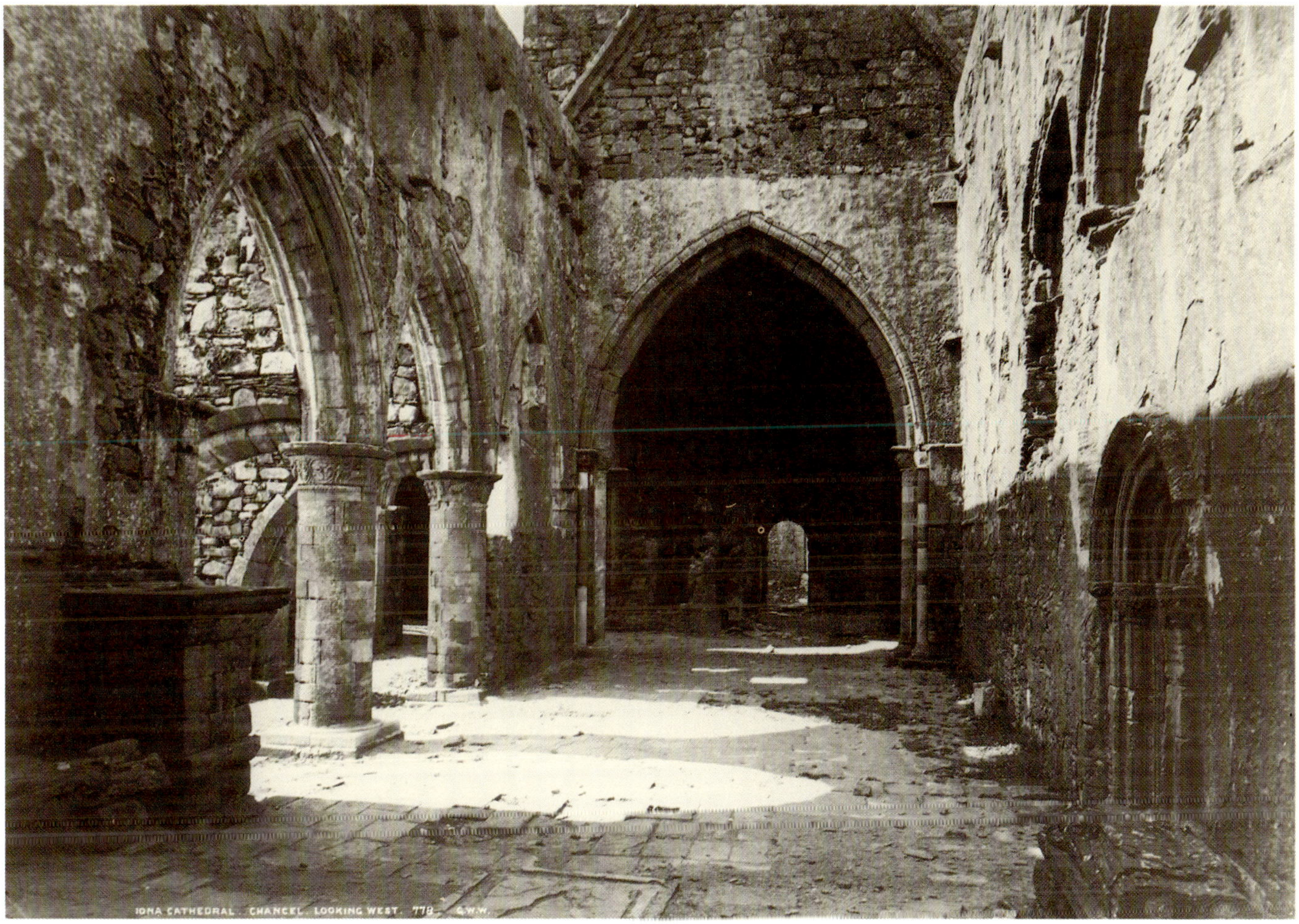

Plate 58 GEORGE WASHINGTON WILSON
Tighnalechan, Aberfeldy
undated

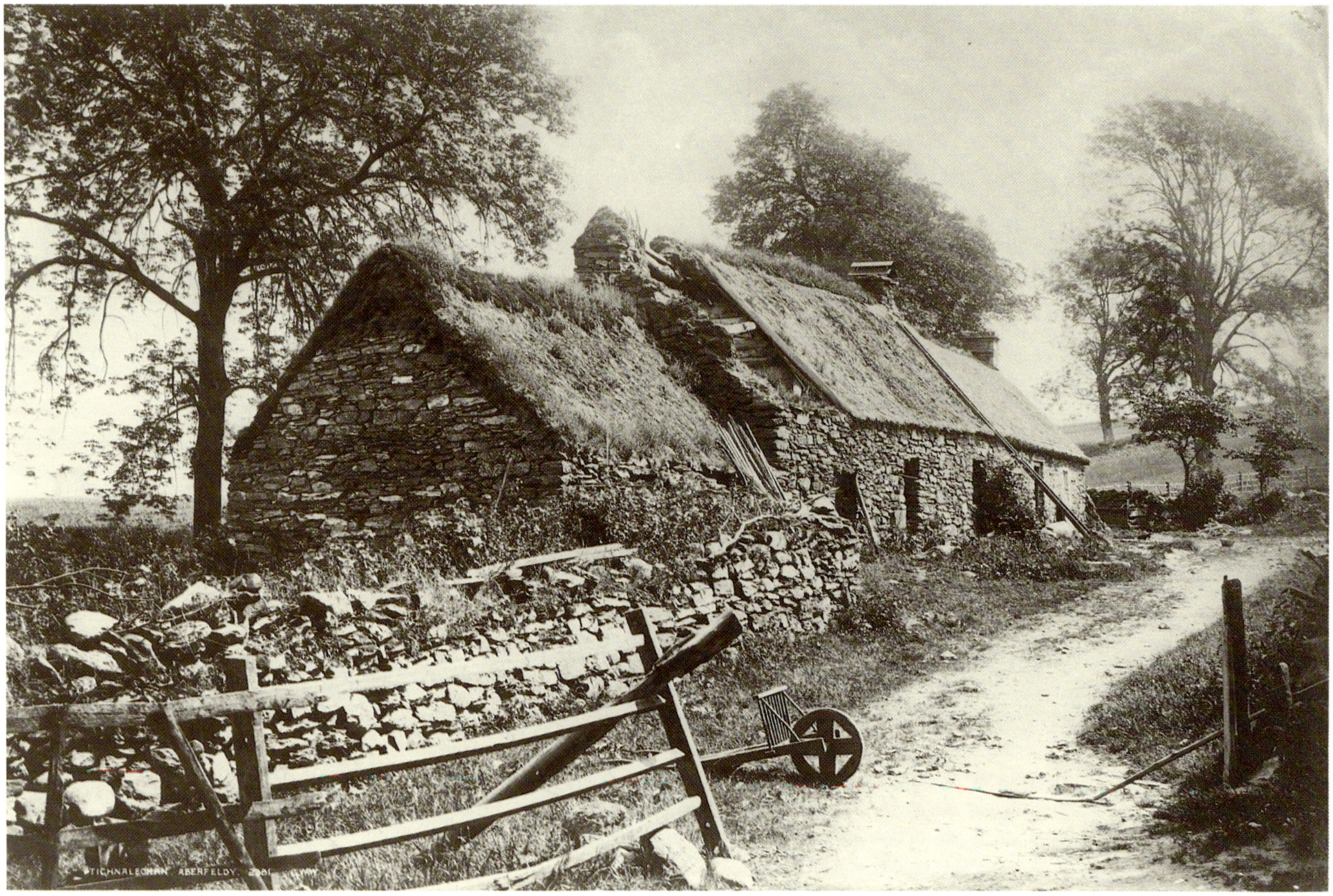

Plate 59 ZANGAKI
Tourists at a Pyramid
undated

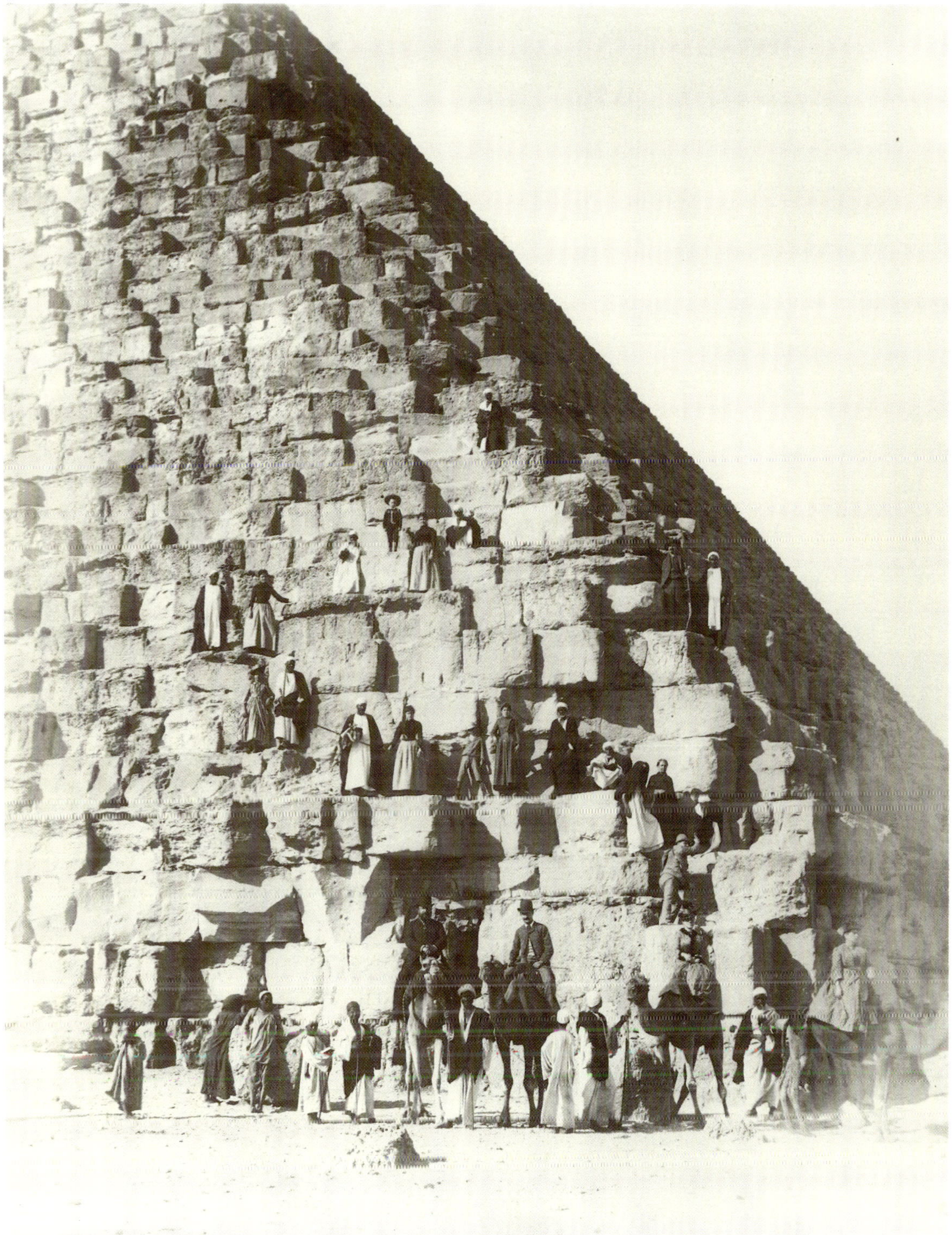

Plate 60 PHOTOGRAPHER UNKNOWN
The Arch of Constantine, Rome
probably taken in the 1850s

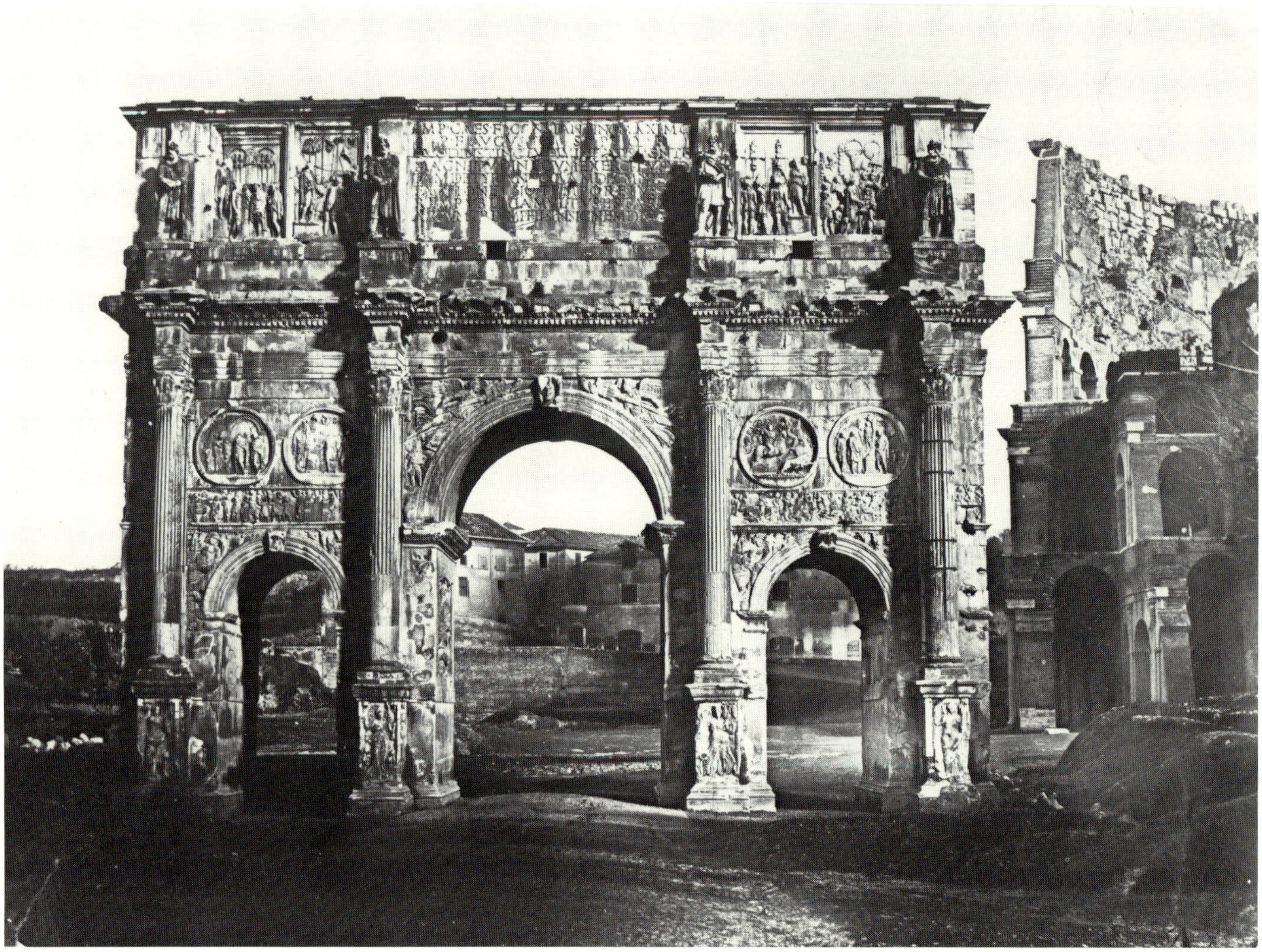

Plate 61 PHOTOGRAPHER UNKNOWN
The Temple of Saturn, Rome
probably taken in the 1850s

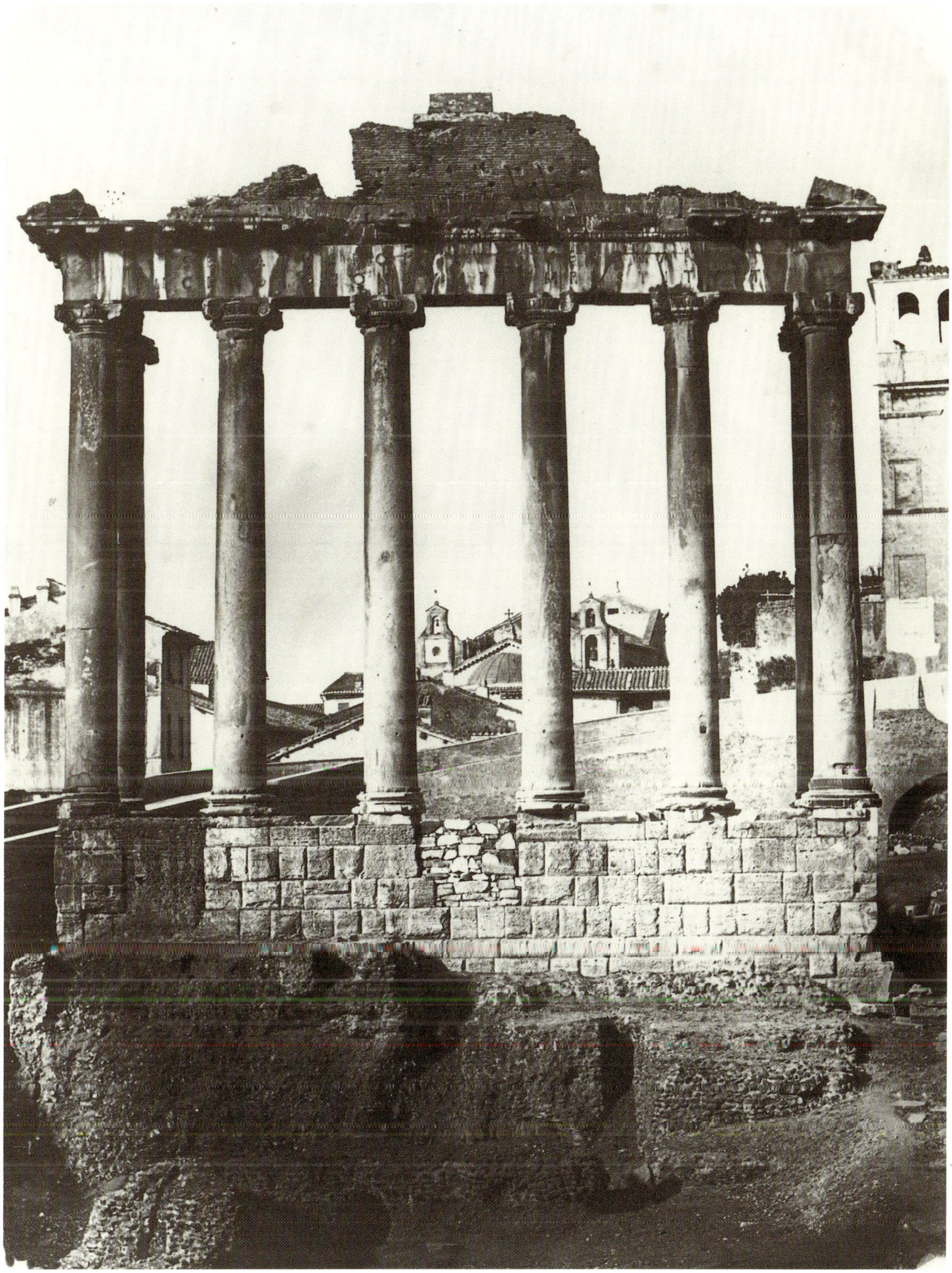

Plate 62 PHOTOGRAPHER UNKNOWN
The Basilica of Maxentius, Rome
probably taken in the 1850s

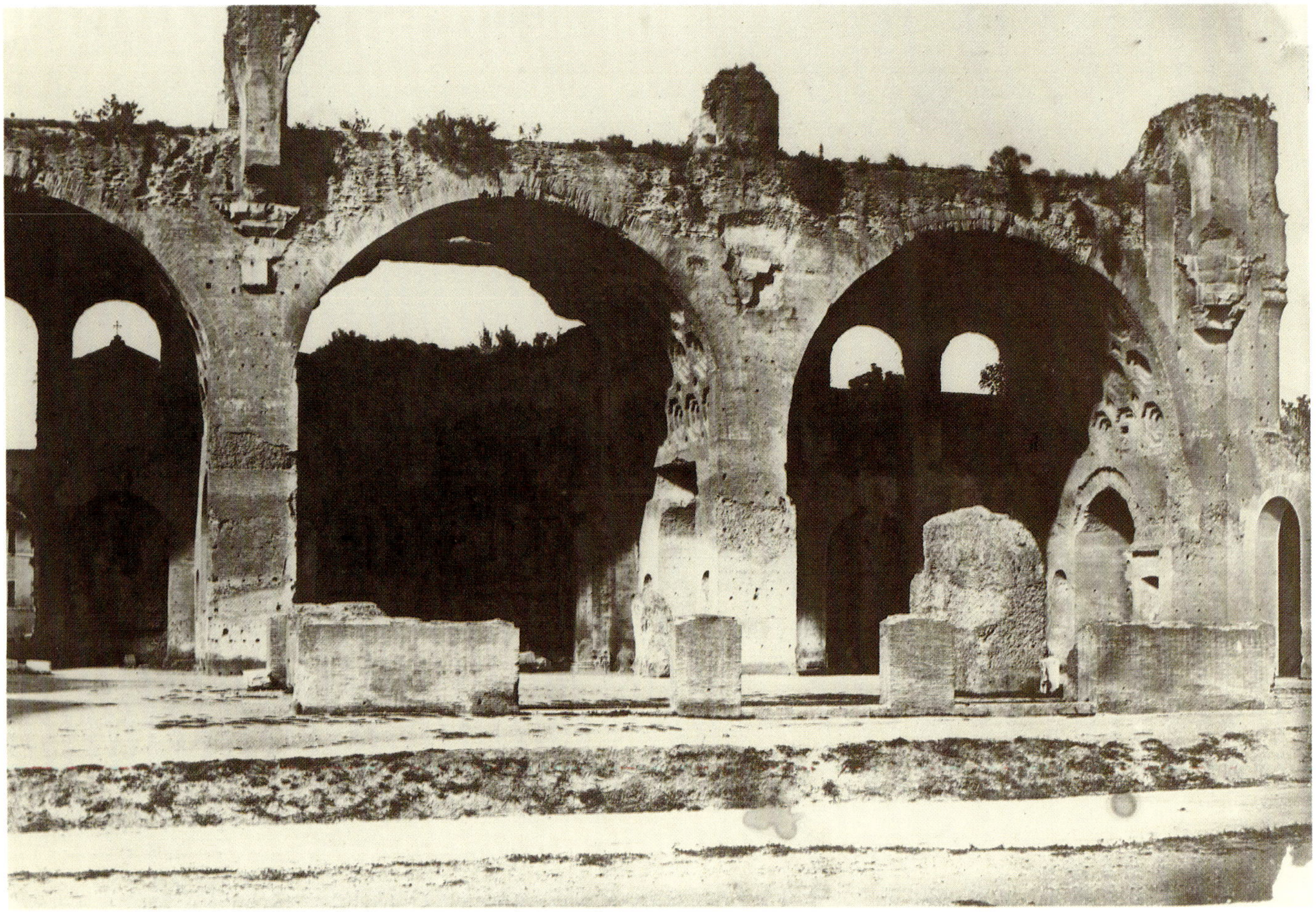

Plate 63 PHOTOGRAPHER UNKNOWN
Two small girls and a pony
about 1900

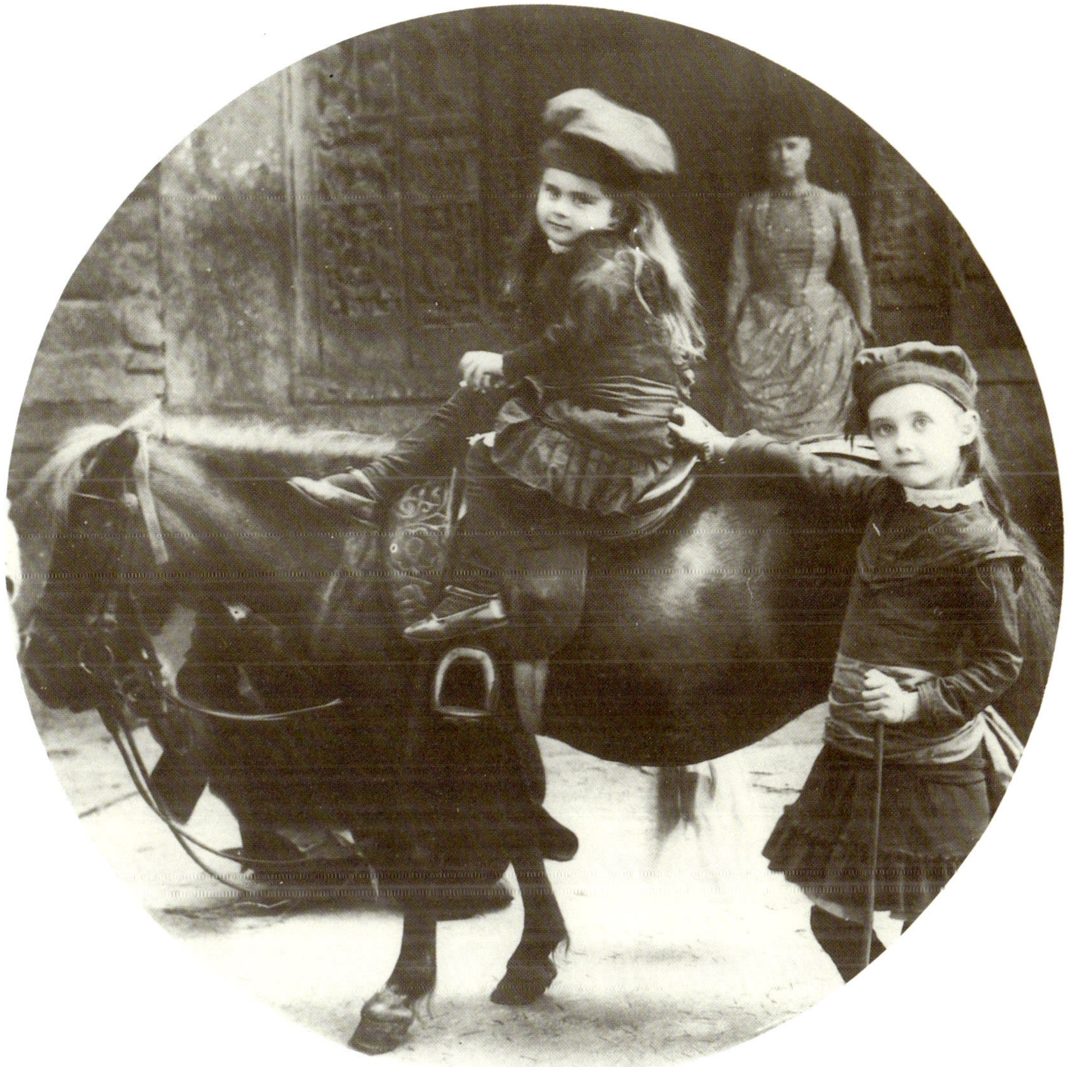

Plate 64 PHOTOGRAPHER UNKNOWN
Niagara Falls in Winter
undated

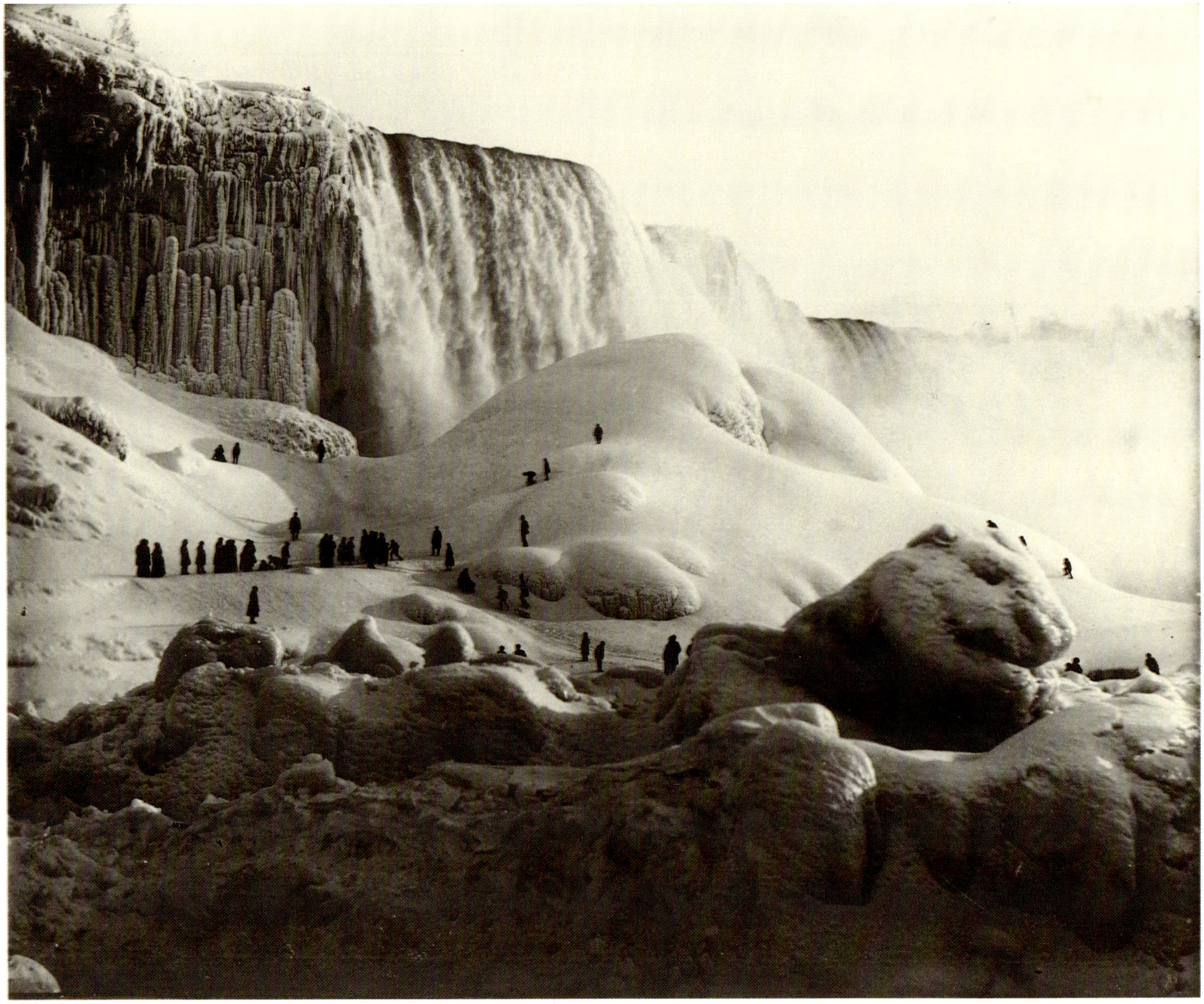

Plate 65 PHOTOGRAPHER UNKNOWN
The Cathedral, Manila
undated

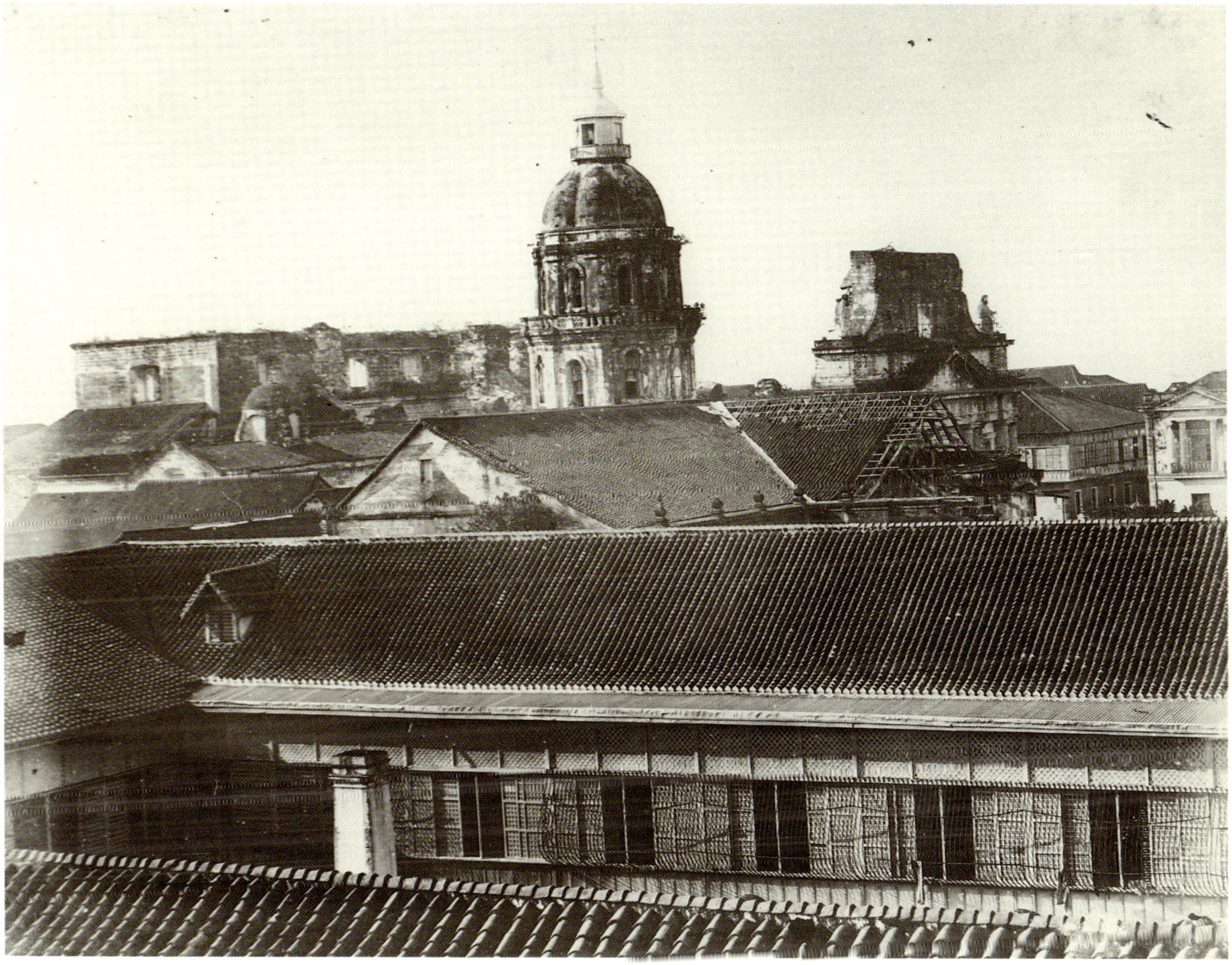

Plate 66 PHOTOGRAPHER UNKNOWN
Sugar Factory, Manila
undated

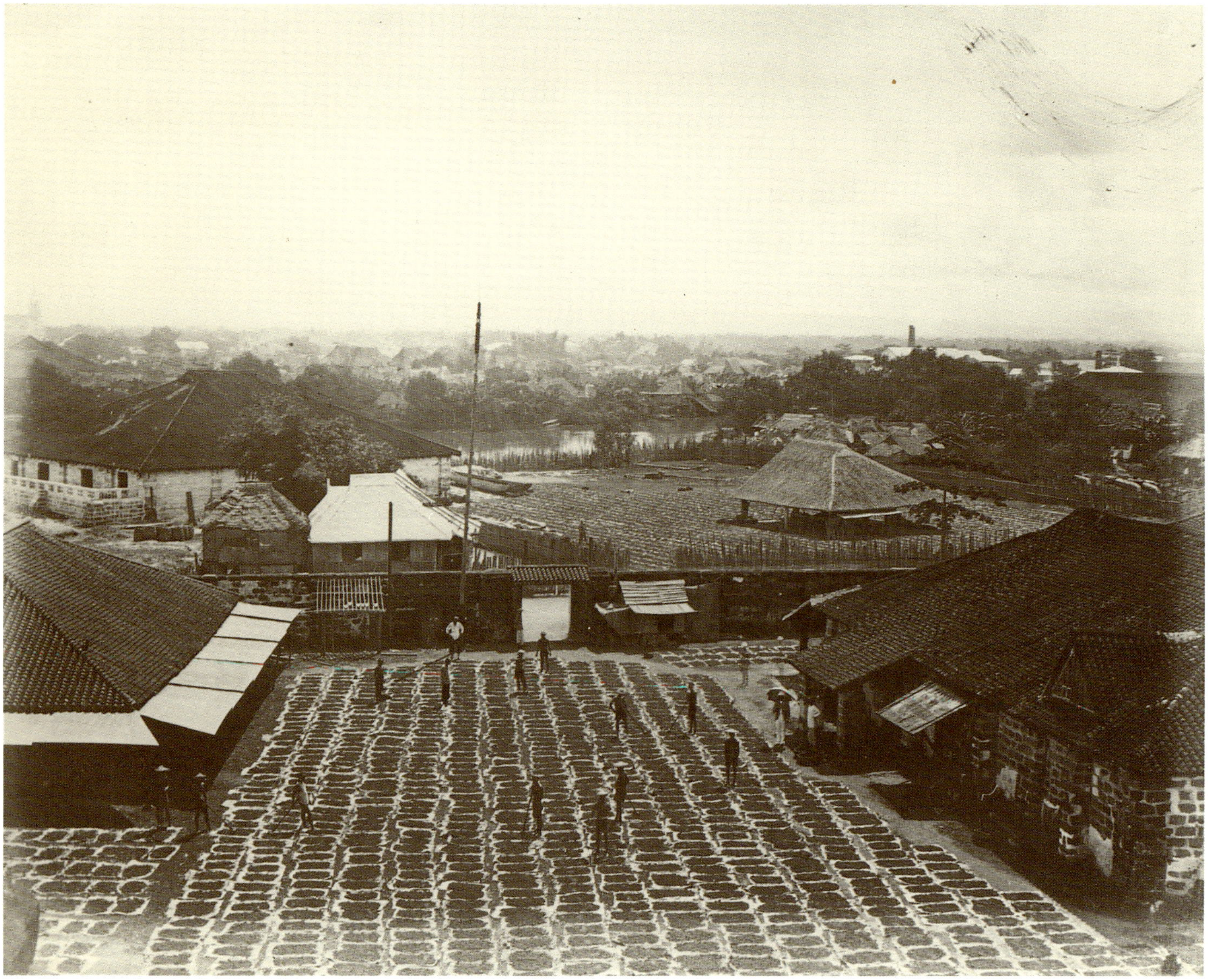

Plate 67 PHOTOGRAPHER UNKNOWN
Corregidor
undated

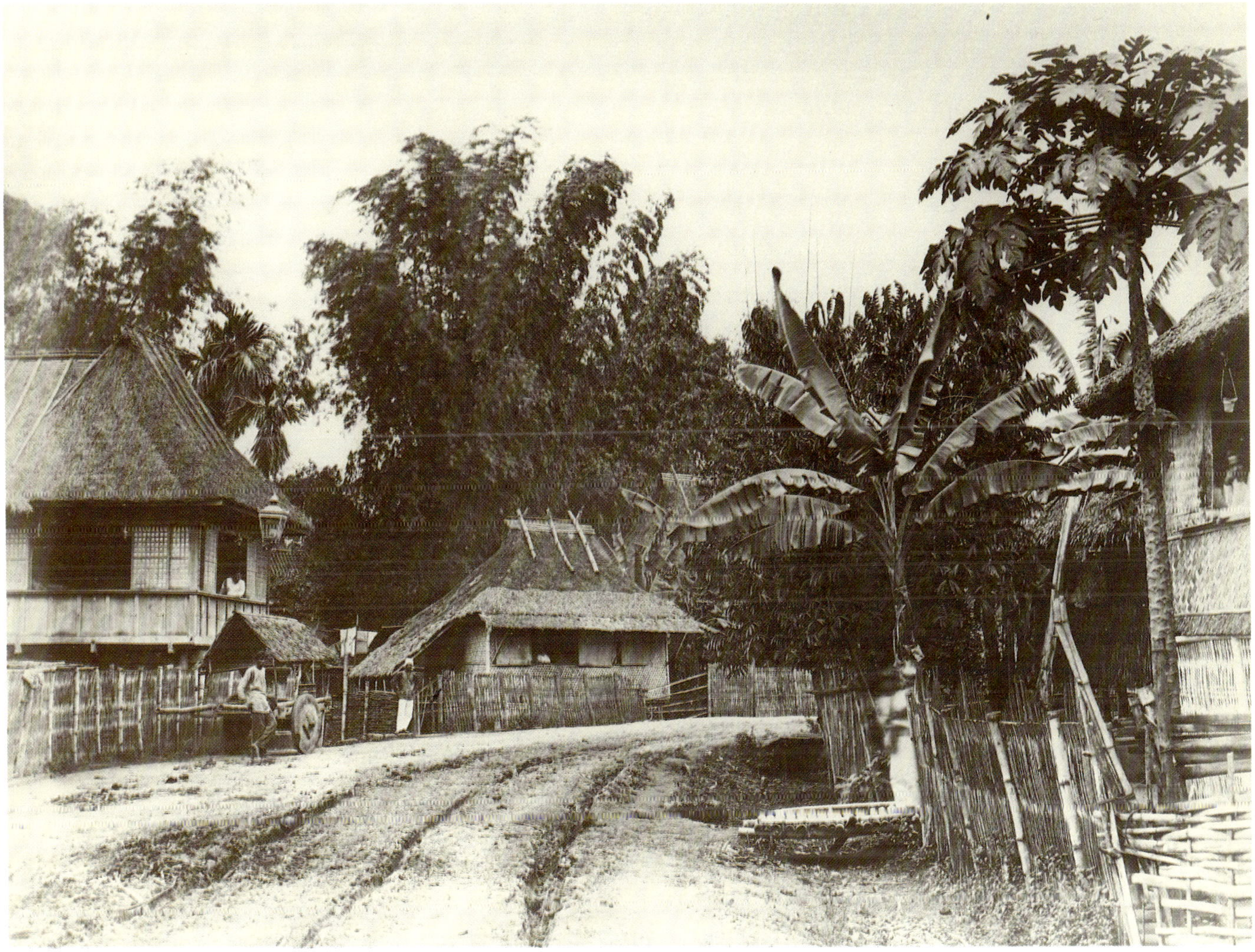

Plate 68 PHOTOGRAPHER UNKNOWN
Syrian Shepherd
undated

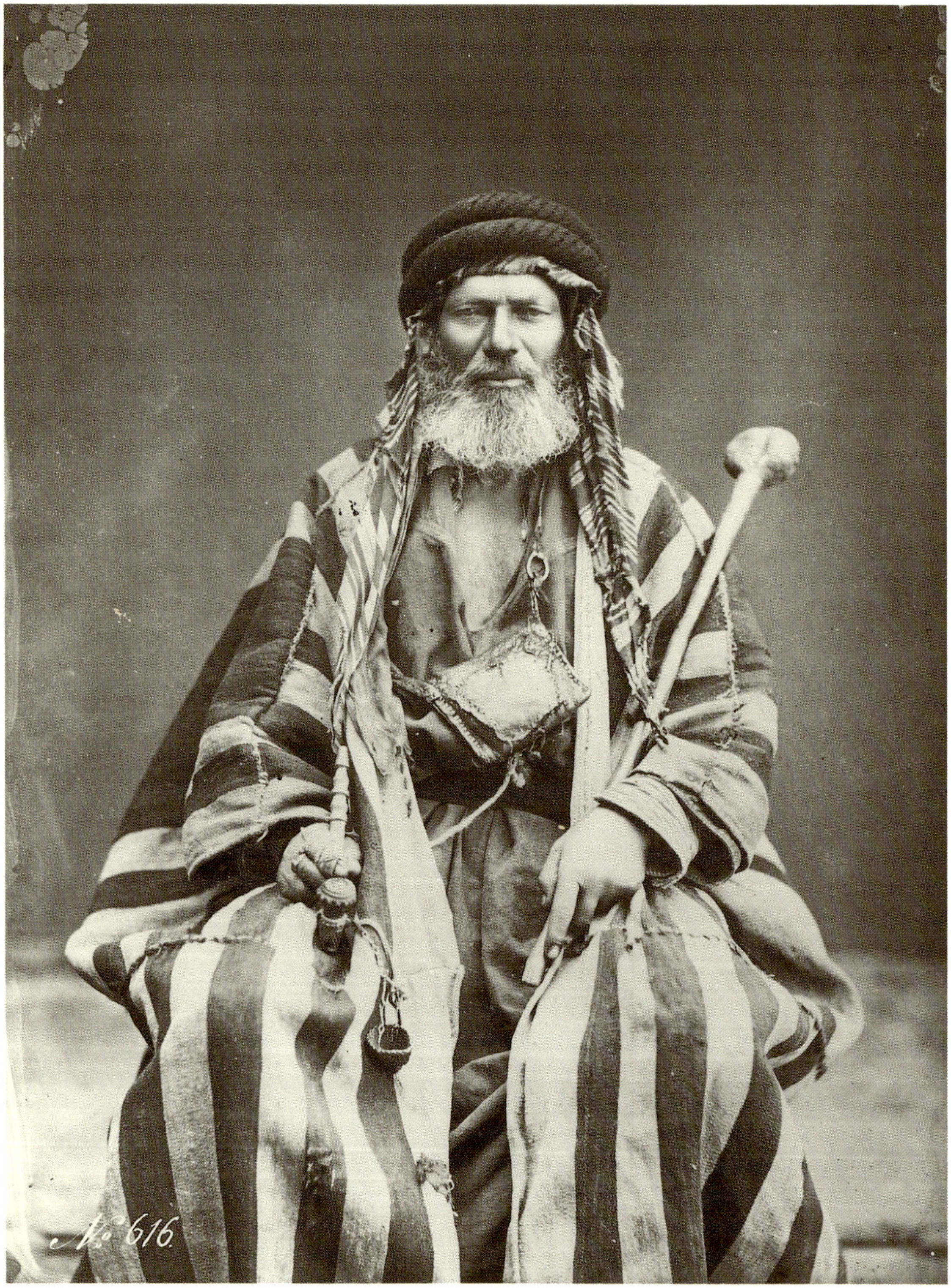

Plate 69 PHOTOGRAPHER UNKNOWN
The Rock, Trichinopoly
undated

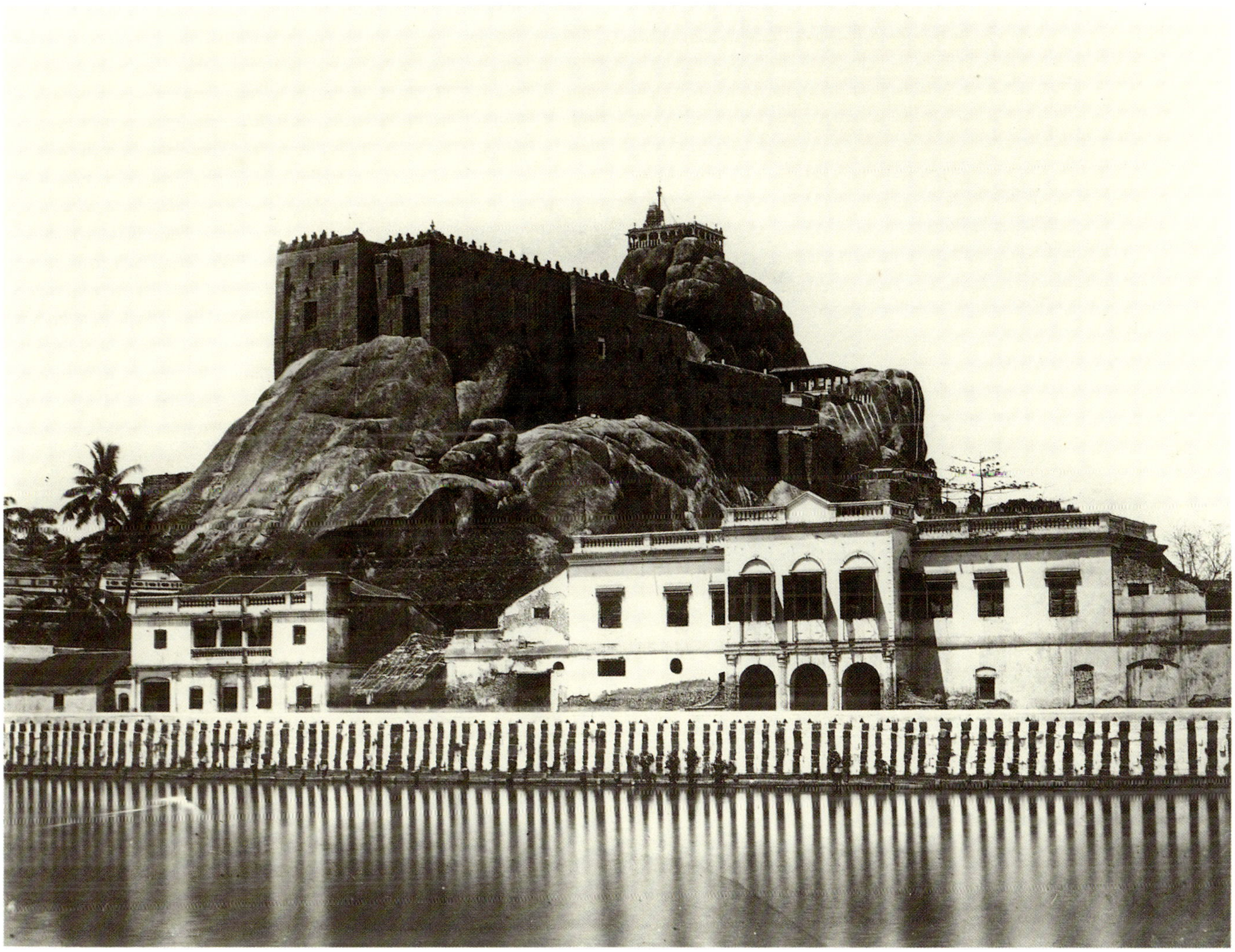

Plate 70 PHOTOGRAPHER UNKNOWN
The Great Pagoda, Seringapatam
undated

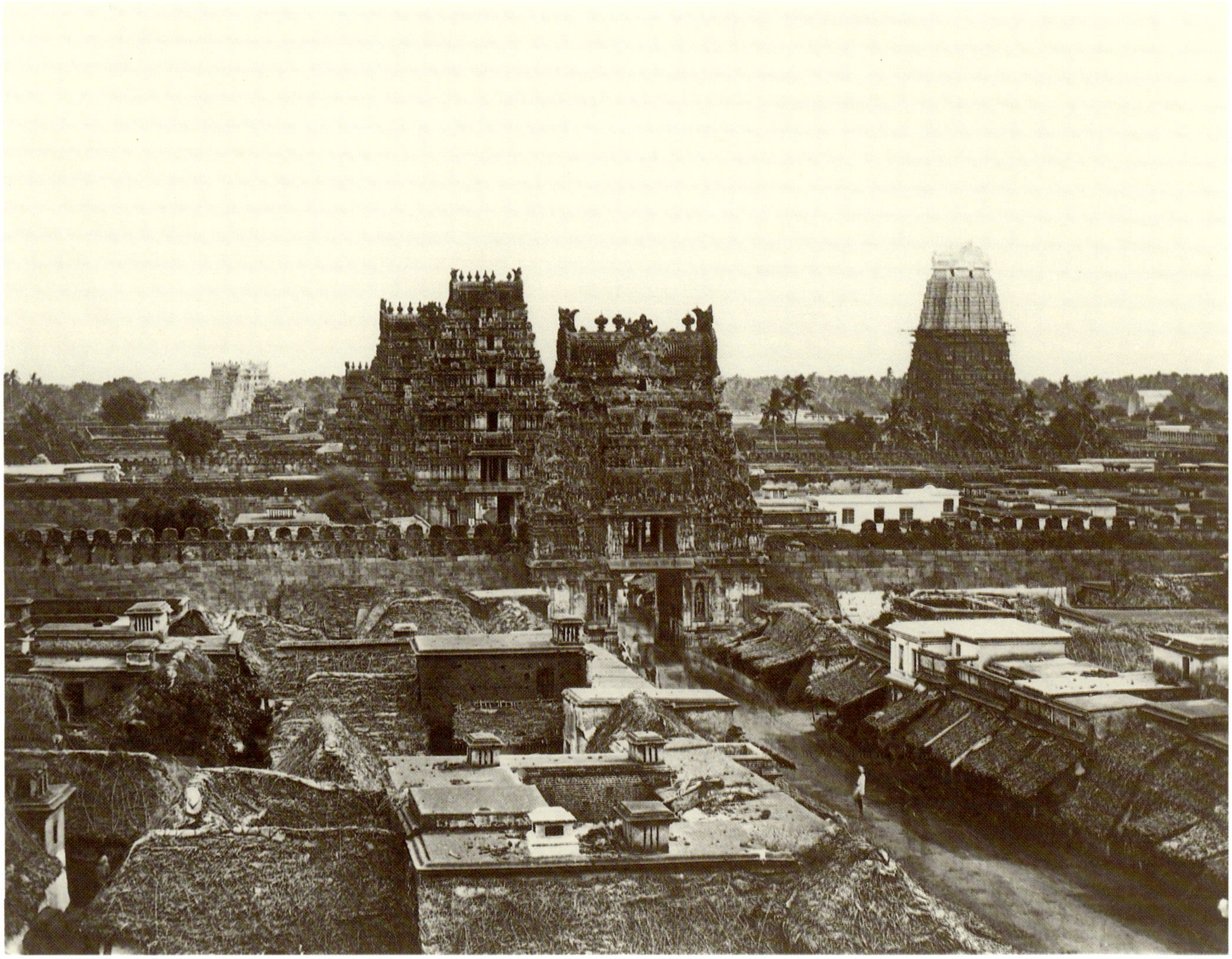

Plate 71 PHOTOGRAPHER UNKNOWN
The Jumma Masjid, Seringapatam
undated

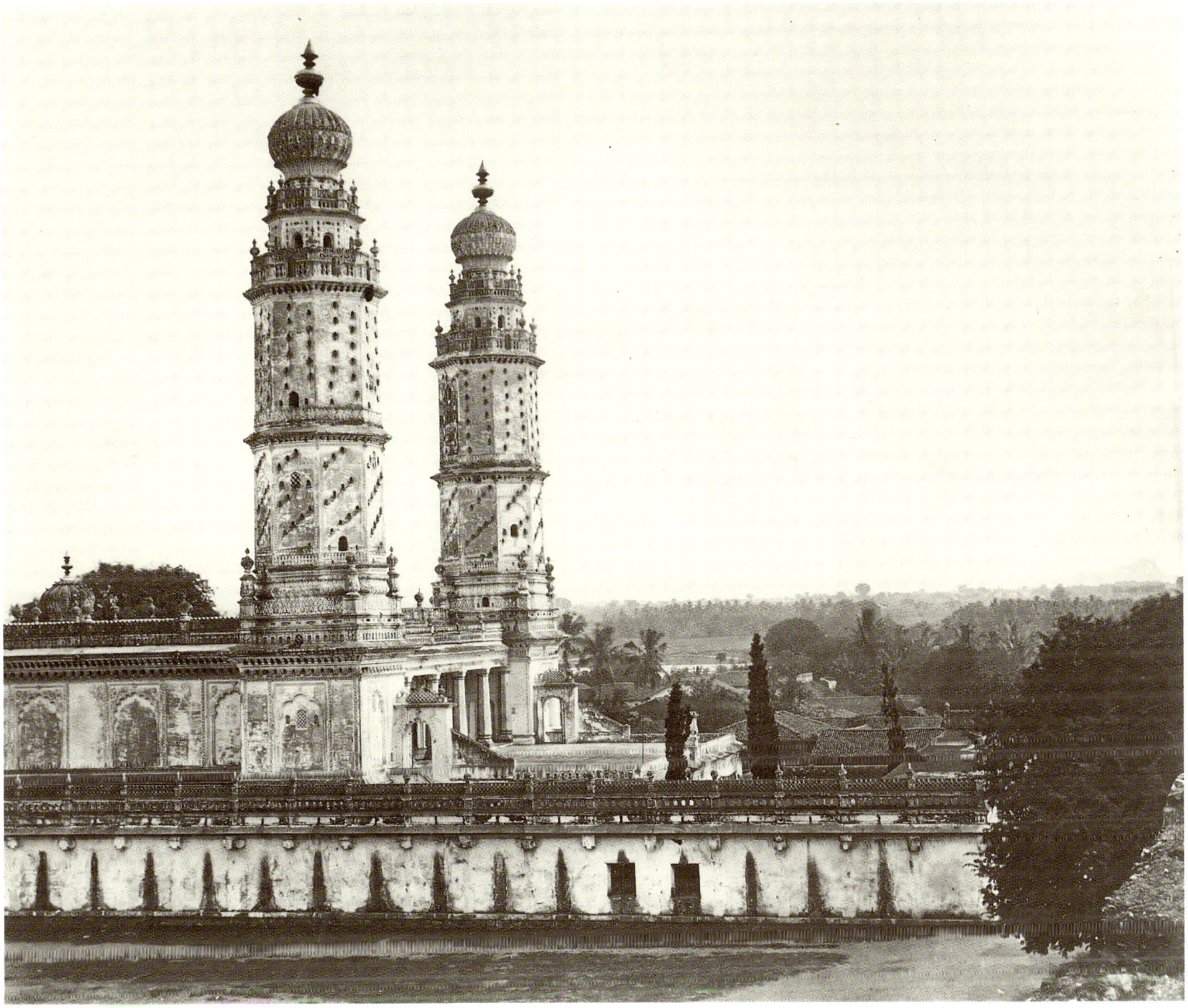

Plate 72 PHOTOGRAPHER UNKNOWN
Mausoleum of Tipu Sultan, Seringapatam
undated

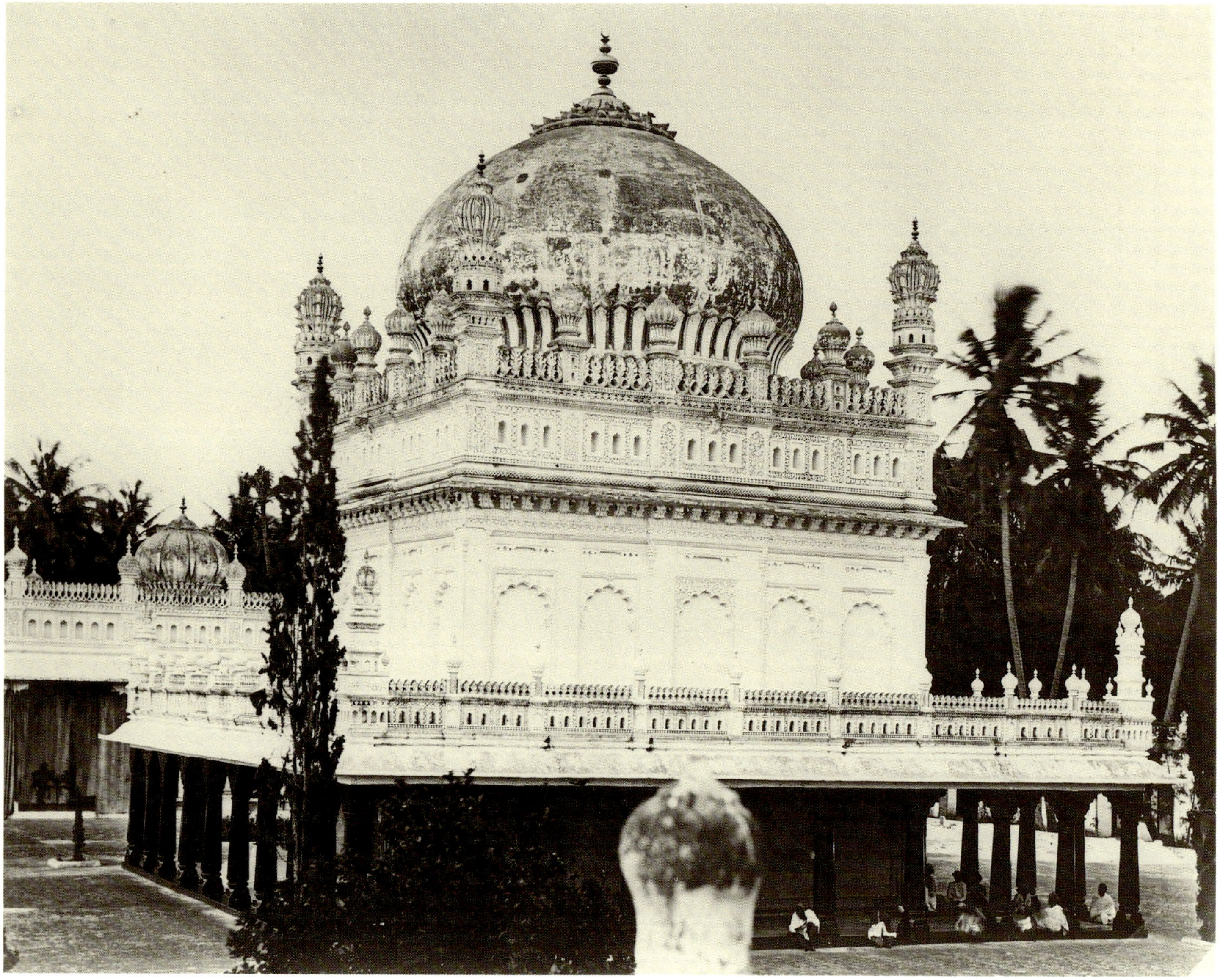

ANNAN & SONS
Scottish

1 *Glasgow Harbour Series No 1*
1894
Platinum print
0.303×0.392
Inscribed in negative: 'AN 11039'; printed on mount: 'Annan & Sons Glasgow'

2 *Glasgow Harbour Series No 3*
1898
Platinum print
0.303×0.390
Printed on mount: 'Annan & Sons Glasgow'

Thomas Annan (1829–1887) founded his photographic studio in Glasgow in 1857. He and his brother, Robert, were joined by Thomas's sons John and James Craig (qv) and the firm became 'Annan and Sons' in 1888. Thomas Annan was a specialist in architectural photography, producing photographs like those published in *The Old Country Houses of the Old Glasgow Gentry* of 1870. He is best known for his *Photographs of the Old Closes and Streets of Glasgow* published 1878–9,[1] (fig 12).

The Clyde Navigation series was a set of eight platinum prints of Glasgow Harbour and Docks taken between 1892 and 1897. Plate 1 shows the north-west corner of the south pier of Princes Dock. Taken in September 1894, it shows the arrangement of concrete cylinders and chock piles, and the building of the south wall of the centre basin on top of the cylinders. Plate 2 shows the Graving Dock, looking outwards from the Head. The last copestone had been laid by the Duke of York on 10 September 1897 and the photograph was taken the following year. While not intended to be 'artistic' in the sense that the photogravures by James Craig Annan (plates 3–6) were, these photographs are compositionally as artful.

[1] The photogravure edition was published in 1900 by James Maclehose and Sons

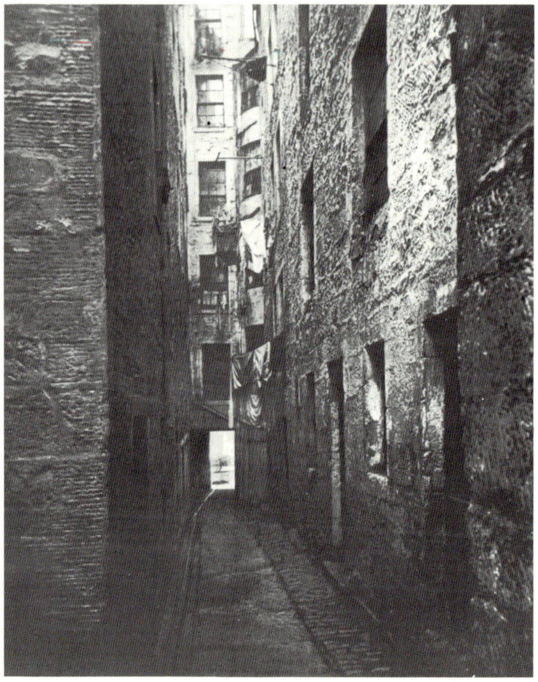

Figure 12
'Close no 148 High Street', Glasgow, 1868
by Thomas Annan

JAMES CRAIG ANNAN 1864–1946
Scottish

3 *A Utrecht Pastoral*
1892
Photogravure
0.221 × 0.288
Signed in pencil: 'A Utrecht Pastoral J C Annan'

4 *A Genoa Harbour*
1894
Photogravure
0.214 × 0.290

5 *Harlech Castle*
about 1908–9
Photogravure
0.230 × 0.322

6 *Miss Dacre*
1906
Photogravure
0.308 × 0.235

James Craig Annan was the son of the Glasgow photographer Thomas Annan (qv). He studied chemistry and natural philosophy before joining the family firm of T & R Annan. In 1883, at the age of nineteen, James Craig Annan was sent to Vienna to study the art of photogravure with its inventor Karl Klic. This process involved the fixing of the photographic image upon a copper etching plate, etching it, inking it, and drawing prints from it. Plates 3 to 6 are examples of photogravures by Annan. While Thomas Annan was one of the most respected photographers in Scotland, James Craig Annan was to gain an international reputation.[1]

In 1892 Annan made a trip to Holland in the company of the painter and etcher D Y Cameron (1865–1945). The resulting photogravures or 'monotones', which were exhibited at the Annan gallery at 230 Sauchiehall Street in Glasgow, show the influence of the Dutch masters, as William Buchanan has observed.[2] *A Utrecht Pastoral* (plate 3) is particularly reminiscent of Hobbema. In 1894, a second trip was undertaken with Cameron, on this occasion to Italy. *A Genoa Harbour* (plate 4) dates from this time. When it was shown at the Photographic Salon of 1909, it was singled out for praise by F H Evans (qv) in his notice of the exhibition. Evans wrote, 'J Craig Annan's work is specially rich in quality and interest; his photogravures are full of fine etching qualities; how fine are the lines made by the horses and masts in No. 57 *A Genoa Harbour*'. Evans also said of plate 5, in the same review:

> '. . . how rich in romantic charm is No. 68 *(The Ruined Castle)*; its colour scheme is extraordinarily strong; the cold dark snow is really felt; note, too, the splendid sense of distance behind the arch over the steps. This is one of those renderings of a subject that make one feel that no one else ought to touch it in that aspect or condition; it is done once and for all.'[3]

Annan was perhaps most admired for his portraiture. The profile study of the diffident *Miss Dacre* (plate 6) invites comparison with the portraits of Carlyle and the artist's mother by James McNeill Whistler (1834–1903).[4] Whistler's graphic work may also have been an influence on Annan. ▷

Annan was a 'pictorialist'—one of that group of photographers which included Coburn (qv), Käsebier (qv), and Stieglitz, which was dedicated to the promotion of the idea of photography as a fine art. The debate about the status of photography in relation to art is still alive, but there is general agreement that James Craig Annan may be considered as one of the greatest photographers of his generation.

[1] Information from William Buchanan, 'The "most versatile and artistic" James Craig Annan', *The Photographic Collector,* vol 5, no 1

[2] William Buchanan, *ibid*

[3] F H Evans, *The Amateur Photographer and Photographic News,* 21 September 1909

[4] Whistler's *Arrangement in grey and black* of 1871 has been suggested as an 'influence' on Annan's *Miss Janet Burnet* of 1883 (by William Buchanan, *op cit*). This would seem equally applicable to *Miss Dacre*

PLATT D BABBITT active at Niagara Falls 1853–1870s
American

7 *Group at Niagara Falls*
about 1855
Daguerreotype, whole plate

The first daguerreotype taken at Niagara Falls was by Langenheim of Philadelphia in 1845. By 1853, Platt D Babbitt had set up his camera on the American side and kept it permanently trained on Horseshoe Falls across Prospect Point. He would produce a daguerreotype of any tourists who came within the sights of his camera and kept still long enough. This proved a profitable enterprise, as the tourists would invariably buy the daguerreotype from him. Babbitt was granted a monopoly by General Porter, the manager of the American side, and he guarded it jealously.[1] A story is recounted of what happened when a Scotsman, William Thompson, attempted to photograph the Falls from Prospect Point: 'Mr Babbitt would not have it . . . Every time Mr Thompson made an attempt to take the cap off the camera for an exposure, Mr Babbitt and his forces would stand between the camera and the Falls swinging large-sized umbrellas to and fro, thus preventing Mr Thompson from getting a picture'.[2]

Babbitt remained at Niagara Falls for over twenty years taking photographs. The numerous daguerreotypes, of which plate 7 is an example, probably date from the 1850s.

[1] Robert Taft, *Photography and the American Scene 1839–89,* 1964, p 96

[2] Beaumont Newhall, *The Daguerreotype in America,* Third revised edition, 1975, p 69, quoted from 'Reminiscences of J J Anthony', *Niagara Falls Gazette,* April 1914

FRANCIS BEDFORD 1816–1894
English

8 *Mer de Glace*
undated
Albumen print
0.165×0.208
Inscribed in ink on mount: 'Mer de glace (Bedford)'

Bedford trained as an architect and lithographic artist. Photography was for him, at first, an extension of these early pursuits. His views of English scenery and cathedrals resulted in a series of royal commissions: to photograph the royal art collection for Queen Victoria; to produce a series of Bavarian views for Prince Albert; and to accompany the Prince of Wales on his tour of the Middle East in 1862 as official photographer.[1]

Plate 8 is a record both of spectacular Alpine scenery and the intrepidity of the men who have made the excursion. The Mer de Glace is a glacier in the French Alps of the Haute Savoie, just north of Mont Blanc. Its name derives from the wave-like formation of its snow and ice. It was first photographed by the French pioneers of mountain photography, the Bisson brothers, who recorded the visit of the Emperor Napoleon III and the Empress Eugénie to the glacier in 1860.[2]

The difficulties faced by photographers at such altitudes and temperatures were considerable. Bisson was often unable to make an exposure at all during his ascent of Mont Blanc in 1862 because the silver crystallized as soon as it came into contact with the cold air.[3] Bedford employed the pre-prepared 'Extra Quick Dry Plates', invented by Dr Hill Norris, which appeared in 1860 and which, it was claimed, were as fast as wet collodion.[4] The advantage of this method was the reduction in the amount of equipment which the photographer needed to transport. The sky in Bedford's photograph was probably superimposed from another negative.

The nineteenth century saw an interest in the Alps on the part of mountaineers, scientists and artists. The first daguerreotype taken in the Alps was a view of the Matterhorn in 1849 by John Ruskin, in whom the interest of the geologist was combined with the romantic inspiration of Shelley's hymn to Mont Blanc:

'. . . The glaciers creep
Like snakes that watch their prey, from their far fountains,
Slow rolling on; there many a precipice,
Frost and the Sun in scorn of mortal power
Have piled; dome, pyramid, and pinnacle,
A city of death, distinct with many a tower
And wall impregnable of beaming ice.'[5]

1 *The Golden Age of British Photography, 1839–1900,* ed Mark Haworth-Booth, 1984, p 83

2 Helmut and Alison Gernsheim, *The History of Photography,* 1969, p 290
L-A and A-R Bisson published their photographs in the album *Haute Savoie. le Mont Blanc et ses glaciers; souvenir du voyage de LL. MM. l'Empereur et l'Impératrice* about 1860

3 *After Daguerre: Masterworks of French Photography (1848–1900) from the Bibliothèque Nationale,* 1980, catalogued by Bernard Marbot, no 24

4 Gernsheim, *op cit,* p 325

5 Percy Bysshe Shelley, *Mont Blanc, Lines Written in the Vale of Chamouni*

SAMUEL BOURNE 1834–1912
English

9 *Mussucks for Crossing the Beas below Bajoura*
1866
Albumen print
0.235×0.291
Inscribed in negative: 'Mussucks for crossing the Beas below Bajoura 1436; signed in the negative: 'Bourne 1436'

10 *The Ki Monastery, Spitti*
1866
Albumen print
0.237×0.295
Inscribed in ink beneath: 'Ki Monastery Spitti'; inscribed in negative: 'Bourne 1460'

11 *Twig Bridge over Spitti River*
1866
Albumen print
0.242×0.230
Inscribed in ink beneath: 'Twig Bridge over Spitti River'; inscribed in negative: 'Bourne 1466'

The landscape photographer Samuel Bourne worked in India from 1863 until 1870. He joined the firm of Robertson and Shepherd (qv) which subsequently became Bourne and Shepherd. By the time Bourne arrived, photography was well established in the sub-continent, with European and native practitioners in all the major centres. Bourne was the first, however, to undertake long and arduous journeys through the Himalayas with a camera. He made three expeditions, taking photographs at unprecedentedly high altitudes. His first expedition took ten weeks, his second was to Kashmir in 1864 and took nine months. Plates 9 to 11 were taken on his third expedition, to photograph the source of the Ganges, in 1866.[1]

Bourne set off from Simla on 3 July 1866, 'having laid in a good stock of provisions and hermetically sealed stores, and arranged them with the cameras, chemicals, glass, tents, bedding, portmanteau and cooking utensils on the backs of sixty strong coolies'.[2] The 'coolies' were to prove (perhaps understandably) recalcitrant on the journey. Bourne also had the foresight to take along large quantities of brandy. This, apart from its obvious palliative properties, had proved indispensable on a previous occasion when the glass chemical containers were broken and empty brandy bottles were substituted thus enabling the photography to continue.[3]

Near the start of the journey, Bourne described the crossing of the river Beas (plate 9):

> 'Presently we had to cross the river, which was here about eighty yards wide, by means of "mussocks", or inflated buffalo skins. These were not new to me; I had crossed rivers upon them before on my journey to Kashmir. But the doctor[4] looked upon them with fear and misgiving, though he was too old a traveller and too much accustomed to the Himalayas to make any scruples about the matter, and forthwith committed himself to their buoyant inflation. I won't say he did not shut his eyes as the steersman pushed off, and he found himself being carried down the stream by the force of the current as rapidly as he was conveyed by the little paddles and feet of the steersman to the opposite bank. However, he stood on terra firma on the other side, while I had yet to cross. Running up the bank about 150 yards the men soon paddled back for me, after which all our coolies and baggage had to be brought across by the same means. This occupied about three hours, one of the loads nearly coming to grief by being carried down close to some rapids below, but was happily rescued by

another mussockman who had discharged his load, and who, seeing the danger, rushed to the rescue in time to save the man and his charge.

While this was going on I grouped a number of the mussockmen with their skins on the river bank, and took a photograph of them, which to those unacquainted with this mode of crossing rivers looks a most mysterious picture.'[5]

Bourne used the wet collodion process—the most inconvenient under such circumstances, as it necessitated coating the glass plates immediately before and after exposure. The tent visible in the photographs was a portable dark room, ten feet square at the base and ten feet high. It appears to have a flap on the side, presumably for ventilation, as working with chemicals at such high temperatures was both hazardous and unpleasant. Bourne boasted that he had obtained good negatives 'even at a temperature of 130°'. For varnishing negatives he used a recipe (unbleached lac dissolved in alcohol with sandarac added) which had been given to him by G W Wilson (qv) and which could withstand great heat.[6]

Bourne persisted in using large 10×12 inch plates despite the fact that it was 'not an easy matter to manipulate large plates successfully, and they involved considerable expense and trouble'.[7] This was because he was primarily concerned with the pictorial quality, and not the mere documentary value of the photographs.[8] Bourne was, therefore, obliged to employ the methods that would ensure the best results. In order to convey an impression of 'the grandeur and effect of the scenes' in the Himalayas, he worked on as large a scale as possible.

It has been said that Bourne's photography depicts India in terms of the Western landscape tradition. The aesthetic underlying these photographs is, inevitably, a Western one, but the 'imperial picturesque' as it has been called, does not preclude an authentic response on Bourne's part to Indian landscape.

In the *Ki Monastery* at Spitti on the Tibetan border for example (plate 10), the subject dominates the photograph. The Buddhist monastery perches among rocks, camouflaged by the sand and stones of the arid terrain whose colours and forms it echoes. Bourne has chosen a viewpoint that exaggerates this symmetry, the line of the building almost mirroring that of the hillside behind. From earth and fire we pass immediately to their antitheses, air and water (plate 11). Bourne describes crossing the Spitti river by means of 'a most villanous bridge, made as usual of twisted twigs, and in such bad order that, near the centre, four feet of it was broken away . . . After getting safely over I could afford to survey it calmly, and took a picture of it with the greatest composure.'[10]

Both of these photographs are remarkable for their depth of focus, detail and tonal range.

[1] Bourne wrote an account of these journeys in *The British Journal of Photography*

[2] Samuel Bourne, 'A Photographic Journey through the Higher Himalayas', *The British Journal of Photography*, 26 November 1869, p 570

[3] *ibid*, 8 February 1867

[4] The doctor referred to was Bourne's travelling companion Dr G R Playfair, the Scottish botanist and geologist, who was the brother of Sir Lyon Playfair, MP

[5] S Bourne, *op cit*, 3 December 1869, p 579

▷

[6] *ibid,* 31 December 1869

[7] *ibid,* 18 March 1870, p 126

[8] Bourne said that his objective was 'purely pictorial', *ibid,* 26 November 1869, p 570

[9] Philip H Egerton, the deputy commissioner of Kangra, had photographed the 'Kee' monastery in the summer of 1863 to investigate an alternative route for the shawl-wool trade (see Gernsheim, *op cit,* p 288). His photograph was used as one of the illustrations of his *Journal of a Tour Through Spitti to the Frontier of Chinese Thibet* of 1864

[10] S Bourne, *op cit,* 14 January 1870, p 16

ARCHIBALD BURNS active 1858–1880
Scottish

12 *The Horse Wynd, Edinburgh*
1871

Salt print from collodion negative
0.234×0.185

Inscribed in pencil, verso: 'No. 3 The booth at the head was a well known book stall'

13 *East Side, Horse Wynd, Edinburgh*
1871

Salt print from collodion negative
0.234×0.185

Inscribed in pencil, verso: 'No. 4 East side Horse Wynd. The two windowed shop on E. side was a haunt of C. K. Sharpe in search of old china bric a brac etc'

14 *The Cowgate, Edinburgh*
1871

Salt print from collodion negative
0.235×0.185

Inscribed in pencil, verso: 'No. 11 In the Cowgate South side between College Wynd and Horse Wynd'

15 *Back of house in College Wynd, Edinburgh*
1871

Salt print from collodion negative
0.185×0.234

Inscribed in pencil, verso: '19a Taken from window in [? North] side of the University. Head of College Wynd. The yard is the site of house where Sir W. Scott was born'

Archibald Burns was a professional photographer working in Edinburgh from about 1858 until 1880. He is best known for his book *Picturesque Bits,* published in 1868. This is an account, illustrated with his own photographs, of the streets and monuments of the historic Old Town of Edinburgh.

Plates 12 to 15 are from a set of twenty-six photographs taken in January or February 1871 for the Edinburgh Improvement Trust as a record of buildings that were to be demolished.[1] The Edinburgh Improvement Act was passed in 1867 and made provision for the removal of old tenements, widening of streets, and general amelioration of social and sanitary conditions in the city. Burns was an appropriate choice as photographer to the Trust. He had, in *Picturesque Bits,* stated the paradoxical nature of the problem—as an antiquarian he found these buildings fascinating and as a photographer he found them picturesque, but he also regarded them as miserable, squalid slums, and therefore advocated their removal:

> 'Unfortunately this [Bull's] close could not be photographed as a whole, which we would have liked, both for its picturesqueness and to give an idea of one of the lowest haunts of misery in Edinburgh. The Census of 1861 revealed that in the old town there are 13,000 families, consisting of 60,000 individuals, living in one-roomed houses—that 1,500 rooms are the abodes, day and night, of from five to fifteen persons. About 120 of these houses have no windows, and 900 of them are cellars. Taking Bull's Close as a sample, one gets somewhat reconciled to the loss of the picturesque, if thereby a better sanitary condition could be induced; and it takes the utmost stretch of the imagination, when looking at such hovels, and their present inhabitants, to conceive of them as the abodes of the gay, the beautiful, and the noble of other days.'[2]

The photographs show the area between the Cowgate, and what is now Chambers Street (see fig 13). The Horse Wynd (plate 12) was 'almost the only descent from the southern suburbs by which a horse could safely approach the Cowgate'.[3] The notice announcing the terms of the Edinburgh Improvement Act is affixed to one of the buildings. The College Wynd was formerly the site of 'an ancient ecclesiastical building referred to by old writers as the *Collegium Sacerdotum*'.[4] On the east side was the site of Sir Walter Scott's birthplace (plate 14).

The photographs are salt prints from collodion negatives.[5] They resemble calotypes, the earlier process used by Hill and Adamson (qv), and they have been given an 'old fashioned' appearance and nostalgic appeal, appropriate to their subject. There may also be an intentional homage to the earlier

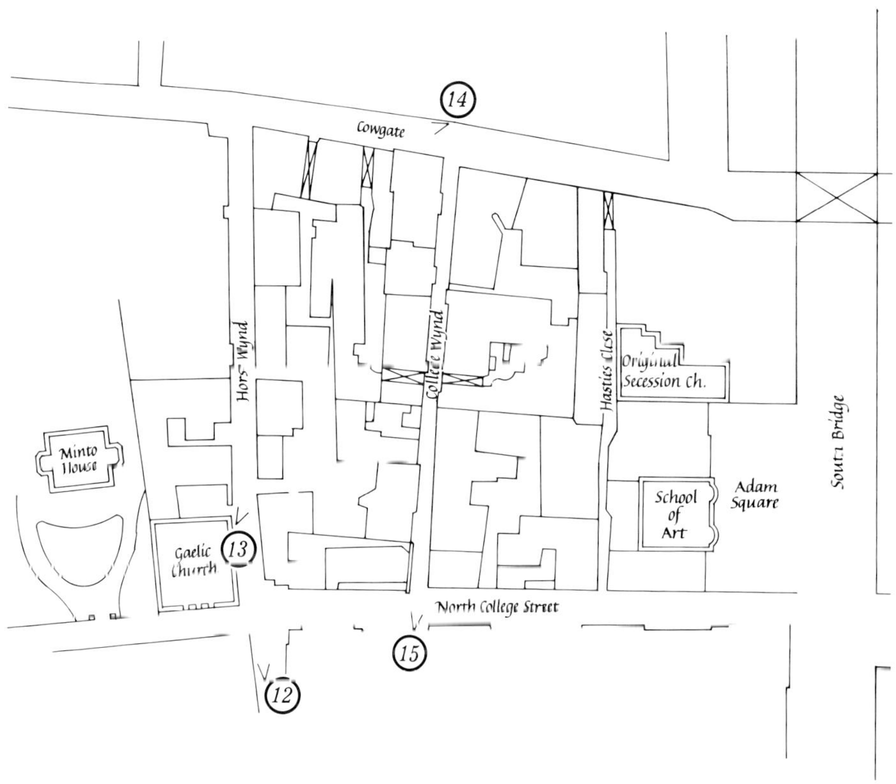

Figure 13
Plan of the area of Edinburgh photographed by Archibald Burns before demolition in 1871, showing his camera sites. (Based on a plan in an album containing Burns's photographs in the Edinburgh Central Library)

photographers, as D O Hill had died in 1870 just before these photographs were taken, and Archibald Burns was using the studio at Rock House, Calton Hill, that had previously belonged to Hill and Adamson. This was also the address, from 1870–1, of Thomas and John Annan.[6] Burns's photographs are comparable in conception and purpose with those taken by Thomas Annan of the streets and closes of Glasgow (fig 12). The Glasgow Improvement Act was passed in 1868 and Annan's photographs date largely from that year. There are similarities, for example, in that the limitations imposed by the subject with its narrow constricted spaces and high buildings, result in raking shots and oblique angles. The similarity in the appearance of the photographs may be more than the result of a common subject. That Burns should have been sharing a studio with Thomas Annan at the time of taking these photographs means that we may see his direct influence at work.

[1] *Minute Books of Edinburgh Improvement Trust,* 7 February 1871 Book II, p 190

[2] Archibald Burns, *Picturesque Bits,* 1868, p 68

[3] Wilson, *Memorials,* vol II, p 104

[4] Archibald Burns, *op cit,* p 50

[5] The photographs may not have been printed by Burns himself. At least one of the negatives seems to have come into the possession of A A Inglis who published it with his own monogram. A set of these photographs in the collection of the National Monuments Record of Scotland, and formerly in the possession of William Chambers, are albumen prints

[6] Burns lived at 22 Calton Hill until 1872, when his address changed to 28 Calton Hill (Rock House). The Annans are listed in the Edinburgh Post Office Directory as living and working at 28 Calton Hill in 1870–1 and 1871–2. Burns, while still living at number 22, is listed in 1871–2 as having his photographic studio at number 28, which means that he must have shared the Rock House studio with the Annans, even if only for a brief period early in 1871

WILLIAM DONALDSON CLARK died 1873
Scottish

16 *The National Gallery and Royal Institution (Royal Scottish Academy) Edinburgh*
about 1858
Albumen print
0.211×0.263

17 *Princes Street, Scott Monument and Royal Institution (Royal Scottish Academy) Edinburgh*
about 1858
Albumen print
0.216×0.275

18 *The Bank of Scotland from Princes Street Gardens, Edinburgh*
about 1858
Albumen print
0.205×0.271

19 *The Lawnmarket—head of the West Bow, Edinburgh*
about 1860
Albumen print
0.216×0.273

20 *The Cowgate Arch of George IV Bridge, Edinburgh*
about 1860
Albumen print
0.211×0.274

21 *Three figures in a tree-lined lane*
about 1864
Albumen print
0.213×0.262

22 *Melrose Abbey, piers of the nave*
1866
Albumen print
0.262×0.210

William Donaldson Clark[1] was born in Ayr, the son of a shipmaster. He had a successful career, beginning as the superintendent of a Dunbartonshire print-works, and ending in Lancashire as 'one of the best calico printers in England'.[2] He was able to retire and furnish 'in a most sumptuous manner'[3] a house in Mayfield Loan, Edinburgh.

However, 'finding time hang heavy on his hands',[4] he acquired the Princes Street premises of the late Alexander Hill, brother of D O Hill (qv), and became a picture dealer, print-seller and publisher. He found 'the retail trade not so congenial as he had expected',[5] and gave it up after a few years. Clark died on 23 April 1873.

Clark was a prolific amateur photographer. He had exhibited with the Manchester Photographic Society, and from 1858 onwards contributed to the annual exhibitions of the Photographic Society of Scotland. Clark's elder brother, Thomas, became professor of chemistry at Aberdeen University, so it is not surprising that William had 'an extensive and accurate knowledge of practical chemistry'.[6] He experimented with various photographic techniques and was an advocate of the collodio-albumen process, a dry collodion method invented by the French chemist Taupenot in 1855. The advantage of this process for outdoor photography was that the plate could be prepared in advance rather than on the spot, thus obviating the need to transport a dark tent and volatile chemicals. The major disadvantage was the long exposure time required.[7]

Clark's results were praised by his contemporaries. When he exhibited views of Edinburgh at Aberdeen in 1859 a critic wrote that they were 'the finest I have seen by that [Taupenot] process'.[8] Clark employed the more popular wet collodion process for his series of Melrose Abbey taken in March to April, 1866. This project—to make a complete visual record of the building—was undertaken with another amateur photographer, John Smith of Darnick. The enterprise indicates Clark's antiquarian interests. Permission was obtained from the Duke of Buccleuch to erect scaffolding in the abbey.[9] This made possible the taking of photographs such as plate 22 which shows the piers of the nave.

A feature of Clark's photography is the frequent inventiveness of the compositions. The ability to select a viewpoint that avoids pictorial cliché is evident in the photographs of Edinburgh. The National Gallery (plate 16) for example looks surprisingly modern. One reason for this originality may have been the assistance he received in selecting his views and framing his compositions from painter friends.[10] The landscape painter, Horatio MacCulloch, was a close friend of Clark's and it is likely that he was one of the artistic mentors.

The photographs also indicate a mastery of tonal effects not only by manipulation of the negative but also through the control of light. The photographs were taken at different times of day. For example, a sunny afternoon was chosen for plate 18, when the effects of aerial perspective would bleach out the distant buildings, rendering the Bank of Scotland more imposing in its apparent isolation.

Clark's treatment of the architecture of Edinburgh is based on the antithesis of classical and gothic. In *Cowgate, George IV Bridge* (plate 20) for example, Roman *gravitas* and order is juxtaposed with medieval picturesque and accidental. Clark is not interested so much in the modernism of the New Town, dedicated to order and uniformity, but rather in the opposing principle of cultural history and diversity that permits the Scott Monument and the Royal Scottish Academy to be side by side and contemporaneous (plate 17).

▷

[1] These photographs have been attributed to W D Clark on the basis of documentary evidence. Plate 20 has been attributed to J G Tunny but there seems to be no firm basis for this attribution

[2] *The British Journal of Photography,* 9 May 1873, p 220

[3] *ibid*

[4] *ibid*

[5] *ibid*

[7] *ibid*

[8] Robert Macpherson, the Scottish photographer working in Rome, described making an exposure of up to two days to take a photograph indoors using this process, and five minutes outdoors on a sunny day

[8] *The Scotsman,* 10 May 1866, p 7

[9] *The Liverpool Photographic Journal,* October 1859. Many of Clark's photographs of Melrose Abbey are now in the collection of the National Monuments Record of Scotland, Edinburgh

[10] *The British Journal of Photography,* 1 May 1863

ALVIN LANGDON COBURN 1881–1966
American born, naturalized British

23 *G K Chesterton*
published in 1913
Photogravure
0.203×0.160

Coburn studied photography in New York with his cousin, F Holland Day, before opening his own studio in 1901. He then worked for a time with Gertrude Käsebier (qv). Coburn worked in London from 1904 to 1909, and again from 1912 to 1918.[1] His *Men of Mark,* published in 1913, was a set of portraits of eminent contemporaries, including George Bernard Shaw, Wyndham Lewis, and this one of G K Chesterton (1874–1936). Coburn describes the occasion on which the photograph was taken in his preface:

> 'Chesterton was staying at Westerham in Kent, and in reply to my letter he said that if I would let him know which train I would come by, that he would meet me at the station, but on my arrival I found the platform deserted except for the boy asleep in the bookstall. As far as I can remember I was the only person to alight from the train. I strolled through the station and out into the road, but still no sign of the object of my quest. A dusty road stretched away into the distance, and as I had no idea of the direction in which to proceed I sat down on my camera in the shade of the station and waited. Presently I perceived a cloud in the distance, and as it approached out of it emerged, like the genie in the "Arabian Nights", a large man in a suit of green knickerbockers who could be no other than the great G K C himself.
>
> As his house was far away on the top of a distant hill, and as my camera was heavy, he proposed that we should adjourn to a nearby field, which we forthwith did, and under a tree I photographed him while he wrote an article for the *Daily News,* on cabbages . . . I doubt if he knew very much of cabbage culture, yet the article was so interesting that I, who carried it back to London and delivered it to the *Daily News,* and as a reward was permitted to read it, forgot to get out of the train when it came to its final stop at Charing Cross. It was written, I remember, on the backs of vivid yellow excursion announcements that we found in the station, and with my fountain pen. It is thus that literary masterpieces are created.'[2]

Coburn used the gum platinum process—a double process that allows a greater tonal range than most and permits the juxtaposition of dark shadows and brilliant highlights. There are no hard edges. Forms are soft and the photogravure has a pastel-like quality. The impression of Chesterton's bulk, which seems to expand beyond the confines of the frame, is moderated by a dissolution of form and softened corporeality. Coburn emphasises pattern-making. He simplifies and abstracts forms. The face is reduced to three tones—a light patch on the right, a middle tone and a dark tone. This reduced means of modelling is reminiscent of painters like Manet. The eyes are lost in shadow, while the rims of the *pince-nez* are caught by the light. The black ribbon establishes the setting of the figure in space. The white shirt, tonally the most dramatic area in the photograph, is anchored spatially thanks to the careful judgement of the surrounding tones. We are given a tonal patchwork that we may choose to recognize as the man Chesterton.

Coburn used his original negatives to make the gravure plates. He printed them himself and thus they have the status of original prints.

[1] Article by Marianne Fulton, *Contemporary Photographers,* 1982, pp 153–4

[2] *Men of Mark,* pp 11–12

JAMES CRIGHTON active 1870s—1880s Scottish

24 *Washing Day, Newhaven*
undated
Albumen print
0.181×0.146
Inscribed in pencil, verso: 'Washing Day Newhaven Jas Crighton'

Little is known about the amateur photographer James Crighton, who exhibited a photograph of *Newhaven Fisher Folk* at the International Exhibition of Industry, Science and Art, held in Edinburgh in 1886.[1] He may be the James Crighton of 'Crighton and Thomson, Wine, Spirit Merchants and Grocers, 77 South Clerk Street, Edinburgh', who was a member of the Edinburgh Photographic Society in the 1870s and '80s.[2]

Newhaven is a fishing village about a mile and a half north of central Edinburgh. The photographers Hill and Adamson (qv) had taken a series of calotypes of Newhaven scenes in the 1840s. These were of fishermen, sailors and, predominantly, fishwives (fig 14). The fishwives were well-established as picturesque local subjects for painters and photographers, so Crighton, in taking this photograph of the women of Newhaven, was drawing on ready-made photographic imagery. The fishwives had been described in 1832 as '. . . singular Amazons . . . of an exceedingly robust frame and constitution [who] carry loads of from one to two hundredweight upon their backs, in creels or willow-baskets, and evince a masculine degree of strength, which is not unaccompanied by manners equally

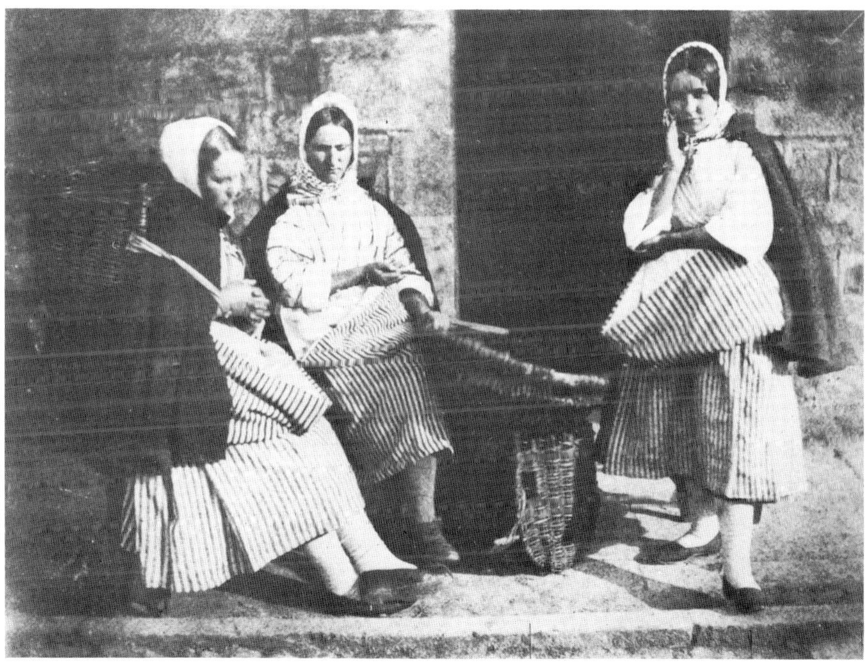

Figure 14
Newhaven Fishwives
by D O Hill and Robert Adamson
Scottish National Portrait Gallery

masculine. There is, indeed, a complete reversal of the duties of the sexes; the husband being often detained at home by bad weather and employing himself as nurse, while the wife is endeavouring at Edinburgh to win the means of maintaining the family.'[3] The women in plate 24 evince this physical strength. They seem very natural before the camera, which is possibly because they were used to visitors to Edinburgh regarding them as one of the local 'sights', and to photographers asking them to pose, with their creels and willow-baskets, as they had for Hill and Adamson.

[1] *Catalogue of the International Exhibition of Industry, Science and Art,* Edinburgh, 1886, no 319

[2] Edinburgh Photographic Society Minute Books, Edinburgh Room, Edinburgh Central Public Library

[3] Robert and William Chambers, *The Gazetteer of Scotland,* vol II, 1832, p 182

WILLIAM ELSMORE & CO active 1897–post 1914
Scottish

25 *School Band*
between 1897 and 1906[1]
Albumen print
0.100×0.145
Printed on mount: 'Windsor Studio, Wm Elsmore & Co Photographers, 19 West Garden St., Corner of City Road, Second St west of St George's X, Glasgow'

Plate 25, showing an infant school percussion band, was taken by William Elsmore, a commercial photographer working in Glasgow. Not all of the children have managed to get into the photograph. The curious black fog that seems to encroach from the lower left corner may be the camera cloth failing to clear the front of the lens. Some of the children seem transfixed by something terrifying to the photographer's right—presumably their teacher! A nice finishing touch is the aspidistra on the front row incorporated to fill a space, according to the aesthetic principle of *horror vacui.*

[1] According to the Glasgow Post Office Directory, Elsmore & Co were at the West Garden Street studio from 1897 to 1905, after which their premises were at 4 St Enoch Square

FREDERICK HENRY EVANS 1853–1943
English

26 *Aubrey Vincent Beardsley*
1893
Platinum print
0.138×0.150
On cover inscribed in ink: 'Aubrey Beardsley Portraits by Frederick Evans—20 sets only—15'
On mount: Stamp of 'Japanese' monogram FHE

Frederick Henry Evans was a London bookseller who took up photography professionally in 1898. Technically, Evans was a purist. He would never touch or alter a negative. He regarded photography as an art, and therefore the ability to see and select the beautiful picture before taking the photograph, not the manipulation of the negative afterwards, was what mattered. He was such a perfectionist that when the material for making platinum prints was unobtainable during the 1914–18 war, Evans gave up photography. His most famous photograph is the 'Sea of Steps' taken in Wells Cathedral in 1903.[1]

It was through Evans that Aubrey Beardsley obtained the commission to illustrate Malory's *Morte d'Arthur.* Beardsley (1872–1898) was one of the leading figures of the Aesthetic Movement, which held that the aesthetic values of civilization and artifice were superior to those of nature and naturalism. He was the editor of the *Yellow Book,* and the illustrator of Oscar Wilde's *Salome.* He died of tuberculosis at the age of twenty-six.

A portrait is always to some extent the result of a collusion between the portrayer and the portrayed. Beardsley has presented himself to the camera, severe in profile, wearing a stiff collar and short hair. His gaunt and pallid face enhances the ascetic air. Prominence is given to his hands which assume a devotional, prayer-like attitude. Evans has chosen the view-point, close and low, which emphasises the 'beak-like' profile. A gothicising portrait is the result. (This is a precursor of the gothic portraits of Edith Sitwell by Cecil Beaton—again the result of a collusion between photographer and subject.) A febrile beauty, lacking in virility and containing elements of the grotesque and the exotic, together with a sexual ambiguity, are all characteristics of the photograph found in Beardsley's own work. Languorous elegance, etiolation, grace and sinuosity, and just a touch of necrophilia, are the stylistic features of Aubrey Beardsley's black and white drawings (fig 15).

[1] Beaumont Newhall, *The History of Photography,* 1982, pp 147–150

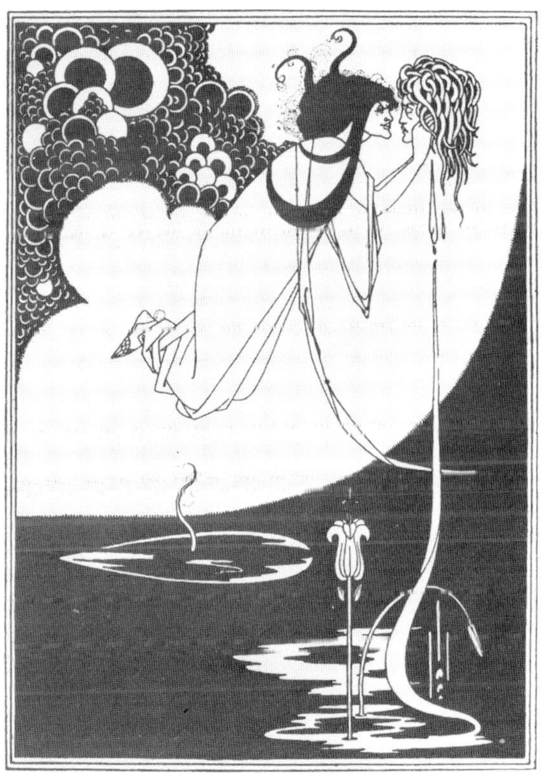

Figure 15
Salome
book illustration by Aubrey Beardsley for Oscar Wilde's Salome

(?)FRANCIS FRITH 1822–1898[1]
English

27 *The Khazneh, Petra*
between 1856 and 1860
Albumen print
0.100×0.152
Inscribed in pencil, verso: '547 El Khasné Petra'

For five hundred years, until the Swiss traveller and Orientalist John Burckhardt rediscovered it in 1812, Petra was a lost city. Deep in the mountains of Jordan, south of the Dead Sea, is the biblical city of Edom, called Petra because it is carved out of rock. The place became one of romantic fascination. It was the subject of the Reverend J W Burgin's Newdigate Prize winning poem—'. . . rose red city, half as old as time . . .'—and the artist David Roberts made a series of drawings of the place in 1829. Photographers followed later.

Of the seven hundred temples, tombs and palaces carved out of stone, the Khazneh, or Treasury, is the best known. It is situated at the entrance to the city, and is only accessible along a tortuous path called the 'Siq'. The date and true purpose of the Khazneh is uncertain. It may have been built in the reign of Aretas III Philhellen (84–56 BC) who, as his name suggests, preferred Hellenistic to native Nabatean architecture. The façade is, on the lower level, like that of a prostyle temple, but with six instead of four columns, entablature and pediment. The smaller Corinthian order of the upper level consists of two pavilions surmounted by broken pediments flanking a kiosk. The whole is carved in the rock and is 130 feet high and 92 feet wide. The photograph gives little impression of this gigantic scale. The Khazneh may have been a temple, but was traditionally believed to have been a repository for treasure. There is an engraving by Léon de Laborde showing an Arab marksman aiming his rifle at the urn, which was said to contain the gold. This practice accounts for the damage to the top of the facade. The photograph shows one of the pillars of the portico missing. This has been restored, though at what date is not known.[2]

[1] This photograph belongs to a set taken in the Holy Land and Middle East. Part of a signature is visible on one of these photographs and would seem to be that of Frith

[2] Iain Browning, *Petra,* 1973

ALEXANDER HENDERSON 1831–1913
Scots Canadian

28 *A Train in the Snow*
undated
Albumen print
0.117×0.192
Inscribed in ink on mount: 'A train in the Snow'; blind stamp on photograph: 'A Henderson Montreal'; inscribed in negative: '2487'

Alexander Henderson was a Scottish accountant who emigrated to Canada in 1855. He worked as a merchant in Montreal where he took up photography as a hobby. His earliest dated photographs were taken in 1858. His main interest was landscape photography, and he published a series of *Canadian Views and Studies* in 1865. Some time after this, Henderson decided to become a professional photographer, and opened a studio in Montreal. For a while in the 1890s he worked as manager of the Canadian Pacific Railway Photography Department.[1]

The photograph of a train immobilized by snow drifts (plate 28), is a good example of Henderson's work. The train, despite its

strength and its plough, has been no match for the snow, which is banked high on either side of it. The light seems to dissolve the funnels and mitigates the hardness of its iron carapace. Its speed has been frozen. The natural elements have frustrated mechanical forces. The photograph demonstrates Henderson's view of nature, which has been called 'romantic', but 'the opposite of dramatic'.[2] If the photograph is poetic, it is like the poetry of Emily Dickinson or Robert Frost—undeclamatory, finding the poetic and the significant in what is familiar and unexceptional. There is a freshness of vision found in Henderson's photography which finds kinship with these poets.

[1] Dennis Reid, *Our Own Country Canada,* National Gallery of Canada, 1979

[2] *ibid*

DAVID OCTAVIUS HILL 1802-1870 and ROBERT ADAMSON 1821-1848
Scottish

29 *Lady Ruthven,*
about 1847
Calotype
0.194×0.153

The partnership of David Octavius Hill and Robert Adamson was one of the earliest and most successful examples of collaboration photography has known. It lasted only between June 1843 and Adamson's premature death early in 1848 but in that time they were able to take some three thousand photographs by the intractable calotype process. The practical photography was Robert Adamson's responsibility and he achieved a remarkably high success rate. D O Hill, who was a landscape and genre painter by profession, arranged the compositions—an exercise he described as being 'as much an effort of the artist as if he was in reality going to paint it'.[1] The results of their work were precisely controlled and rich in tone.

The calotype of Lady Ruthven (1789-1885) is at first sight an imitation of a fashion plate, designed to show how well a dress can look from behind.[2] No part of Lady Ruthven, not even her hands or the back of her head, is visible and the photograph could be described as a bonnet, a shawl and a dress. But Lady Ruthven was a strong-minded, cultured woman, very outspoken and with a close knowledge of art—not an elegant clothes-horse for a ladies' journal. It is unlikely that either she or Hill would have been thinking in terms of fashion plates and it is more likely that they were simply thinking of an elegant impersonal picture—a photographic figure study that might be used by a painter in a larger composition. This calotype is remarkable also because it was apparently taken at a late date: datable photographs by Robert Adamson are rare after mid-1846. Hill wrote to Lady Ruthven in December 1847, 'I send you impressions of some of the calotypes done the last day your Lp. and Lord Ruthven called here. Lady Haddo's and Miss Baillie's are not what in better circumstances we could hope—and so I may say of your own & Lord Ruthven's portraits—yet yours especially, indicates what could be done in this direction, with good sitters, good backgrounds & good sunshine. Indeed with these appliances a wonderful little family gallery might be made in a few days & to such uses I do not doubt the Calotype will come.'[3] By December 1847, Robert Adamson had returned to his home in St Andrews after some months' illness, so the calotype of Lady Ruthven may be one of the last photographs he took.

[1] MS letter from D O Hill to David Roberts, March 1845, in a private collection, quoted in S Stevenson 'Cold buckets of ignorant criticism: Qualified success in the partnership of David Octavius Hill and Robert Adamson' *The Photographic Collector,* vol 4, no 3, Winter 1983, pp 336-9

[2] The comparison is made by Roy Strong in Colin Ford and Roy Strong, *An Early Victorian Album. The photographic masterpieces (1843-1847) of David Octavius Hill and Robert Adamson,* 1976

[3] Draft MS letter in the Royal Scottish Academy

EUGENE CLUTTERBUCK IMPEY
1830–1904
British

30 *The Kootub, near Delhi*
Albumen print
0.302×0.249

31 *Ulwur, The Cenotaph of Rao Raja Bukhtawur Singh*
Albumen print
0.228×0.298

32 *A Bheestie or water-carrier with his Bullock*
Albumen print
0.150×0.197

33 *Bullocks yoked to a cart*
Albumen print
0.150×0.194

34 *Rajpoots playing Pucheesee*
Albumen print
0.208×0.170

35 *Portrait of Thakoor Lukhdeer Singh, Rajpoot of Ulwar*[1]
Albumen print
0.195×0.155

Eugene Clutterbuck Impey was born in Paris in 1830 of a British father and French mother. He took a degree at Oxford before joining the 5th Bengal Native Infantry in 1851. Impey served during the Indian Mutiny of 1857 before being appointed political agent in Ulwur in 1858. Impey remained in India until his retirement in 1878, and died in 1904.[2]

It is likely that Impey learned photography at Addiscombe Military Academy.[3] Plates 30 to 35 are illustrations from *Delhi, Agra and Rajpootana,* published in 1865.[4] Photography may have been part of Captain Impey's official duties, but his photographs, like those of Linnaeus Tripe, far exceed the requirements of a mere topographical and architectural survey. Plate 31 shows the mosque at Ulwur, which Impey calls 'a very striking instance of the Hindu Cenotaph . . . picturesquely placed at the foot of a range of hills . . . the terrace and pavilions are of red sandstone, but the centre is of white marble streaked with black'.[5] The mosque is placed centrally and photographed on the angle for a strong pyramidal effect. *The Kootub, near Delhi* (plate 30) was the earliest mosque in India. It had been converted from a Hindu temple, to commemorate the defeat of the last Hindu king of Delhi, Prithiraj (1191–93 AD). The photograph shows the northern corridor of the inner enclosure—'pure Jaina, of the tenth or twelfth century, if not earlier'. The pillars are 'of great richness and beauty . . . and here and there a Jaina figure or emblem has escaped mutilation'.[6] Impey has chosen a view along the corridor. The repeating pattern of pillars and lintels is made box-like by the shadows cast along the floor. The contrast on the two front piers on the left has been heightened by the use of black on the negative.

In the portrait of Thakoor Lukhdeer Singh (plate 35) Impey provides maximum visual interest. The quilted garment follows the contours of Thakdoor's ample form, generating 'baroque' linear patterns; the silk catches the light; jewels, sword and shield add ornament. The neutral background concentrates attention on the figure. As well as skill, Impey's originality and humour may be discerned in *The Bullocks* (plate 33).

[1] All of these photographs were taken between 1858 and 1865

[2] Buckland, *Dictionary of Indian Biography*

[3] G Thomas, 'Colonel E C Impey and his Indian Connection', *History of Photography*, vol 7, no 3, July-Sept 1983

[4] This book was illustrated with 82 plates by 'Captain E C Impey, Bengal Staff Corps'. It is thought that only 25 copies were published. Two other copies are in the British Library (information from G Thomas, *op cit*)

[5] Captain E C Impey, *Delhi, Agra & Rajpootana*, 1865

[6] *ibid*

GERTRUDE KÄSEBIER 1852–1934
American

36 *Miss Minnie Ashley*
published April 1905[1]

Photogravure
0.222×0.172

Born Gertrude Stanton in Des Moines, Iowa, Käsebier married and had three children before training as a painter. Her interest in photography dates from about 1893 when she went to Germany to acquire a knowledge of chemistry. On her return to America she established a studio on Fifth Avenue, New York. Her meeting with Alfred Stieglitz (1864–1946) led to the founding of the Photo-Secession in 1902, with Alvin Langdon Coburn (qv), Edward Steichen, Clarence H White and others. The 'pictorialists', as they came to be known, were concerned with the aesthetics of photography, the exploration of photographic subject-matter, and light as a means of expression. Gertrude Käsebier was the first woman to become a member of the 'Linked Ring', which was the British equivalent of this group.[2]

Stieglitz published a set of six photogravures by Käsebier in his *Camera Work* in 1905, of which the portrait of *Miss Minnie Ashley* (plate 36) is one. Stieglitz said of her, 'Mrs Käsebier is, beyond question, the leading portrait photographer in this country. Her pictures are broad, full of colour and harmony, and above all, have the great charm of a keen artistic feeling and temperament.' He added somewhat patronisingly, 'their strength never betrays a woman'.[3]

[1] *Camera Work,* no 10, April 1905

[2] Information from Weston J Naef, *The Collection of Alfred Stieglitz,* the Metropolitan Museum of Art, 1978

[3] *Camera Notes,* 3 July 1899, p 24

POW KEE active in the 1880s
Chinese

37 *Hankow during floods*
1887

Albumen print
0.222×0.291

Inscribed in pencil, verso: 'No. 202—Your old house during the flood 1887'

38 *Fishing, Hankow*
1884

Albumen print
0.208×0.283

Inscribed in pencil, verso: 'Concession from sand bank in the river Winter of 1884'

Hankow is a port on the left bank of the Yangtze River, at the confluence with the River Han. It is in the Hupeh province of China. After the Opium Wars, Hankow was opened to foreign trade by the Treaty of Tientsin of 1858, and the British concession was obtained in 1861. The main export from Hankow was black tea.[1]

Plate 37 shows Hankow during the floods of 1887. Flooding was a regular occurrence. The neo-classical buildings are evidently the residences of British merchants around the *bund,* which was the commercial centre and where the largest concentration of Westerners was to be found. The Chinese photographer has chosen a subject of Western interest and treated it in a manner that is not noticeably Oriental. The buildings are at odds with the chaos of improvised walkways, and the busy, somewhat cluttered composition of what is man-made contrasts with plate 38 which is, both in content and conception, more obviously poetic. It is tranquil, visually less eventful, carefully arranged. A group of Chinese people, some fishing, stand on a sand-bank, and are reflected in the water.

There is empty space above and below them and their reflections are as substantial as themselves. The equilibrium of the composition depends upon the relationship and balance of solid and void. The slow water, and the absence of incident and anecdote in the presentation of the people, alludes to the more harmonious balance in nature which Chinese philosophy as much as its art celebrated.

[1] Rhoads Murphey, *China Meets the West: the Treaty Ports,* 1975

(?) A O KNOBLAUCH active about 1909

39 *Pitch and Toss*
1909
Carbon print
0.165×0.217

Inscribed in ink on mount: '[?] A O Knoblauch 09 Pitch & Toss'

Plate 39 is a scene of street life, showing children at play. The grouping of the children is either fortuitous or artful. The compact group on the left is framed by the busy shop window, whose lettering forms an arch over their heads. The boy on the right is separated from the others by the shadowy, starkly geometrical doorway behind. The tossing of the coin, the pitching forward of the boy as he does so, and the visual caesura of the little girl serve to link all the figures together, and unify the composition.

Such urchin-like children, bare-foot, dirty and unkempt, would not have been an unfamiliar sight in Edinburgh or Glasgow early this century. They would be pathetic were it not for a sense of indomitable self-assurance suggested by their poses, particularly that of the boy looking down, hands on hips. Such children have their predecessors in Dickens's Artful Dodger, Mark Twain's Tom Sawyer and Bastien-Lepage's gamin in *Pas Mèche* (fig 16).

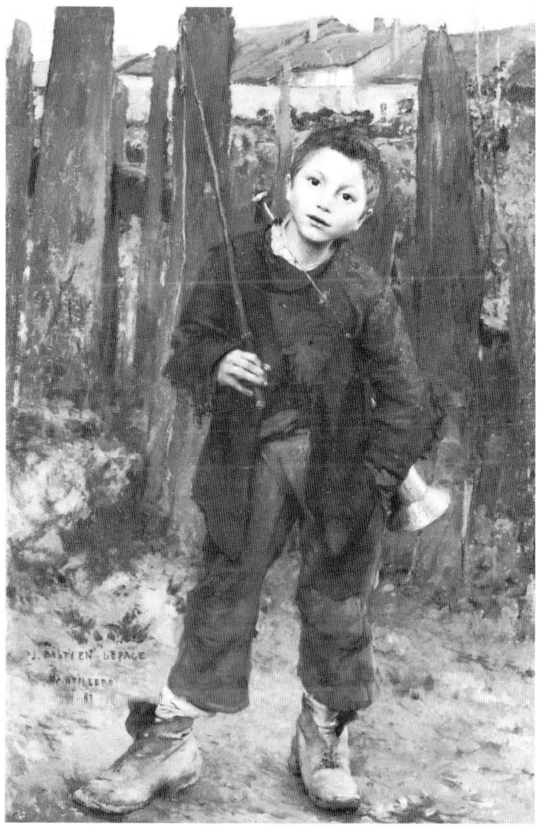

Figure 16
'Pas mèche', 1882
oil painting by Julien Bastien-Lepage
National Gallery of Scotland

JOSEPH LAWTON died 1874
British, working in Ceylon

40 *Waterfall with figures*
about 1870–4[1]

Albumen print
0.236×0.275

Inscribed on mount in ink, verso: 'For Aunt Mary'; 'Waterfall on [?] Retratenne our new estate JG'; printed on mount: 'Colombo Exhibition 1870 Gold Medal awarded for best photographers to J. Lawton & Co, photographers to H.R.H. the Duke of Edinburgh, Kandy'

The photographer Joseph Lawton emigrated to Ceylon (Sri Lanka) in the 1860s. He opened a studio at Kandy in 1866. Lawton's most important surviving work is a series of views of the ancient ruins of Ceylon undertaken for the Committee of Ancient Architecture in 1870–1 to illustrate a government survey. This commission adversely affected Lawton's health and he died in 1874.[2]

Ceylon had been controlled by the Portuguese and the Dutch before becoming a British Crown Colony in 1796. Situated in the Indian Ocean, en route to Australia, India and the Far East, it was an ideal trading position. A large British colonial population settled on the island as tea, coffee and tobacco planters.

The two Europeans in plate 40 pose beside the waterfall on their estate. They have climbed up the rock face in their stocking-feet, accompanied by a native guide who wears Western dress but who climbs barefoot. The young men survey their surroundings from the high vantage point with a proprietorial and rather languid satisfaction.

The length of the exposure necessary has rendered the water as a continuum rather than frozen in an instant.

[1] The photograph may have been taken after Lawton's death by C Robinson who worked for Lawton's widow until the firm closed in 1881

[2] J Falconer, '19th Century Photography in Ceylon', *The Photographic Collector*, vol 2, no 2, 1981

F-J MOULIN active 1850s–1860s
French

41 *A Game of Chess in Algeria*
1856

Albumen print
0.162×0.224

Inscribed in pencil, verso: 'Arabs of the interior of Algeria at play in cafe. SS 'The Southerner', Sept 21st 1863, Algiers. MJ Butcher'

F-J Moulin worked as a photographer in Paris between 1851 and 1869. He was praised by contemporaries for the skill of his 'artistic' productions, particularly his genre scenes—'real life' recreated in the studio. Moulin visited North Africa in 1856. He arrived in Algeria in March carrying a letter of introduction from the Minister of War. *A Game of Chess in Algeria* (plate 41) was taken during this visit, which lasted eighteen months.[1]

A popular taste in France for exotic Middle Eastern or 'oriental' subjects had been fostered by artists in the early nineteenth century. Eugène Delacroix, the leading French Romantic painter, went to North Africa in 1832 and found inspiration for works like *Algerian Women* of 1834 which conveys the enervated sensuality and luxury of the harem. His *Arab Chess Players* in the National Gallery of Scotland (fig 17) may be compared with plate 41. Moulin's photograph is contemplative, the stillness of the figures denoting concentration, and even the young boys who are learning the game watch, still and silent. Delacroix in his treatment of the subject has heightened the drama, making expressive gesture and agitated robes signify intellectual excitation and the cerebral combat that is taking place.

The difference between the Delacroix and the Moulin exemplifies the contemporary debate about the relative status of art and photography. The critic and poet Baudelaire saw painting as essentially a product of the imagination, capable of enhancing our faculties of judgment and feeling. Photography, on the other hand, he regarded as a mechanical means of reproducing objects, more akin to science than art.[2] Later in the century, the Impressionist painters were to reject the notion of truth expressed through the medium of the creative temperament in favour of the ostensibly objective, literal truth of the camera.

[1] *After Daguerre: Masterworks of French Photography (1848–1900) from the Bibliothèque Nationale*, 1980, catalogue Bernard Marbot

[2] Charles Baudelaire, *Salon*, 1859

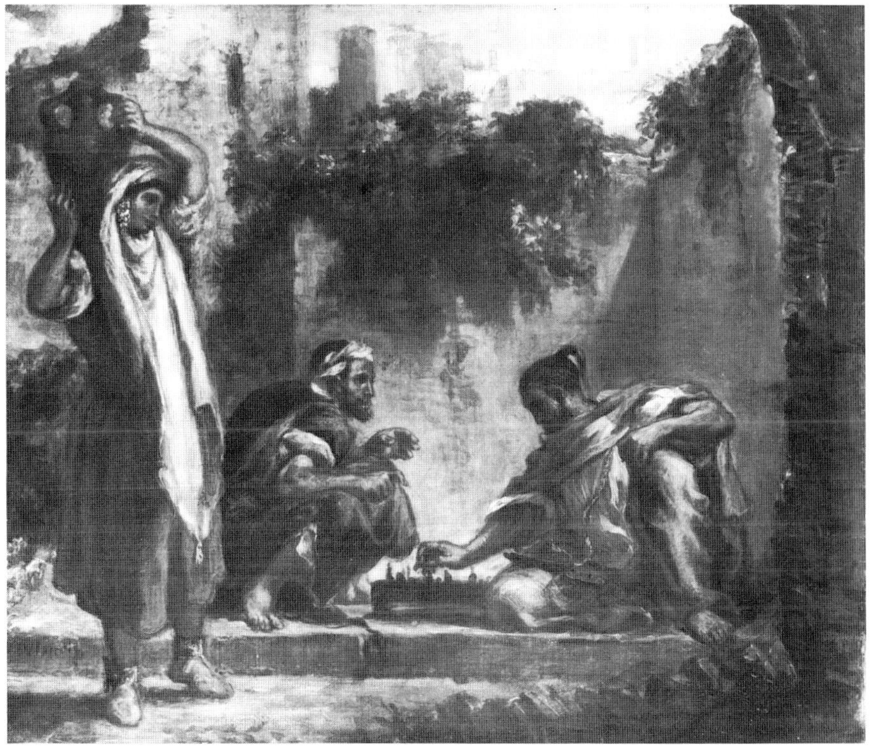

Figure 17
Arab chess players
oil sketch by Eugène Delacroix
National Gallery of Scotland

A NOACK active 1880s
Italian

42 *Boy with Cow*
undated
Albumen print
0.207×0.279
Inscribed in negative '6445'

Plate 42 belongs to a series called 'Costumi della Liguria' by A Noack of Genoa. The photographs represent the people and life of the region and depict types rather than individuals. As bucolic scenes of shepherds and cowherds they are traditional subjects for painters, and as representations of peasants at work they reflect the nineteenth-century Realist movement in art.

JOHN PATRICK 1830–1923
Scottish

43 *St Margaret's Loch, Edinburgh*
undated

Albumen print
0.192×0.279

Inscribed in negative: '598 Skating, St Margaret's Loch, J Patrick'

John Patrick was a professional photographer who worked in Wemyssfield, Kirkcaldy in Fife before moving to Edinburgh. He was also an amateur painter, and his studio at 52 Comiston Road was 'the haunt of many at home and abroad of literary and artistic temperament'.[1] Patrick seems to have had no head for business as his career ended in financial disaster. According to his daughter, he was 'bereft of all through no fault of his own, unless not having money-sense is a fault'.[2]

Plate 43 shows St Margaret's Loch in Holyrood Park, Edinburgh, frozen over, and people skating on the ice. The figures are diminutive silhouettes—Lowry match-stick men out of their time—but with a rugged, magnificent background rather than an industrial one. The spectral ruin that stands on the crag above is St Anthony's chapel.

[1] Jessie Patrick Findlay, letter to James Pittendrigh MacGillivray, 7 May 1924, National Library of Scotland

[2] *ibid*

THOMAS RODGER 1833–1883
Scottish

44 *Walter Little Gilmour*
about 1858

Albumen print
Oval, 0.240

Inscribed in ink on mount: 'T Rodger'; inscribed in pencil, verso: 'From the coll. of Gilmour of the Inch'; blind stamp on mount: [?] IN LUCE VITA EST Thomas Rodger Calotypist St Andrews

Thomas Rodger was born in St Andrews, Fife, in 1833. He was taught photography by Dr John Adamson, lecturer in chemistry at St Andrews University. Rodger was studying medicine in Glasgow when Robert Adamson (qv), John's younger brother, died in 1848. Rodger was encouraged by Dr Adamson to take up photography as a profession.[1] He set up his studio in St Andrews in 1849 and had a long and successful career. His portraiture was particularly distinguished and widely admired.

Plate 44 is a portrait of Mr Walter Little Gilmour, in golfing attire. Gilmour was a member of the Royal and Ancient Golf Club of St Andrews from 1836 until 1883.[2] He appears with a group of golfers in a calotype taken by Dr John Adamson in about 1858,[3] and this photograph would appear to have been taken at about the same time. It is a strong, unselfconscious portrait of this craggy individual.

Rodger disclosed some of his trade secrets in an article in 1857.[4] He said that he always used a Ross and Lerebours lens, had a north-east light in his studio, made exposures of 5 to 30 seconds, and used different developing solutions for photographs of men and women. He explains that by altering slightly the formulae for his chemical baths he could produce markedly different results. That used for photographs of women, for example, would avoid rapid transitions from shadow to light, registering subtle gradations through mid tones and thus create a soft modelling of forms. Rodger's success was in part due to his expertise in the manipulation of chemicals (his early days as laboratory assistant to Dr Adamson had evidently been a useful apprenticeship). The clarity with which a variety of textures—flesh, iron, tweed—are registered exemplifies the technical mastery that sets Rodger's portraits apart from the majority of contemporary studio photographs.

[1] Helen Cook, 'An Artist of the Camera', *Scots Magazine*, January 1977

[2] Letter from Bobby Burnet Esq, Historian to the Royal and Ancient Golf Club of St Andrews

[3] Royal Museum of Scotland, in album formerly owned by Dr John Adamson. Used to illustrate *The Life of Tom Morris*, W W Tulloch, 1907

[4] *The British Journal of Photography*, 21 May 1857

(?) CHARLES T SCOWEN active 1870s–1890s
British, working in Ceylon

45 *Singhalese woman*
undated
Albumen print
0.152×0.110

46 *Singhalese woman*
undated
Albumen print
0.145×0.106

Plates 45 and 46 were taken in Ceylon and show Malay women, or possibly the same model, in different costumes.[1] The photographs are more than anthropological or ethnographical studies whose purpose was to indicate racial characteristics. They are far from scientific or clinical in their depiction of the beautiful sitters. They are also markedly different from each other. Both are posed out of doors, but plate 45 is set in a lush arbour in strong sunlight while the other, plate 46, is in a more sombre grotto-like setting. The latter is monumental and her contemplative inward-looking pose contrasts with the girl in plate 45 who wears robes of lighter, softer material, adopts an elegant posture and gazes out disarmingly at the viewer. The beauty of the woman in plate 46 is darker and nobler—perhaps intended to convey the notion of the 'noble savage' as the 'primitive' appears naturally Michelangelesque.

The photographer may have been Charles T Scowen. Scowen arrived in Ceylon in the early 1870s. He had a studio in Kandy by 1876 and a second in Colombo by the 1890s. His photographs have been judged 'often technically and compositionally superior' to those of Skeen (qv) and Lawton (qv), his contemporaries in Ceylon.[2] Scowen is praised especially for his 'beautifully lit and simply composed studies of racial types'[3] of which these photographs may be examples.

[1] Malays constituted a large proportion of the population of Ceylon in the nineteenth century. They had been introduced by the Dutch for military purposes. J Falconer, '19th Century Photography in Ceylon', *The Photographic Collector*, vol 2, no 2, 1981

[2] *ibid*

[3] *ibid*

CHARLES SHEPHERD active 1860s
British

ARTHUR ROBERTSON active 1860s
British

47 *Bheesties, Delhi*
between 1862 and 1868
Albumen print
0.180×0.214
Inscribed in negative: 'Shepherd & Robertson, Photo'

48 *Chohan Rajpoots, Delhi*
between 1862 and 1868
Albumen print
0.189×0.235
Inscribed in negative: 'Shepherd & Robertson, Photo'

The photographic firm of Shepherd and Robertson was established at Agra in 1862. Samuel Bourne (qv) joined it in 1864 when it had moved to Simla. The firm, later called Howard, Shepherd and Bourne continued until 1870.[1] These photographs by Bourne and Shepherd must pre-date 1868, as they were used to illustrate Forbes Watson's anthropological and ethnographical work, *The People of India* published that year.

Bheesties, Mussulmans, Delhi (plate 47) shows a group of water-sellers. They carry water in skin bags or mussucks and are identified by Forbes Watson as Muslim. They wear skull caps rather than turbans. The figure in the foreground carries a brass cup, used to serve water. Many of the Bheesties served with the British army in India and were praised for their bravery in battle. Forbes Watson says, 'They go into action with their corps, supplying water under the hottest fire. Many a wounded or dying soldier has been relieved in his agony of thirst by these gallant fellows. . .'[2] Kipling's Gunga Din was a regimental Bheestie. The poem's narrator is a British soldier who describes Gunga Din:

'With 'is mussick on 'is back,
'E would skip with our attack,
An' watch us till the bugles made "Retire",
An' for all 'is dirty 'ide
'E was white, clear white, inside
When 'e went to tend the wounded under fire!'

Finally, the soldier states that his assumption of racial superiority was false:

'Though I've belted you and flayed you,
By the livin' gawd that made you,
You're a better man than I am, Gunga Din.'[3]

Plate 48 shows a group of Chohan Rajpoots. The Rajpoots were the highest secular Hindu caste. The Chohans, descendants of warrior princes, claimed the highest position amongst the Rajpoot clans. They adhered to strict caste and marriage laws, preserving their purity of descent from the ancient Aryans. Forbes Watson describes them as 'six feet and upwards in height, and stout in proportion, with strikingly handsome features, fair complexions, and grey eyes'.[4] The soldiers in the photograph all carry swords. The one on the right has a circular shield made of hardened leather; the one next to him is a 'matchlock man'. The composition is based on the opposition of black and white—the dark circle of the shield, the white costumes, and dark figures all set against the alternating dark and light of the building behind.

In both photographs the background is blurred, probably due to the limited focal length of the lens used, but the effect is a happy one as it serves to throw into sharp focus the foreground figures. Plate 48 is more formally posed than the *Bheesties* which looks like an uncomposed 'snapshot'. The figures are casually grouped, and move about, ostensibly unaware of the presence of the camera. Given the length of exposure time required, this cannot have been the case, so it is the photographer's skill that creates the impression. This also distinguishes them from the majority of anthropological photographs of the time.

[1] Ray Desmond, *Victorian India in Focus*, HMSO, 1982, p 3

[2] Forbes Watson, *The People of India,* 1868, vol IV, no 189

[3] Rudyard Kipling, *Barrack Room Ballads,* 1892

[4] Forbes Watson, *op cit*, no 199

W L H SKEEN & CO active 1860s–1903[1]
British, working in Ceylon

49 *Two Singhalese Girls*
undated

Albumen print
0.275×0.218

Blind stamp in negative: 'Photographers W.L.H. Skeen & Co., Colombo, Ceylon'; inscribed in ink on mount, 'Cingalese Girls'

50 *Bamboos*
undated

Albumen print
0.219×0.271

Blind stamp in negative: 'Photographers W L H Skeen & Co., Colombo, Ceylon', inscribed in ink on mount: 'A group of Bamboos'

51 *The Devil's Elbow, on the way to Kandy*
undated

Albumen print
0.277×0.219

Blind stamp in negative: 'Photographers W L H Skeen & Co., Colombo, Ceylon'; inscribed in ink on mount: 'The Devil's Elbow, on the way to Kandy'

William Louis Henry Skeen was the son of a photographer, William Skeen, who had founded a studio in Colombo, Ceylon (Sri Lanka). He was trained at the London School of Photography and returned to the family business in about 1862.

The firm recorded every aspect of life on the island, specialising in photographs documenting coffee cultivation. Plate 49 may be one of the series produced in 1880 of thirty photographs illustrating the new tea industry. It shows two plantation workers, one holding a woven pannier in which the tea leaves were collected. The photograph has been taken from close range using a lens with a shallow depth of field (the girls are in focus while the tree immediately behind them is out of focus).

Plate 50 is a spectacular photograph of the giant bamboos in the Peradeniya Botanical Gardens in Colombo. The natural 'gothic' arch formed by the bamboos is emphasised, and a figure has been introduced for scale.

The railway that connected Colombo with the interior and Kandy was about 75 miles long. It crossed mountainous country and the section called the 'Devil's Elbow' (plate 51) was, as its name suggests, particularly tortuous. The train looks toy-like as it unsteadily negotiates the bend in the track. Skeen has taken a low view-point which induces a vertiginous sense of the sheer drop down and the steep rise of rock above.[2]

[1] W L H Skeen died in 1903. The firm continued until the 1920s, renamed F Skeen & Co

[2] Information from J Falconer, '19th Century Photography in Ceylon', *The Photographic Collector*, vol 2, no 2, 1981

ISAAC WEST TABER 1830–1912
American

52 *Chinese Butcher & Grocery Shop, Chinatown, San Francisco*
1887
Albumen print
0.193×0.244
Printed: '3111 Chinese butcher & grocery shop, Chinatown S.F. Taber Photo., San Francisco, Cal.-1887'

Isaac West Taber was born in New Bedford, Massachusetts in 1830. At the age of fifteen he went to sea. In 1849 he joined a gold rush party bound for San Francisco. Taber was to find his fortune, not in gold but in pigs! He bought a thousand pigs in the Marquesas Islands and sold them, at a handsome profit, to the prospectors. After this coup, he tried gold mining and then farming for a while, before returning to New Bedford at the age of twenty-four.

At about this time photography became a serious interest. Taber opened his first gallery in Syracuse, New York. The quality of his work was such that his reputation reached San Francisco where, in 1864, the firm of Bradley and Rulofson invited him to join them. Taber did so, and worked for them until 1871, when he decided to open his own gallery. He ran this successfully until the earthquake of 1906, when Taber lost all his glass plates—20 tons of view negatives and 80 tons of portrait work.[1]

Another victim of the 1906 earthquake and the fires that swept through San Francisco in its wake, was the old Chinatown. The Chinese quarter occupied twelve city blocks at the foot of Nob Hill. Its streets were full of temples, bazaars and shops like the one in plate 52. San Francisco had a large Chinese population, over 24,000 in 1890, though this halved over the next decade partly due to discriminatory legislation and anti-Chinese feeling.

In Taber's photograph, all the figures watch the camera intently, aware that they are the objects of its scrutiny and curiosity. The directness of their gaze is slightly disconcerting. The strict frontality and formality of the composition adds to the distancing effect, which is clearly intended by the photographer.

[1] Robert Taft, *Photography and the American Scene, 1964* p 355; Ralph W Andrews, *Picture Gallery Pioneers 1850–1875,* p 63; Letter from William F Stapp, Curator of Photographs, Smithsonian Institute, Washington DC

WILLIAM HENRY FOX TALBOT
1800–1877
English

53 *The Scott Monument under Construction*
1844
Calotype
0.196×0.158
Inscribed in ink on mount: 'View taken in October 1844 HFT'

Fox Talbot was the inventor of the calotype process. This process, patented by Talbot on 18 February, 1841, introduced the principle of the development of the latent image. From this image in negative any number of positives could be made. Talbot was, in this sense, the originator of photography as we understand it today.

Plate 53 is a calotype taken by Talbot of the Scott Monument in Edinburgh during its construction. It is one of a series of thirty-two calotypes by Talbot, published in *Sun Pictures in Scotland* in 1845. The photographs, which include views of Abbotsford and Melrose Abbey, all seem to relate to Sir Walter Scott. The monument in Edinburgh, designed by George Meikle Kemp, was completed and the scaffolding removed on 13 January 1845. Talbot probably took the photograph in October 1844.[1] The incomplete and scaffold-clad monument had been the subject of a calotype by Hill and Adamson (qv), and so could be considered a photogenic motif. Talbot tended to choose subjects that were both intrinsically and formally interesting. He liked forms that would create and measure space in the photograph; and the scaffolding, climbing its way up the structure, would have appealed. This is not the only occasion on which Talbot photographed such a motif, as the *Nelson Monument under Construction* of 1843 shows (fig 18). Talbot would have considered the romantic associations of the Scott Monument an intrinsic part of the content of the photograph.

[1] Talbot was in Edinburgh in this month. He had strong Edinburgh associations and was a frequent visitor. He owned a house at 13 Great Stuart Street from 1864 to 1872 so that he would have a permanent base in the Scottish capital

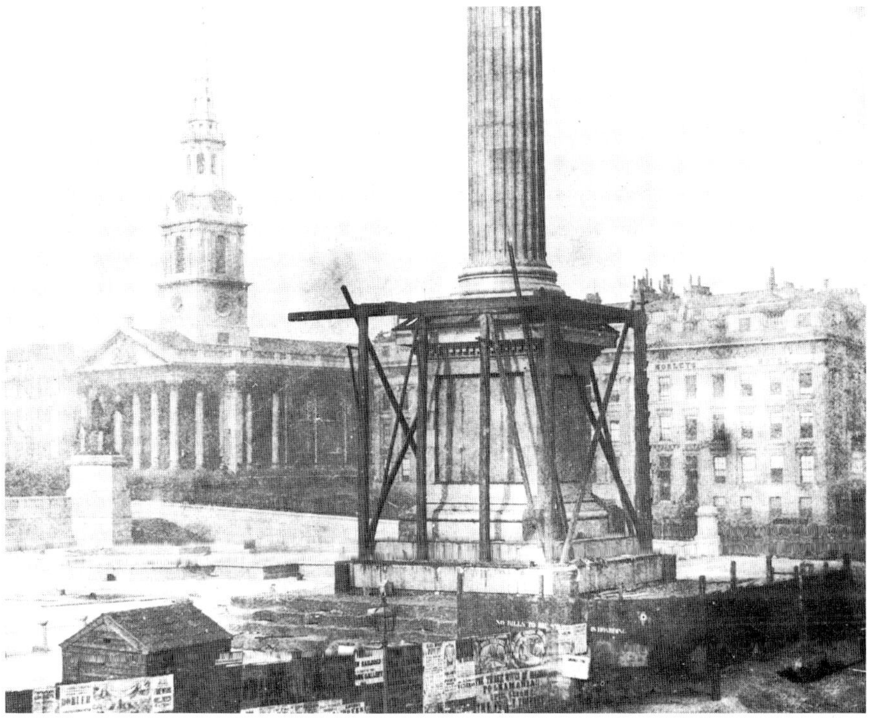

Figure 18
Nelson's Column under construction, 1843
by William Henry Fox Talbot
Science Museum, London
(Fox Talbot Collection)

JAMES VALENTINE 1815–1880
Scottish

54 *Ben Lomond from Luss*
undated
Albumen print
0.188×0.292
Inscribed in the negative: 'Ben Lomond from Luss (Mist Effect) 2026. J.V.'

55 *Staffa, the Clam Shell Cave*
undated
Albumen print
0.190×0.231
Inscribed in the negative: 'Staffa, the Clam Shell Cave 274 JV'

James Valentine belongs to the second generation of Scottish photographers. After studying photography in Paris, he established a studio in the Murraygate, Dundee, in 1856. His father had been a manufacturer of wood blocks for linen printing and James Valentine had originally trained as an engraver and designer of illustrated envelopes—the precursors of the picture postcard.

By the 1870s Valentine's of Dundee and Wilson's of Aberdeen (qv) were the two largest photographic establishments in Scotland. Both dealt largely in Scottish topographical views and both made photography into an industry, realising its commercial possibilities. At his death, Valentine was employing forty people who were producing three thousand prints a day. For the most part, this 'production-line' photography resulted in competent though unremarkable mementos of places visited or read about—inexpensive because mass-produced. On occasion, however, Valentine demonstrates his not inconsiderable skill and judgment as a photographer, as in these examples of his work. Plate 54 is an elegiac scene of the loch at what seems to be twilight or early morning. In fact this is the result of the length of exposure that was necessary to achieve the desired mist effect. At a time when it was virtually impossible to register clouds, the white mist against the dark mountain gives the impression of a dramatic sky.

The Clam Shell Cave (plate 55) gets its name from the strange columns and spirals of basalt, formed by volcanic action. Staffa has strong romantic associations. Fingal or Finn MacCool was the hero, according to ancient legend, who built the Giant's Causeway and lived in Fingal's Cave with his son, Ossian. The 'translation' of the ancient Celtic poems of Ossian by James Macpherson in 1760, the poem *Lord of the Isles* by Sir Walter Scott of 1815, the overture *Fingal's Cave* by Mendelssohn and the visit by J M W Turner in 1831 perpetuated the interest in the legend and the place.

GEORGE WASHINGTON WILSON
1823–1893
Scottish

56 *View in Leith Docks*
undated
Albumen print
0.166×0.239
Inscribed in negative: 'View in Leith Docks 294 G.W.W.'

57 *Chancel, St Mary's Cathedral, Iona*
undated
Albumen print
0.161×0.236
Inscribed in negative: 'Iona Cathedral Chancel looking West 778 G.W.W.'

58 *Tighnalechan, Aberfeldy*
undated
Albumen print
0.187×0.286
Inscribed in negative: 'Tighnalechan Aberfeldy 2381 G.W.W.'

George Washington Wilson was the son of a farmer. He left school at the age of twelve and served his time as a carpenter before deciding to become a painter. After training at art schools in Edinburgh and London he returned to Aberdeen in about 1850. It may have been the need to supplement his income as a teacher of drawing and painting that made Wilson join the photographic business of John Hay junior in 1853. By 1855 Wilson had opened his own studio, and by the 1860s was one of the most prolific and successful photographers in Scotland. He was patronised by Queen Victoria and won international acclaim as a landscape photographer. By the 1880s Wilson was 'the world's largest publisher of photographic views and lantern slides'.[1] Like Valentine of Dundee (qv) Wilson introduced the principle of the division of labour into his photographic 'factory': the preparation of plates, taking of photographs, enlarging and printing were all done by different employees.

Plates 56 to 58 demonstrate Wilson's compositional skills. The subjects—sailing ships, picturesque ruins and rustic buildings—are all familiar motifs in painting. Wilson's artistic training is evident. He looks for natural compositional devices such as the path that leads the eye into the picture (plate 58), the *contre jour* effect of the ships' masts silhouetted against the sky (plate 56), and the play of light and shadow across the motif (plate 57). Wilson is also able to make the apparently arbitrary cropping and framing by the camera into a pictorial virtue (plate 56). As well as technical mastery, Wilson's ability to produce formal coherence out of the visual multiplicity and chaos that is the real world is evident in these photographs.

[1] Information from Roger Taylor, *George Washington Wilson, Artist and Photographer*, 1981

[2] Helmut and Alison Gernsheim, *The History of Photography*, 1969, p 402

ZANGAKI active 1880s–1890s
(?) Egyptian

59 *Tourists at a Pyramid*
undated
Albumen print
0.280 × 0.220
Inscribed in the negative: 'Zangaki'

The photograph of a group of European tourists at a Pyramid was taken by a commercial photographer working in the 1880s and 1890s called Zangaki. The sightseers, possibly on one of Cook's tours, have reached the pyramid by camel. Male and female Egyptian guides have assisted them to climb some way up the pyramid where they pose for their photograph. Men in jackets, collars and ties, women in full length dresses, and a child in a sailor suit, pause, hand in hand with their guides, to face the camera. The apparent breaking down of the social and cultural inhibitions of the time results in a strangely affecting image.

PHOTOGRAPHER(S) UNKNOWN
(?) French

60 *The Arch of Constantine, Rome*
probably taken in the 1850s
Salt print
0.183 × 0.248
Inscribed in pencil, verso: 'Arch of Constantine'

61 *The Temple of Saturn, Rome*
probably taken in the 1850s
Salt print
0.231 × 0.174

62 *The Basilica of Maxentius, Rome*
probably taken in the 1850s
Salt print
0.169 × 0.248
Inscribed in pencil, verso: 'Temple of Peace'

One of the uses of photography, immediately recognised and advocated, was the recording of ancient and decaying monuments. Countless views of Rome were taken in the early years of photography. These had both an archaeological and an artistic motive. The subject of the ruins of ancient Rome has been a constant in Western art since the Renaissance. They have inspired laments for fallen civilisation, thoughts of the transience of human achievement, the vanity of pride and the mutability of time, and meditations on the theme of death and decay. As the vehicle of such ideas, Rome's ruins had been the motif of innumerable paintings and, inevitably, became the subject of even more photographs.

The Arch of Constantine (plate 60) was built to commemorate the Emperor's victory over Maxentius at the battle of the Milvian Bridge in 312 AD. In the building of the triumphal arch were incorporated columns and reliefs from earlier buildings. The inscriptions are clearly legible in the photograph. The Basilica of Maxentius (plate 62) was one of the major buildings in the Forum. The photographer has exploited the strong contrasts of light and shadow created by the massive arches. The Temple of Saturn (plate 61) consists of eight Ionic columns of granite. These form a 'grid' through which we see the buildings beyond, including the church of Sts Martina and Luca by Pietro da Cortona.

All these photographs are remarkable for their clarity and the precision of their detail. The purplish tint of plate 61 indicates that it has been gold-toned, a process that adds richness to the print.

PHOTOGRAPHER UNKNOWN

63 *Two small girls and a pony*
about 1900
Albumen print
Circular, 0.119

This is presumably an amateur photograph —a curiously direct portrait of two small girls with luminous eyes, open wide in a bright sun, with their mother standing watchful in the background. Also just visible, crouching down behind the group, is a figure holding the pony's bridle to keep it still.

PHOTOGRAPHER UNKNOWN

(?) American/Canadian

64 *Niagara Falls in Winter*
undated
Albumen print
0.192×0.235
Inscribed in ink on mount: 'Niagara Falls in Winter'

We are firstly struck by the strangeness, the almost lunar quality of this frozen landscape. The extreme elemental condition of the waterfall seems inimical to the life of the diminutive people. But these penguin-like figures are not the victims of destructive and wanton natural forces. They are tourists who wander at will in the snow, and for whom the sublime experience of a critical confrontation with tremendous Nature has been replaced by a mere frisson of excitement, an enjoyable thrill.

There were many photographers, both on the American and the Canadian side of Niagara Falls, producing innumerable views. The best of these photographers was a Scots Canadian, William Notman (1826–91). This well-crafted and original composition may be an example of his work.

PHOTOGRAPHER UNKNOWN
British

65 *The Cathedral, Manila*
undated

Albumen print
0.217×0.278

Inscribed in ink on mount: 'The Old Cathedral No 7 all the old cathedral was pulled down when the new one was built, except the tower which was ruined in the 1880 earthquakes'

66 *Sugar Factory, Manila*
undated

Albumen print
0.217×0.278

Inscribed in ink on mount: 'No 13 Sugar Factory Mats of Sugar Sundrying'

67 *Corregidor*
undated

Albumen print
0.210×0.282

Inscribed in ink on mount: '17 Bamboo Banana Palm'

These three photographs are part of a larger group mostly taken in Manila in the Philippines. Notes written on the photographs suggest that the photographer was a member of a firm referred to as 'S B and Co' which was based in Manila.

The photographer had a conventionally-trained eye for the picturesque noticeable in the picture of the village street (plate 67) which he has treated in a manner strikingly similar to George Washington Wilson's photograph of Tighnalechan (plate 58). He had also a strong interest in pattern and clearly enjoyed the repetitive abstractions of the mats of drying sugar and tiled roofs, which he exaggerated in plates 65 and 66 by using a low-angled sun.

PHOTOGRAPHER UNKNOWN

68 *Syrian Shepherd*
undated

Albumen print
0.229×0.172

Inscribed in negative: 'No 616'; inscribed in pencil on mount: 'Syrian Shepherd'

Plate 68 is one of a series of photographs showing the distinctive costumes and physiognomies of Arabs from different countries in the Middle East. The sitter, in this case a Syrian shepherd, is anonymous. As he is meant to represent a generic type, the photographer has chosen a frontal, static pose with no movement or facial expression. While the picture is not intended as a portrait of an individual, nevertheless the way in which the stern-featured man sits upright, gazing steadily at the camera, holding his club as if it were a sceptre, makes for a strong patriarchal image. The broad stripes of the shepherd's cloak are also felicitous, adding a bold, decorative element which enlivens the picture. The photographer may not have been familiar with Western art, but the photograph is reminiscent of the self-portraits in fancy dress and Biblical costume of Rembrandt.

PHOTOGRAPHER UNKNOWN
(?) British

69 *The Rock, Trichinopoly*
undated
Albumen print
0.181 × 0.238
Inscribed in pencil, on verso: 'Rock and Temple'

70 *The Great Pagoda, Seringapatam*
undated
Albumen print
0.185 × 0.242
Inscribed in pencil, verso: 'Pagoda, near Trichinopoly, Madras Presidency'

71 *The Jumma Masjid, Seringapatam*
undated
Albumen print
0.214 × 0.258
Inscribed in pencil, verso: 'Mohammedan Mosque'

72 *Mausoleum of Tipu Sultan, Seringapatam*
undated
Albumen print
0.212 × 0.262
Inscribed in pencil, verso: 'Tippoop Tomb, Seringatam'

Trichinopoly (Tiruchirapalli), the ancient capital of the Chola kingdom, lies on the sacred Cauvery River. In the nineteenth century it formed part of the Madras Presidency, and was the scene of hostilities between the French and British during the Carnatic Wars. The granite Rock (plate 69) stands, 273 feet high, inside a fort. It is a sacred place and is crowned by a Dravidian temple and shrine to Ganesa. Trichinopoly was fortified by the Naiks of Madura, who used Trichinopoly as their capital, in the seventeenth century. Viswanatha Naik built the Teppakulam—the large masonry tank or reservoir at the foot of the Rock.[1]

Seringapatam (Srirangapatan), an island three miles long on the Cauvery River, was the capital of Mysore, a native state of Southern India. Its name derives from a temple of Vishnu, Sri Ranganatha which is one of the seven sacred places of Hinduism[2] (plate 70). The temple or 'Great Pagoda' was founded in 894 by one of the Ganga kings, Tirumalayya, and covers a larger area than any other temple in South India. The photograph was taken from the top of the Raya Gopuram—the foundations of an unfinished tower—and shows the line of Gopurams. Linnaeus Tripe took a photograph of this view from the same spot in 1858.[3]

Plates 69 to 72 show the sacred and secular monuments of the islands, particularly those relating to the story of Tipu Sultan, which is also the history of the brief, though momentous involvement of the British in the destiny of Mysore and the history of India in the eighteenth century. Tipu Sultan was the legendary 'Tiger of Mysore', so called because of the tiger imagery associated with his court and with his personal cult. His father was Hyder Ali, the Muslim adventurer who usurped the throne and became one of the most powerful princes in India. They were both fiercely anti-British. Tipu withstood a British siege in 1792. On 23 February 1792 he assembled all his principal officers in the Jumma Masjid or Great Mosque (plate 71), to seek advice before signing the treaty surrendering his two young sons as hostages to Lord Cornwallis.[4] In 1799, during a second British assault, Tipu was killed. Plate 72 shows the Gumbaz or Mausoleum which Tipu had built for his father and where he and his wife were buried. It stands in the Lal Bagh or 'Red Garden', Tipu's favourite garden retreat. ▷

The photographs are remarkable both for their quality as prints and strength of composition. The photographer had a strong sense of design and interest in pattern, and maximised visual interest whether in the stripes formed by the variegated wall of the tank and its reflections in plate 69 or the intricately carved designs on the *Jumma Masjid*. The photographs also have a great depth of field. There is a sense of distance without a concomitant loss of detail, which may have been the result of using a dry, rather than a wet, collodion process.[5]

1 *The Imperial Gazetteer*

2 Letter from Mrs P Kattenhorn, the British Library, India Office Library & Records

3 Captain L Tripe, *Photographs of Seringham,* 1858, plate 2

4 Letter from Mrs P Kattenhorn

5 Bourne notes 'how much better a dry process will render distance that is more or less shrouded by haze than the wet'. Samuel Bourne, 'A Photographic Journey through the Higher Himalayas', *The British Journal of Photography*, 26 November 1869 p 570